Debrett's

ETIQUETTE & MODERN MANNERS

Debrett's

ETIQUETTE & MODERN MANNERS

EDITED BY ELSIE BURCH DONALD

PREFACE BY SIR IAIN MONCREIFFE
OF THAT ILK, BT

Webb & Bower

This edition reprinted in 1990 by
Webb & Bower (Publishers) Limited
5 Cathedral Close, Exeter, Devon EX1 1EZ
in association with Debrett's Peerage Ltd
73–77 Britannia Road, London SW6

Distributed by the Penguin Group
Penguin Books Ltd, Registered Offices:
Harmondsworth, Middlesex, England
Penguin Books Australia Ltd, Ringwood, Victoria,
Australia
Penguin Books Canada Ltd, 2801 John Street,
Markham, Ontario, Canada L3R 1B4
Penguin Books (NZ) Ltd, 182–190 Wairau Road,
Auckland 10, New Zealand

First published in Great Britain in 1981 by
Debrett's Peerage Limited

ISBN: 0–86350–366–7

Printed and bound in Great Britain by
Billing and Sons Ltd

Contents

Acknowledgements

Those who helped

□We wish to thank the following people, firms and organizations for their help in the preparation of this book:

□Mr Brian Abethail at The Mansion House; Lady Elizabeth Anson, Party Planners; Mr Michael Bannister, MFH; Mr Brinsley Black; Mr Nicholas Bull; Miss Lucie Clayton, Lucie Clayton Secretarial College; Major R.A.G. Courage, M.V.O., M.B.E.; Mrs Anne-Marie Cox, Belgravia Bureau; Captain Maldwin Drummond; Mrs Kenneth Edwards; Alice, Lady Fairfax-Lucy; Mr Stephen Green, Curator of Lord's Cricket Ground; Mr F.J.Haggas, Joint Master of the West Norfolk Hunt; Mr Peter Hargreaves; Miss Jay Harris; Lord Henley; Mr George Howard; Mr M.V. Kenyon, M.V.O.; Mrs Norman Lamont; Mr George Lawson, Press Officer of Henley Regatta; Miss Marjorie Lee, Press Officer, Dorchester Hotel; Mrs Jeremy Maas; Mr T. Neate, Smythson of Bond Street; Rev. Kenneth Nugent, S.J.; Lady Ropner; Mr Harold Rosenthal, Opera Magazine; Mr D.M.A. Scott, The Worshipful Company of Goldsmiths; Miss Sophie Scarisbrick; Mrs S. Sproule; Rev. J. Sunshine; Mr Robert Wade; Rev. Andrew Walmisley; Miss Audrey Wild, General Synod of the Church of England; Mrs. Digby Willoughby; Mr and Mrs John Woodward.

□Berry Bros and Rudd Ltd.; The Clerk of Information Services at the House of Lords; Thomas Goode Ltd.; Huntsman Ltd.; Knightsbridge Nannies; London Domestics Ltd; Lines Agency; Moss Bros Ltd.; PDC Graphics Ltd.; The Press Office and Master of the Household, Buckingham Palace; The Press Office of the All England Club; The Press Offices of Glyndebourne Festival Opera, The Royal Opera House, Covent Garden and the Savoy Hotel; R. Twining & Co. Ltd.

Authors of chapters

□Jane Abdy, Chapter Eight; Jonathan Abbott, Chapter 15; Judy Allen, Chapters Nine—13; Iain Finlayson, Chapter 16; Sibylla Jane Flower, Chapters One—Five; Joan Jenkins, Chapter 14; Anna Sproule, Chapters Six and Seven.

Preface

☐When as Chairman of Debrett, I was consulted about the need for us to publish this book, my first thoughts were to thank goodness I haven't had to write it myself, but that there is certainly a demand for one.

☐My own attitude has always been simple. As a child, I was taught that the good fairy Do-As-You-Would-Be-Done-By should be emulated. But adult observation soon reinforced the lessons of history that the fairy was slightly mistaken: a zealous 'do-gooder' who 'knows best' often causes people present inconvenience 'for their own good,' distressing them now for some future pie in the sky they may not prefer. The true spirit to emulate is that of Do-As-They-Would-Be-Done-By, whether one agrees with them or not.

☐Confucius felt that if there was a correct mode of behaviour prescribed for every possible situation, the everyday stress and grind of human contacts would as it were be oiled to everybody's benefit. Survivals from such former codes can be fun, such as the custom in Guards Officers' Messes of wearing one's uniform cap at meals derived from the pre–1914 custom of a man wearing his hat in his own house or club but not in other people's.

☐To me, manners should be natural. The object is to put everybody at their ease, whatever their age or rank. This has sometimes to be played by ear and needs tactful observation, as even Queen Victoria discovered: she was served first and as soon as she put down her knife and fork everybody's plate was removed. Nobody told the Queen that everyone had not finished, until one dinner at Windsor Lord Hartington called to the footman to bring him back his plate, whereupon Her Majesty enquired into and stopped the custom.

☐Ever since the publication of *Debrett's Correct Form*, we have been asked to supply an up-to-date guide to the everyday conventions of the present day. This carefully vetted publication is the answer.

Iain Moncreiffe of that Ilk
Albany Herald of Arms

In halle, in chamber, ore where thou gon,
Nurtur and good manners makyth man.

Urbanitatis, 1490

If spitting chance to moove thee so
Thou canst it not forbeare,
Remember do it modestly,
Consider who is there.
If filthiness or ordure thou
Upon the floore doe cast,
Tread out and cleanse it with thy foot,
Let that be done with haste.

Booke of Demeanour Richard Weste 1619

Behaviour is the garment of a mind and ought to
have the conditions of a garment. For first, it ought
to be made in fashion; secondly, it should not be
too curious or costly; thirdly, it ought to be framed
as best to set forth any virtue of the mind and
supply and hide any deformity; and lastly, and
above all, it ought not to be strait, so as to confine
the mind and interfere with its freedom in business
and action.

Francis Bacon

The lowest and poorest people in the world expect good breeding from a gentleman, and they have a right to it; for they are by nature your equals, and are no otherwise your inferiors than by their educations and their fortune. Speak to them with great humility and with *douceur*, or else they will think you proud and hate you.

Lord Chesterfield

He is no gentleman! He divides his coat tails when he sits down.

George IV of Sir Robert Peel

It is almost a definition of a gentleman to say he is one who never inflicts pain.

Cardinal Newman

Introduction

Books on manners

☐Books about etiquette and good manners have a long history. They have concentrated for the most part on four topics, treating one or more of them in accordance with the mood of the time.

☐The first topic, much out of fashion today, is parental advice. The very oldest book in existence contains the pharaoh Ptah Hotep's instructions to his son on personal conduct and this tradition is more recently known to us through Lord Chesterfield's letters to his son. But modern youth does not welcome immersion in the sagacious reservoirs of its progenitors and many parents feel too unsure of their pools of wordly wisdom to offer a dip.

☐The second topic, equally out of place, is advice on the arts of wordly success, including the rules of statecraft. This was epitomised in the most famous of all courtesy books, Castiglione's manual for rising Renaissance youths, *The Courtier*, a classic of literature if no longer a safe guide to gentlemanlike behaviour.

☐In England in the 15th and 16th centuries there appeared a number of books on 'civility'. These were guides to deportment, dress, bearing and conversation derived from precepts of universal good taste rather than fashion. They were greatly influenced by Erasmus's *De Civilitate* in which character, personal habits and appearance were treated as interrelated. They included details like how to fold a napkin and lie in a bed; and cautioned against spitting and breaking wind at table. Personal habits and cleanliness clearly offered great scope to the reform-minded of the time.

☐The fourth and final topic, akin to civility, is custom. Custom too involves rules of dress, deportment and table manners, but it focuses on acceptable behaviour at a particular time and place rather than on universal precepts. So, civility requires that dress should not be ostentatious; custom that women wear hats at Ascot.

☐The rising middle classes of Victorian and

Edwardian England were obsessed with nuances of social customs which marked the social elite, and a plethora of manifestos on etiquette tried to keep them informed. But the elite kept changing the rules. The tremendous importance given to these endless rites that seemed almost to be invented to confuse the *arriviste* (and to some extent were) caused a reaction against formal tradition and etiquette—and books about them—that has continued to the present day. 'Who needs a book on manners; anything goes nowadays,' is a familiar cry.

Defining manners   □Before the advantages of a contemporary book on manners can be given, the nature of manners themselves must be looked at. Innumerable observations exist on this subject from pithy epigrams to carefully reasoned moral treatises, but all boil down to the fact that good manners mean showing consideration for others—a sensibility that is innate in some people and in others requires considerable inculcation.

□Whatever its sources, however, its purpose is to enable people to come together with ease, stay together for a time without friction or discord, and leave one another in the same fashion. This is the essence of all civilized behaviour and, on the face of it, hardly sounds difficult. But though thoughtfulness and kindliness are parts of our characters, so too are irascibility, selfishness, intolerance and suspicion. Furthermore, a great deal of social life is not inherently pleasant; undertaken rather for business or other special reasons, it strains affability. Just as important, it is not the nature of the species to be fully at ease in unfamiliar surroundings, or among strangers; a secure footing is needed to promote ease and relaxation. This is the role of custom and of courtesy: the first stimulates personal confidence and reduces misunderstandings, the latter reassures us that our associates mean to be friendly.

Purpose of this book   □Today social customs are greatly simplified and remarkably flexible; expressions of courtesy are more informal, often gaining spontaneity because of it; formal tradition too is modified and generally reserved for ceremonial occasions at which it happily serves to reinforce and remind us of links with the past. But easing conventions does not mean that 'anything goes'. The ground rules are as important now as ever, perhaps more so when so many social encounters are haphazard; but it is crucially important that these rules be available to everyone and that they be adaptable to all economic backgrounds.

□Etiquette and Modern Manners seeks to accomplish this in three ways: by giving detailed information about ceremonies and events which are part of the British tradition, by removing as 'dead wood' obsolete conventions, and by establishing as 'correct form' useful new practices that have emerged to suit new circumstances. This involves recording changes in a variety of activities ranging from ordinary entertainments like dinner parties to expectations in courtship and new rules of courtesy in business. Our aim is to construct an improved framework that will increase opportunities for convivial interchange without restricting the pleasures of self-expression and individuality.

Special note   □To simplify desciptions, the feminine gender has been used throughout the book to refer to those activities which were traditionally performed by women, for example, the role of hostess. The masculine pronoun has been applied in references to mankind in general as well as to instances which by tradition fall into the male province. Therefore, the presiding figure at a dinner party is the 'hostess' or 'she' and the guest, though male or female, is 'he'. Readers must of course make their own substitutions where relevant.

Note to 1990 edition   ☐In the nine years since this book was first published, some new trends have developed in both social and business life. For instance, first names are becoming established practice everywhere and today almost no one needs be offended by what used to be thought a step over the boundary between friendliness and familiarity. Equally, titles and prefixes are fast disappearing from envelopes: many people, particularly the young, find 'Esquire' a silly anachronism, though Ms continues to flourish in written address to women. Another trend is the ingenuity used in planning social affairs: invitations are apt to come in all sorts of novel forms, and even traditional ceremonies — weddings, funerals — are often boldly adapted to suit personal needs and wishes. Such innovations are to be welcomed, saving as they do ritual from the ever-present threat of emptiness; though innovators must take care always to avoid changes that could cause confusion or embarrassment to others.

☐But the most rapid changes of all are taking place in business, where electronics and an economic boom have outstripped many established customs and, at the same time, created new areas where they are required. Few of us, for example, want to hear dinky tunes on telephones or watch video advertisements in post office queues; we feel harassed by sonic bleeps in Underground lifts and are maddened when addressed like idiots by credit card computers. As technology develops, business too needs to remember that if something is likely to cause annoyance to anyone, then it isn't really beneficial.

Elsie Burch Donald
Editor

1 BIRTHS AND THE CEREMONIES OF CHILDHOOD

☐It is still customary, whether a family has religious views or not, to initiate children into the religious life that is traditional in that family. This usually involves special ceremonies, often ancient in origin, whose function is to introduce the infant and, later, the adolescent, formally into the society (and its responsibilities) as well as to explain the articles of faith peculiar to that sect. The initiation ceremonies included here are the Anglican, Roman Catholic and Jewish, but most religious denominations have comparable rites and anyone who is likely to be a participant and wishes to know beforehand what is expected should telephone the church, mosque or the religion's administrative headquarters for details.

BIRTHS

☐The birth of a child is almost always a happy occasion. The majority of babies are born today in hospitals and members of the family and close friends will be aware of the imminence of the event and eagerly await the news.
☐As soon after the baby has appeared as is practicable, the father should telephone the grandparents, others immediately concerned, close friends and anyone who has been particularly solicitous in the last weeks.
☐Visitors should check carefully before arriving at the hospital that it is convenient to call. Mother and child may be sent telegrams, letters, cards and flowers at the hospital. Gifts, other than for the baby from close friends, are not expected.

Announcing

☐Announcements may be placed by letter or telephone in the Births column of national and local newspapers.

Examples

Martin.—On October 3rd, at the Knightsbridge Hospital, London, to Mary, the wife of Robert Martin —a daughter.

14

Martin.— On 3rd October 1980, at the Knightsbridge Hospital, London, to Mary and Robert—a daughter, Anne.

Martin.— On October 3rd, at 27 Wellington Street, London, to Mary (née Grant) and Robert—a daughter.

Single mothers

☐Most newspapers will publish announcements of the birth of a child to an unmarried woman.

Smith.— On 6th October 1980, at the Knightsbridge Hospital, London, to Mary—a son.

Special notices

☐The social editors of *The Times* and *The Daily Telegraph* invite certain people who have placed notices in the Births column to make a further announcement on the court and social pages. This entry is made free of charge. If no invitation is received, a notice may be submitted in writing for publication in the paper and paid for in the usual manner. The wording is as follows:

Mrs John Smith gave birth to
a daughter in Oxford on April 17

Registering a birth

☐A birth must be registered in England and Wales within a period of 42 days at the office of the Registrar of Births for the district in which the birth took place. The father or mother of the child may register this as one signature only is required.
☐If a child is born in England and Wales to unmarried parents and the father wishes to have his name entered in the register both parents must attend for the registration. Alternatively, the father

may make a statutory declaration on a special form obtainable from the registrar, which must be witnessed by a solicitor or commissioner of oaths. A mother can re-register a birth if she subsequently obtains an affiliation order.

Scotland ☐In Scotland a period of 21 days is allotted for registration with due allowance made for illness or other misfortune. The birth may be registered at the office of the registrar for the district in which the birth took place or in which the mother lives. ☐For unmarried parents, the same regulations apply as in England and Wales, if both parents attend at the registrar's office. If the father is unable to attend and wishes to have his name entered in the register, he must obtain a special form on which to make the statutory declaration; this must be witnessed by a justice of the peace or a public notary.

CHRISTENINGS ☐The early Christian church attached great importance to the sacrament of baptism. For this reason, many of the churches of Europe had their own baptisteries, small detached buildings, generally octagonal in shape, and often with richly decorated interiors.
☐Inside each baptistery was a large basin into which water gushed from a fountain. This was the setting of the baptismal ceremony. Anyone wishing to be baptized who had undergone the rigorous instruction required by the church, immersed himself in the water and was held by the bishop under the fountain for the initiation ceremony; he then climbed out of the basin and was handed a long, white robe, a symbol of the spotless purity of the newly baptized; he was then anointed and made his way to the basilica to be greeted by the congregation.

Infant baptism ☐As time went by, infant baptism became almost universal in the Christian church. The ritual rebirth through water and the Holy Spirit survives in the pouring of water over the forehead of the child by the priest and in the white robe in which the child is clothed.

☐Both the *Book of Common Prayer* and Roman Catholic doctrine refer to the regenerative nature of baptism, and for this reason it has been the custom of both churches to allow children to be brought by their parents to be baptized before they are old enough to profess the Christian faith. But this is done on the understanding that baptized children will receive a Christian upbringing. In the new liturgies of both churches, great emphasis is placed on the responsibilities of parents and godparents and these are outlined by the priest at the beginning of the ceremony.

Planning the ceremony

☐The ceremony takes place in the parish church of the parents, or where they normally worship. As soon as this is decided, the parish priest should be approached. If the parents are not church-goers and the priest is a stranger, it is not difficult to find out his name (it may well be written on the board outside the church). He should be telephoned so that an appointment can be made for a discussion on the religious background to the parents' request, the choice of liturgy and a suitable date for the ceremony to take place.

☐Most clergymen welcome an opportunity to christen a child and will be glad to do so provided that the parents sincerely intend to give the child a Christian upbringing.

Friends in Holy Orders

☐Some families have a friend or relation in Holy Orders whom they would like to officiate at the christening. This will require the permission of the parish priest of the church in which the ceremony is planned to take place. If he is well known to the family, he may be asked informally, but if he is not, a letter outlining the reasons for asking another clergyman to perform the ceremony is more courteous than a telephone call and should be undertaken as soon as possible.

17

Time of ceremony: Church of England	☐In recent years, the Church of England has emphasized its preference for administering baptism within the principal Sunday service. At Morning or Evening Prayer the baptismal ceremony takes place at the end of the second lesson and in the Holy Communion service, after the sermon. ☐*The Book of Common Prayer* and the canon law of the church require that a child should be baptized into the church in the presence of the worshipping congregation. However, baptism can also be administered at a separate ceremony attended by the family, the godparents of the child and close friends grouped informally round the font. This takes the needs of the mother and child into account, creates an unforgettably intimate occasion and avoids the unfortunate mix of infants and the older generation at prayer. ☐This form of private baptism is discouraged by the church and a clergyman may refuse to conduct such a service. However, there are many others who will be only too happy to officiate at the ceremony if this is desired, provided that the goodwill of the parish priest of the parents is obtained. ☐Some parishes have reached a compromise on this point: private baptism will be administered on condition that the parents will bring the child to a subsequent service for a public blessing. ☐Thus the arrangements for a Church of England baptism depend upon whether the ceremony takes place at a morning or evening service, the times of which will vary from parish to parish, or at a private ceremony, which by tradition takes place in the afternoon.
Time of Ceremony: Roman Catholic	☐The Roman Catholic Church has retained the traditional form of private baptism which can take place at any time by arrangement with the priest. Baptism may also be carried out during Mass.
Arrangements before the ceremony	☐After the details of the ceremony have been worked out with the priest, the parents must decide whether to invite friends and relations. If the

baptism is private, it is customary to have a small gathering around the font: parents, grandparents, godparents, other members of the family and some close friends. All foregather in the parents' house or some other suitable meeting place and proceed together to the church or, if this is impracticable, meet at the church.
☐The family is generally responsible for decorating the font with flowers although this detail should be checked with the clergyman concerned. The priest will distribute the form of service for the participants.

Godparents   ☐These are selected by the parents and may be members of the family or close friends. Under canon law of the Church of England a boy has two godfathers and one godmother and a girl two god-mothers and one godfather. In the Roman Catholic church a child has one godfather and one godmother. In practice these numbers are frequently exceeded.
☐Both churches require the godparents to be baptized, confirmed and practising Christians and in the course of the new liturgies of each church, the godparents are asked explicitly to express their own faith. The Roman Catholic church will permit in certain circumstances a baptized and practising Christian 'from a separated Church or community' to act as a godparent provided that the other is a Catholic. The Church of England is equally flexible.
☐It is a great compliment to be invited to stand as a godparent to a child, and a thoughtful godparent is a precious gift for a child to acquire at birth.

Declining   ☐Potential godparents should be approached in good time. If anyone refuses to stand, this must be accepted gracefully and thankfully for the child's sake. It is quite in order to decline and better to do so than to accept and ignore any further responsibility once the christening is over.

Proxies   ☐A godparent who is unable to attend the christening ceremony may ask a friend to stand proxy. Alternatively, the parents will make the arrangements with someone whom they know will be present.

Duties

☐In the Church of England it is customary for a godmother to hold the child at the font until the priest takes over; in the Roman Catholic church the mother holds her child throughout the ceremony. All godparents join with the parents in the responses.

☐The duties of the godparents do not end with the ceremony and traditional christening gift. As the child grows, the link forged at baptism should become a bond; only the godparent can ensure that this occurs.

Church of England ceremony

☐The liturgy from which the variant services in use today derive is set out in the *Book of Common Prayer* (1662).

☐The service begins with prayers and a reading from the Gospel of St Mark followed by a brief commentary, the promises by the godparents, including the renunciation of the devil and all his works, and the Apostles' Creed; then follows the blessing of the water, the naming of the child by the godparents, the baptism and the signing of the cross on the child's forehead; the concluding prayers include the request addressed to the godparents to ensure that the child is virtuously brought up as a Christian and later confirmed.

☐The *Alternative Service Book,* 1980 contains the initiation services which include the service of baptism (*Series 3*) and, in addition, *Series 2,* which has been authorized by the General Synod for use until further notice.

Alternative Services Series 2

☐This simplifies the presentation and the language of the earlier liturgy.

☐There are some variations. The directions to the parents and godparents on a Christian upbringing are outlined in the preface and spoken by the priest at the start of the service. The elaborate renunciation of the devil is reduced to the simple question: 'Do you renounce evil?' and the priest asks the parents and godparents to profess their own faith.

☐There is one additional ceremony. At the signing of the cross on the child's forehead, the priest gives to one of the parents or godparents a lighted candle saying to the child, 'I give you this sign, to show that you have passed from darkness into light'.

☐This service is authorized for use until further notice.

Alternative Services Series 3

☐This service is in modern English; the structure and the presentation closely resemble that of Series 2. Both services are designed to simplify the rite and drastic pruning makes them suitable for inclusion in Morning or Evening Prayer or the Holy Communion services.

Roman Catholic ceremony

☐The Roman Catholic rite of baptism is more elaborate than that of the Church of England. It has been revised and restructured since the Second Vatican Council and is divided into three parts beginning with the preparatory rite.

☐The first words are addressed to the parents and godparents. The child is welcomed into the Christian community by the priest who traces on its forehead the sign of the cross and asks the parents and godparents to do the same. A reading from the Gospel is followed by a brief homily and prayers, including a single prayer of exorcism no longer addressed to Satan but to God. The priest anoints the child on the breast with oil of catechumens (the oil of salvation) and lays his hand on the child.

☐The second part of the ceremony consists of the conferring of the sacrament, the blessing of the water, the renunciation of Satan by parents and godparents, and their threefold confession of faith. This is followed by the baptism throughout which the mother holds her child.

☐After the baptism, the child is anointed with chrism (oil blessed on Maundy Thursday) on the

crown of the head.
☐The concluding ceremonies form the third part;
the child is clothed with a white garment and the
father or godfather lights a candle from the paschal
candle held by the priest: 'Receive the light of
Christ'. The rite of Ephphetha may follow here in
which the priest touches the ears and mouth of the
child, but this is optional.
☐Finally, the Lord's Prayer is recited, the priest
blesses the mother who holds the child in her arms,
then the father, and lastly the entire assembly. The
threefold blessing ends the ceremony.

Baptism during Mass

☐The rite of baptism may also be carried out
during Mass. The introductory rite, as above,
replaces the penitential rite of the Mass. The
baptism takes place following the homily after the
gospel.

After the ceremony

☐It is customary to invite the officiating clergyman,
the godparents, family and friends to some festivity
afterwards, depending on the time of day.
☐Christening parties are generally small, informal
affairs in the parents' house. If the christening takes
place in the morning a lunch party would be
appropriate; private baptism in the early afternoon
is generally followed by tea and christening cake or,
later in the afternoon by a drinks party.

Christening presents

☐These are given to a child by parents, godparents
and close members of the family—grandparents for
example. Presents are not expected from others
although friends who visit the mother and child in
hospital may bear a small gift.

Suitable gifts

☐The golden rule in choosing christening presents
is probably to think in terms of the future and not
of the present. A gift of money is appropriate and
antiques of all kinds, including silver, porcelain and
glass, maps, prints and books are suitable. Wine is
a traditional gift and port, claret and burgundy can
be purchased for laying down for the future.

Jewellery remains a most desirable present for girls.
☐One old country custom that deserves to be
encouraged is the planting of trees to commemorate
an event such as a christening.

Announcing a
christening

☐Christenings may be announced on the court and
social pages of *The Times, The Independent* and *The*
Daily Telegraph at the advertised rates, but this is
increasingly rare. Notices are submitted to the social
editor in writing.

Example

The infant daughter of
Mr and Mrs John
Harris was christened
Alice Mary by the Rev
George Roberts at the
Church of the Holy
Trinity, Ryde, on Satur-
day, April 13. The
godparents are Mr Robert
Grant, Mrs Hugo Edwards
and Mrs Anthony Smith
(for whom Mrs John
Parker stood proxy).

Dress

☐Dress at christenings tends to be elaborate.
Godmothers will almost certainly wear hats and
dresses suitable both for church and the festivities
after the ceremony.
☐Men wear suits.
☐Christening robes are by ancient tradition always
white and often they are handed down through
several generations. Sometimes the costume
includes a white baby's bonnet.

BERIT MILAH

☐It is the Jewish law that at the age of eight days,
male infants are taken by their parents to be
circumcised. This is a religious ceremony presided
over by an official trained to perform the rite, a
mohel.
☐Guests are invited to attend.
☐The child is held by his godfather during the

operation and a special prayer is said by the father. Afterwards, the *mohel* recites prayers and blessings over a cup of wine and the child is given a name. ☐Some Reform Jews dispense altogether with the ceremony surrounding the operation. In their congregation, it is customary for babies of both sexes to be brought to the synagogue for a blessing. This is usually incorporated into the service on the Sabbath.

FIRST COMMUNION ☐This precedes confirmation in the life of a Roman Catholic child. The simplest instruction at school or in the parish is given by the priest who administers the sacrament to a number of children at a special Mass.
☐This takes place at the impressionable age of seven or eight; the white dresses and veils worn by the girls add to the excitement and sense of occasion. The ceremony is usually followed by a party.

CONFIRMATION ☐A child is confirmed as soon as he is old enough to be instructed in the Christian faith and to renew for himself the vows taken by his godparents on his behalf at baptism. The rite bestows on the baptized the grace of the Holy Spirit and strengthens the recipient to lead a Christian life.

Church of England ☐It is customary to confirm children between the ages of twelve and fourteen. Parents are responsible for arranging that the child receives instruction either at school or from his parish priest.
☐Confirmation is administered by a bishop to each child in the form of a prayer and the laying on of his hand.
☐The ceremony may take place at school, or if the child is prepared in his home parish he will join others at what is generally an annual ceremony. Each child is accompanied by a godparent—a baptized and confirmed Christian but not necessarily one of the baptismal godparents—as a witness of the confirmation. Parents may act in

this capacity.

☐The child's first communion follows as soon as possible after confirmation and may be incorporated in the confirmation service.

Roman Catholic ☐The age for confirmation varies according to the diocese, but the responsibility for bringing the child to be confirmed lies with the parents. Instruction, as for first communion, is given at school or in the parish in which the child lives or worships.

☐The confirmation ceremony is a family occasion with the parents participating. In addition, each child has a sponsor who accompanies him throughout the ceremony and should be, if possible, the baptismal godfather or godmother.

☐Confirmation takes place within the Mass or at a separate ceremony. It is usually administered by a bishop although in certain cases a priest may do so. The rite is simple. Each child kneels before the bishop. He extends his hands over the child and prays. He dips his right thumb in the chrism (oil blessed on Maundy Thursday) and traces the sign of the cross on the child's forehead.

Jewish ☐The Reform synagogue has instituted a confirmation ceremony for the children of its members. Both boys and girls take part, reciting passages from the scriptures and pledging their faith in Judaism.

☐To ensure that the nature of the ceremony is fully understood, sixteen or seventeen years is the usual age for confirmation. Bar-mitzvah does not necessarily preclude confirmation and some boys celebrate both rites.

☐The social festivities surrounding bar-mitzvah do not occur at confirmation; there is no banquet, and presents —other than one or two of a religious nature—are not given.

BAR-MITZVAH ☐A male child is called up in the synagogue to the reading of the Torah on the first possible occasion

after his thirteenth birthday. This follows a period
of religious instruction which begins when he is of
school age.
☐The ceremony symbolizes the boy's attainment of
maturity and demonstrates in public his new role as
a full member of the community. The joyful nature
of the occasion is reflected in the atmosphere of the
morning service on the Sabbath when a bar-mitzvah
is celebrated. Frequently a special sermon is
delivered by the rabbi. Great emphasis is laid on
the nature of the responsibilities the boy assumes,
particularly with regard to his family and to the
Jewish community. He is urged to observe the
commandments of the Torah in his own life and to
pass on his knowledge of the Law to succeeding
generations. This is an important occasion in Jewish
family life. A banquet is held for relations and
friends either on the day of the bar-mitzvah or on
the following day.
☐Formal invitations are issued to the banquet. It is
the custom for all guests to give presents.

2 ENGAGEMENTS TO BE MARRIED

Historical background

☐The promise to marry or give in marriage was known in the past as a betrothal. This was a ceremony which went back to biblical times and was considered for centuries as binding as marriage itself.

☐A girl's betrothal was frequently arranged to serve a dynastic end with property and money involved. This led to great abuse and the Church was forced at one time to forbid the betrothal of children under the age of seven.

☐The essence of the bethrothal ceremony was the giving of a ring by the man to the woman in the presence of a priest and other witnesses. The betrothal could be dissolved by mutual consent but public betrothal signified a pledge to marry, hence the disappointed lovers throughout history who have resorted to the courts for redress.

☐Elaborate betrothal ceremonies no longer take place in Britain but vestiges of this ancient tradition remain. The pledge has been absorbed into the marriage service; the words 'Thereto I plight thee my troth', which occur in both the Church of England and the Roman Catholic liturgy, are echoes of the formal ceremony of the past. And the custom of giving a ring at the time of betrothal as a symbol of the pledge to marry has survived as part of the engagement ritual.

☐Today, the announcement of an engagement is a public expression on the part of two people of their intention to marry.

PROHIBITED MARRIAGES

☐It is as well for a couple who are related to one another to check that they are legally entitled to marry.

☐The *Book of Common Prayer* contains a list of relationships considered too close for marriage. They are as follows:

☐A man may not marry his mother, daughter, father's mother, mother's mother, son's daughter, daughter's daughter, sister, father's daughter, mother's daughter, wife's mother, wife's daughter, father's wife, son's wife, father's

27

father's wife, mother's father's wife, wife's father's mother, wife's mother's mother, wife's son's daughter, wife's daughter's daughter, son's son's wife, daughter's son's wife, father's sister, mother's sister, brother's daughter, sister's daughter.
☐A woman may not marry her
father, son, father's father, mother's father, son's son, daughter's son, brother, father's son, mother's son, husband's father, husband's son, mother's husband, daughter's husband, father's mother's husband, mother's mother's husband, husband's father's father, husband's mother's father, husband's son's son, husband's daughter's son, son's daughter's husband, daughter's daughter's husband, father's brother, mother's brother, brother's son, sister's son.

Legal revisions

☐The above remained the law of the land until widened by the Marriage Acts of 1907 and 1921. These permit a man's marriage to his deceased wife's sister, deceased brother's widow, deceased wife's brother's daughter, deceased wife's sister's daughter, father's deceased brother's widow, mother's deceased brother's widow, deceased wife's father's sister, deceased wife's mother's sister, brother's deceased son's widow and sister's deceased son's widow.
☐The Marriage (Enabling) Act of 1960 permits a man to contract a valid marriage with the sister, aunt or niece of his former wife and the former wife of his brother, uncle or nephew provided that both parties are domiciled in Great Britain.
☐The civil acts apply similarly to women.

Religious restrictions

☐Church of England and Roman Catholic clergymen may refuse to solemnize a marriage between two people whose degree of relationship is considered too close by their respective churches but is acceptable to the civil authorities; a Registrar of Marriages, on the other hand, is bound to marry any couple legally entitled to do so.

28

☐A rabbi will advise on relationships considered incestuous in Jewish law.

**ANNOUNCING
ENGAGEMENTS**

☐Many people today who announce their engagements do so in a traditional manner: parents and close friends are told first, followed by a formal notice in a newspaper. Others prefer to announce their intentions informally or keep them firmly to themselves. The old and well-tried method has many advantages and will induce the maximum of goodwill on the part of parents who are generally grateful for an unequivocal statement on the intentions of their offspring.

☐Social pressures on a couple to announce their engagement have lessened, but more personal ones from family and friends remain; silence, until a firm decision on future plans has been made, is always preferable to a hasty announcement followed by a sad retraction.

☐Those who have lived together for some time may prefer to announce their forthcoming marriage shortly before the event takes place, instead of their engagement.

**Length of
engagements**

☐Long engagements are trying experiences. If for one reason or another no date can be fixed for the wedding, it is probably better to postpone any announcement until plans have been finalized. Engagements vary greatly in length, depending generally on the arrangements that must be made both before marriage and for the day itself. It is difficult to generalize but six months is probably an ideal length for an engagement.

**Announcing to
parents**

☐Parents should be told as soon as possible whatever their likely reactions. It was rare in the past for a girl to accept an offer of marriage from a man who was unknown to her family; even today an engagement is more often than not an event that has been anticipated by parents. But if they have not met their prospective son- or daughter-in-law, it is tactful whenever feasible to arrange a meeting before any question of an engagement or marriage is raised.

☐It is customary for a young man to have an informal talk with the girl's father on the subject of finances and prospects before any announcement is made. Parents expect this small act of courtesy, and their feelings at what is an emotional time should be taken into account whenever possible.

☐A man informs his own parents of his plans; his parents write immediately to his fiancée whether she is known to them or not. (See 'Contact between families'.)

☐If an engagement is welcomed by the parents, there is no difficulty; if hostility is anticipated, it is better to abide by the rules at this stage than to court further opposition. Any breach of family ties is bound to strain a relationship and the outcome of divided loyalties is rarely predictable.

Contact between families

☐It is customary for the bridegroom's parents (usually his mother) to write at once to the bride's parents. The letter should express pleasure at the engagement and, if the two parties are not personally known to each other, a desire to meet before the wedding takes place. The letter should be answered without delay.

☐If it is not possible for geographical or other good reasons to meet for dinner or lunch, the bridegroom's parents may suggest a weekend visit.

Announcing to family and friends

☐In the past, it was customary for a girl's mother to inform relations and close friends of the family of her daughter's engagement before any public announcement was made. Now the task is generally shared. The young man is responsible for informing his own relations and friends.

☐It is most important to ensure that members of the family, godparents, benefactors and certain close friends are told before there is any chance of them hearing the news at second-hand; no subsequent action can make up for this neglect.

Second marriages   ☐Widows and widowers write to the parents of
their deceased spouse before they announce their
engagement. Those who are divorced do so if
relations are amicable. This contact is essential,
however, where children are involved so that
grandparents are aware of the changed
circumstances.

Public   ☐Engagements are formally announced in the
announcements   forthcoming marriages column on the court and
social pages of *The Times, The Independent* and *The
Daily Telegraph*, or in *The Guardian*, the *Jewish
Chronicle, Scotsman* and many local newspapers. The
text of the court and social page announcements
must be submitted to the social editor in writing and
be signed by one of the parties or by a parent.
☐It is customary for the bride's parents to arrange
and to pay for this announcement to appear. The
particulars include the names and parentage of the
betrothed, and usually their addresses. However,
some people refrain from adding addresses.

Examples   **Mr E.R. Smith
and Miss J.R. Greene**
The engagement is
announced between
Edward, second son of
Mr and Mrs E.L. Smith
of 14 Cumberland
Square, London SW1,
and Julia, only daughter
of Major R.A. Greene
of Spring Cottage, Stone,
and the late Mrs Greene

**Captain G.T. Aitken
and Miss R.E. Harris**
A marriage has been
arranged and will shortly
take place between
Captain George Aitken,
Royal Lowland Fusiliers,

son of Colonel R.E.
Aitken DSO and Mrs
Aitken of The Priory,
Edinburgh, and
Rosemary, daughter of
Mr and Mrs R.H.
Harris of 21 Eaton
Road, London W1

**Dr R.B. Jones
and Miss E.F. Lee**
The forthcoming
marriage is announced
between Richard, son
of Mr and Mrs Robert
Jones of Old House,
Portmadoc, and
Elizabeth, youngest
daughter of Dr Edward
Lee of 10 Market Place,
Aylesbury, and Mrs
A.H. Ward of 5 The
Drive, Brighton

Second marriages ☐If a person who has been widowed or divorced for
some time plans to remarry, an announcement of
the engagement is made if desired in the
newspapers. (Those waiting on a divorce to remarry
do not formally announce their engagement.)

**Mr R.N. Grant
and Mrs N.A. Richardson**
The engagement is
announced between
Robert, son of Mr and
Mrs F.R. Grant of 5
Belgrave Square, London
W1, and Nicola Anne,
youngest daughter of Mr
and Mrs E.R. Baker of
12 The Grove, London
W11

Magazines ☐There are several magazines that publish photographs of engaged couples. For many years, *Country Life* has devoted its frontispiece to a photograph of an engaged girl.
☐Photographs should be submitted to the editor of the magazine selected with the appropriate information about the couple enclosed.

LETTERS OF CONGRATULA-TION ☐The announcements will bring letters of congratulation which should be answered as soon as possible. The letters are addressed either to the girl or to her fiancé but not jointly. This may necessitate two letters.
☐The replies provide a good opportunity to let people know of any wedding plans already made; if the wedding is to be a quiet occasion now is a good time to make this clear.

CELEBRATIONS TO MARK THE ENGAGEMENT ☐These may be formal or informal as circumstances dictate. It was customary in the past for the bride's parents to arrange and to pay for a celebratory dinner to which the parents of the fiancé would be invited. This remains the most agreeable way to celebrate an engagement and an ideal opportunity to bring the two sets of parents together. The dinner party takes place on the day the announcement is made or shortly afterwards. The nature of the celebration is explained to the guests when they are invited; presents are not expected. If the health of the couple is drunk, this is proposed by the girl's father.
☐A similar entertainment may be given by the young man's parents. These are generally intimate, family occasions.
☐Both sets of parents may decide to hold a drinks party in their respective houses to celebrate the event, and to introduce their future son- or daughter-in-law to a wider circle of friends than would be possible at a dinner party.
☐Frequently, an engaged couple will hold a more informal party themselves or have one given for them.

Invitations to engaged couples

☐Invitations to social events during the course of the engagement should include both parties whenever possible.

ENGAGEMENT PRESENTS

☐The girl receives her engagement ring and gives a present to her fiancé. This may take the form of gold cuff-links, a watch, a signet ring (if he does not possess one), reflect some particular interest or add to a collection (a book, a drawing or water-colour, a snuff box), according to individual taste.

Engagement rings

☐Engagement rings have a longer history than wedding rings; for thousands of years they have symbolized the pledge to marry. The Romans used iron betrothal rings sometimes set with precious stones, but by the fifteenth century the diamond was established as the favourite choice for a betrothal stone and remains so to this day.

Symbolism and superstition

☐Gemstones have been invested through the ages with all kinds of properties, magical and otherwise. Rubies were considered symbols of intense devotion, helping their wearers to resist the temptations of the flesh and to obtain honour and respect; sapphires were symbols of undying affection and emeralds of hope, inducing in their wearers chastity in both body and speech. The amethyst was thought to give protection against nightmares and drunkenness; moonstones were supposed to bring luck; and the turquoise to grow pale in the presence of poison. The opal has always had a sinister reputation and a gift of pearls is still thought to bring tears.

Conventions of style

☐Many early betrothal rings have survived, some bearing the most delightful inscriptions engraved on the inside. The harlequin ring was popular in late Victorian and Edwardian times; this was composed of different stones whose initial letters spelt out a word. 'REGARD', produced by a sequence of ruby, emerald, garnet, amethyst, ruby and diamond is an example; Queen Alexandra's engagement ring in similar fashion spelt 'BERTIE'.

□In the last hundred years, rings have assumed a fairly conventional pattern—a half hoop of diamonds, a solitaire diamond or a stone set in a circlet of diamonds. The stone may be a precious stone—a diamond, ruby, emerald or sapphire—or one of the many attractive semi-precious stones.

Choosing an engagement ring

□The choice of stone and style, antique or modern, is made by the girl and paid for by the man. He may ask a jeweller to make a selection in a given price range from which the girl may make her choice. But there are so many rings on the market that the girl may prefer to be given an indication of what she can spend and look at a far wider range in a number of different shops. Antique rings are popular and there are some gifted modern jewellery designers at work.

PHOTOGRAPHS

□Photographs are part of the traditional engage-ment ritual. As they tend to adorn the drawing-rooms of parents, parents-in-law, grandparents and aunts for a very long time indeed, it is essential to select a good photographer. The easiest way is probably to glance through the pages of one of the magazines that feature the work of society photographers; each photograph will be credited with a name. The photographer's secretary will give an idea of the fees involved and advise on suitable dress.

BREAKING AN ENGAGEMENT

□This is an ordeal that is always embarrassing and painful, particularly when two people belong to the same circle of friends. But the sooner this is faced, the better. *No explanation is necessary.*

□It is customary for the girl to announce that the engagement is broken. The girl's mother may wish to make an announcement in the newspapers; this was common practice in the past where an engagement had been announced formally, and such announcements still appear from time to time. However, this is by no means obligatory.

□Parents inform members of the family and close friends may be written to or telephoned with the news.

Press announcement

□If an announcement in the press is thought necessary, a notice is placed on the court and social pages. Notices must be submitted in writing to the social editor and signed by both parties.

The marriage arranged between
Mr Robert Smith and Miss Elizabeth Jones
will not take place.

When invitations have been sent

□If wedding invitations have been sent out, notes are sent stating simply that the ceremony will no longer take place; these may be worded formally and printed, or written informally. Guests should be telephoned if there is not time enough to inform them by post (See also 'Cancellation of Wedding', Chapter Three).

Return of presents

□The engagement ring and any presents that have passed between the couple are returned. All wedding presents should be carefully packed and returned to the donors with a letter of thanks.

3 WEDDINGS

☐The organization of a large wedding is such a daunting task that the mixed reaction of many newly-engaged couples to the prospect is hardly surprising.

☐Some brides-to-be have no doubts at all about their capabilities and relish every detail of the intricate arrangements, whereas others are lucky enough to have a member of the family or a friend who is only too happy to shoulder much of the burden.

☐More men than women appear to favour a register office wedding on the grounds that ceremony is kept to a minimum. But a registrar standing by his desk lacks the significance of a clergyman at his altar and this thought, with the tendency of plans to snowball, often results in a larger wedding than was envisaged at the outset—in a church or synagogue and with all the traditional accompaniments. Such an occasion makes a splendid start to married life whether there are 15, 50 or 500 guests, and, in retrospect, the hard work and the efforts of everyone concerned to make the day memorable will appear very worthwhile.

LEGAL POINTS

☐The legal minimum age for marriage in the United Kingdom is 16, but anyone between the ages of 16 and 18 who wishes to marry in England or Wales must obtain the written consent of their parents or legal guardian; this parental consent is not required in Scotland.

☐A couple related to each other who wish to marry should check that their relationship does not fall into a category forbidden by civil or religious law (see 'Engagements', page 27).

Authorized ceremonies

☐A marriage is authorized to take place by various means of which the three following are the most usual: first, according to the rites of the Church of England; second, according to the rites of other religious denominations and with the certificate of a civil superintendent registrar of marriages;

third, at a civil ceremony in a register office
conducted by a superintendent registrar of
marriages without any religious service.
☐If a marriage takes place outside a church of the
Church of England, the building must be registered
for the purpose *except* in the case of the Jewish
community and among members of the Religious
Society of Friends (Quakers) who are not bound by
this law and are permitted to conduct marriages
wherever they wish to do so.

Witnesses ☐A marriage must be witnessed by at least two
people aged 18 or over and by either the Church of
England clergyman conducting the service, or in the
case of marriages in other denominations and in
civil marriages, by an 'authorized' person, that is
the registrar, his deputy, or a clergyman authorized
to do so by the registrar.

Exception ☐Jews and the Quakers are not required to obtain
this authorization.

RELIGIOUS AND ☐Churches, synagogues and registry offices all
CIVIL have requirements and codes of eligibility that must
REQUIREMENTS be met before a marriage ceremony can be
performed. These usually involve residential
stipulations, declarations of religious affiliation and
licences.

Church of England ☐The vicar or curate of the church chosen for the
wedding should be contacted before any other
plans are made or dates fixed. There are various
steps that need to be taken before the marriage can
be solemnized and he will explain these and make
certain that the couple are entitled to marry and
have, or will provide, the necessary legal
qualifications. He will also wish to have two
or three talks on the nature and meaning
of Christian marriage.

Eligibility ☐As far as the requirements of the church are
concerned, one or other should have been baptized

into a Christian church (not necessarily the Church of England) but if neither has, and a church wedding is desired, adult baptism is a possibility that can be discussed with the clergyman.

Divorced persons

☐The marriage of a divorced person is not permitted if the former spouse is still alive.

Choice of church

☐By tradition, a marriage takes place in the bride's parish church. However, this is a matter of sentiment, not law, and there are alternatives such as the bridegroom's parish church or one in which either the groom or the bride has worshipped for long enough to place his or her name on the electoral roll.

☐If a church with which the couple have no links is chosen, a London church perhaps, it is necessary for one of them to establish 'residence' in the parish for 15 days.

The publication of banns

☐A marriage can take place in the Church of England by one of several means but this is the most popular and straightforward method. The clergymen of the parishes of both the future bride and bridegroom read out the banns during a service in their respective churches on three successive Sundays; anyone in the congregation with doubts about the qualification of the couple to marry is asked to give his reasons.

☐The couple must continue to live in the parishes concerned during the three weeks in which the banns are read.

☐The clergyman who performs the wedding ceremony will require a certificate from the clergyman of the other parish stating that the banns have been read and that no objection to the marriage has been received.

☐As soon as this has been established to the clergyman's satisfaction, the couple may be married by arrangement with him on any day between the hours of 8am and 6pm during the course of the following three months.

Second reading □The banns must be read a second time if the three-month period is exceeded.

Fees for publication of banns □Fees are payable for the publication of banns, the certificate of banns and to the clergyman for conducting the marriage ceremony.

Marriage by common licence □This is an alternative to the reading of banns and enables a marriage to take place at one day's notice.
□Residential qualifications are still needed but these are not so strict: only one party need establish residence in a parish for 15 days immediately prior to the application.
□The vicar of the parish may grant the licence himself, or give the address of the nearest surrogate for granting marriage licences in the diocese, or of the Faculty Office; this licence must be applied for in person and is valid for a period of three months.
□Fees are payable for the licence and to the clergyman for conducting the ceremony.

Marriage by special licence □Special licences are issued in exceptional circumstances and enable a marriage to take place at any time and place. These are issued on the authority of the Archbishop of Canterbury through the Faculty Office.
□Residential qualifications are not necessary and the building in which the ceremony takes place need not be registered for marriages (eg a private chapel or a hospital).
□Fees are payable at the Faculty Office and to the clergyman conducting the ceremony.

Certificate of the superintendent registrar of marriages □The superintendent registrar of marriages (the civil authority) may issue a certificate that technically enables a couple to marry in church without the calling of banns. This remains, however, entirely at the discretion of the clergyman who may insist that the couple also procure a common licence.
□Application may be made to the superintendent

registrar in whose district one or the other has lived for the seven days immediately before the notice is entered by the registrar. If the couple do not live in the same district, application must be made to the superintendent registrars in both.

☐Twenty-one clear days will elapse between the day on which the registrar enters the notice in his notice book and the day on which he issues the certificate.

☐The marriage may take place, as far as civil law is concerned, within three months *from the day on which it was entered.*

☐Fees are payable for the civil certificate and to the clergyman conducting the ceremony.

Church of Scotland

☐The reading of banns in the Church of Scotland has been abolished and application to the civil registrar must be made.

Marriage in the Church of Scotland

☐The registrar issues a Schedule of Marriage as soon as the civil regulations outlined below have been met.

☐After the ceremony, the Schedule must be signed by the bride and bridegroom, the clergyman and two witnesses of at least 14 years of age. This Schedule is then returned within three days to the registrar.

Roman Catholic

☐The priest of the parish church in which the marriage is planned to take place will need, in normal circumstances, a minimum of two or three months to ensure that the couple are adequately instructed in the step that they are about to take, and to complete the paper-work required by the church.

☐He will wish to see copies of the baptism and confirmation certificates of both parties before filling up the pre-nuptial enquiry forms.

☐The party who is not marrying in his or her own parish church must receive permission for the marriage to take place in another church and obtain what is known as a letter of freedom.

41

☐Banns are read only if both parties are Catholics.

Mixed marriages ☐The preference is always for Catholics to marry each other but the Catholic Church has modified its views on marriage between Catholics and non-Catholics in recent years particularly in cases where the non-Catholic partner is a Christian.
☐However, a Catholic is still required to obtain special dispensation to marry a non-Catholic. This dispensation can now be obtained from a parish priest.

Marrying in a non-Catholic church ☐If a Catholic wishes to marry a non-Catholic in a Christian church according to the rites of that church (the Church of England, for instance), dispensation must be obtained from a bishop.
☐In return for this dispensation, the Catholic partner must agree to preserve his faith, to respect his partner's faith and to do all in his power 'within the unity of the marriage' to have all his children baptized and brought up in the Catholic Church.
☐The priest will wish to see the non-Catholic's baptism certificate and to arrange the necessary course of instruction.

Civil requirements ☐As soon as arrangements have been finalized with the priest, the certificate of the superintendent registrar of marriages must be obtained from the register office (see pages 43–45).

Jewish ☐Jewish weddings usually take place in a synagogue but as the Jews are not required to marry in buildings registered for the purpose, the use of a secular building is also permissible.
☐Marriages do not take place between sunset on Friday and sunset the following day (the Sabbath), on the Day of Atonement or on any other major festival or fast day. Sunday is the most popular choice.

Civil requirements ☐In all cases, the certificate of the superintendent registrar of marriages must be obtained from the register office (see below and pages 44–45).

The Religious Society of Friends (Quakers)

☐ The registering officer of each Monthly Meeting will give advice and information to those wishing to marry and he will issue the forms that must be completed.

☐ An announcement of the intended marriage is given at the Sunday morning meetings of which the couple are members. If no objection is received by the registering officer, arrangements for the marriage can go ahead.

Civil requirements

☐ The certificate of the superintendent registrar of marriages must be obtained from the register office (see below).

Civil marriages in England and Wales

☐ There are many people who have no religious affiliations and prefer to be married at a civil ceremony. This is a straightforward proceeding at which vows are exchanged before a superintendent registrar of marriages.

☐ This matter-of-fact approach to marriage is not acceptable to everyone, but those who are divorced and are debarred by their church from a religious ceremony for as long as the divorced partner is still alive have little choice.

Application

☐ The superintendent registrar's office (this is listed in the telephone directory under Registration of Births, Deaths and Marriages) will supply an application form. Names, ages, addresses, details of the marital status and occupations of the couple, the office in which they intend to be married and their residential qualifications must be entered. If either of the parties has been divorced, a copy of the decree absolute must be produced, and the death certificate of a spouse if either is a widow or widower.

Registrar's Certificate

☐ The superintendent registrar will issue a certificate with or without licence depending on the length of time before the wedding takes place (22 days or one clear day).

This registrar's certificate is not required before a Church of England wedding takes place but is obligatory in every other instance of marriage in this country.

Superintendent registrar's certificate without licence

□To qualify, both parties must have established a place of residence in a district for seven days immediately preceding the giving of notice to the registrar.
□The notice may be given by either party but if they live in different districts notice must be given to the superintendent registrar of each district.
□The building in which the marriage is to take place must be specified in every notice of marriage.
□A period of 21 clear days must intervene between the day on which the superintendent registrar enters the notice in his notice book and the day on which he issues his certificate. The marriage may take place by appointment within three months from the day on which the notice was entered by the superintendent registrar.

Superintendent registrar's certificate and licence

□To qualify, both parties must be in England and Wales or usually reside there on the day the notice is given; only one notice is required and this may be given by either party, one of whom must have lived in the registration district where notice is given for the 15 days immediately preceding the giving of notice. The marriage must take place in that district and in the building specified in the notice. One clear day (other than a Sunday, Christmas Day or Good Friday) must intervene between entry of the notice and issue of the certificate and licence. The marriage may take place by appointment within three months from the day on which the notice was entered.

Marriage by registrar general's licence

□This licence enables a person who is seriously ill and not expected to recover to be married in a house or hospital. The superintendent registrar of marriages will explain what evidence is required before a licence can be granted.

Civil marriages in Scotland

□A civil marriage is authorized by publication of notice at the registrar's office of the district in which the parties live.

□To qualify, a person must have his or her usual residence in Scotland, or have lived in Scotland for 15 clear days immediately preceding the application to the registrar. If one party lives in England or Wales, a superintendent registrar's certificate without licence is valid in Scotland and is applied for in the usual way.

□Forms must be signed in the presence of two householders who sign as witnesses. The notice remains on view for the subsequent seven days; if no valid objections to the marriage are received by the registrar, he will issue a Certificate of Publication. This enables a marriage to take place in the following three months.

□In certain emergencies, a sheriff's licence is granted which is valid for ten days.

THE ARRANGEMENTS

□Two decisions must be made at the outset that will influence every detail of the arrangements. The first concerns the nature of the wedding ceremony—whether it is religious or civil—and the second, the size and scope of the reception.

Type of ceremony

□The bride and bridegroom alone decide whether they marry in a church, a synagogue, a meeting house or a register office; they may belong to the same denomination, which simplifies the decision they have to make, or they may not, which calls for one or the other to compromise. If this proves difficult, the problem should be resolved with as little parental interference as possible.

The reception

□The question of the reception, however, is by long-standing tradition the responsibility of the bride's parents and they should be consulted before anyone else.

□The bride will have an idea of what her parents can afford and she should take her fiancé fully into her confidence on this point. There may be no financial problems, in which case the bride's parents will make themselves responsible for the arrangements and payments which fall by tradition to them. But it is unfair to press parents of slender means to provide a lavish celebration that they cannot afford. However, most parents enjoy their prerogative in this respect and as many bridegrooms and brides today are prepared to contribute to the costs of the wedding, the final sum should not be prohibitive.

The date □The bride and bridegroom have their own worldly responsibilities which they take into account first. Dates are then discussed with both sets of parents, the person officiating at the wedding and the organizers of the reception.
□Spring and summer weddings are the most popular choice, for the abundance of flowers and the chance of warmer weather make a more agreeable prospect than the rain and the ice of autumn and winter.
□Weddings in Lent are usually avoided in the Church of England and the Roman Catholic Church.
□The idea that May is an unlucky month for weddings ('Marry in May, rue for aye') is an ancient superstition.

The time □The most popular time of day for a wedding is the early afternoon. This gives plenty of time for the bride to have her hair done, the flowers to be arranged and the food made ready and also for the guests to assemble, particularly if they have long distances to travel.
□A convenient time for country weddings is 2.30pm on a Saturday: this allows for a service of three quarters of an hour and a reception of two — two and a half hours, the bride and bridegroom leaving about 5.30pm and the guests soon after.
□Town weddings on weekdays frequently begin later, between 3pm and 5pm, with a reception held at a time when everyone can attend without

disrupting a working day.

☐In the past, weddings were not permitted to take place after noon; thus, a morning wedding was followed by a wedding breakfast. But in the course of this century, the hour was advanced to 3pm and later to 6pm (as it now stands) with the result that the old form has been entirely superseded by the modern custom of holding an afternoon or early evening reception.

Responsibilities

☐As soon as the date, the time and the place of the wedding service and the reception have been decided upon, the other arrangements can be put in motion. These, summarized below, fall by tradition into two groups: those made (and paid for) by the bridegroom; and those made by the bride and her parents (and paid for by her father).

The bride and bridegroom's joint responsibilities

☐They plan the wedding service with the clergyman and help to draw up a list of wedding guests; they decide about wedding present lists.

The bride's responsibilities

☐She arranges the decoration of the church and discusses the music with the organist; she chooses her bridesmaids, pages and their dresses, also her own dress, trousseau and 'going away' outfit; she books a hairdresser.

The bridegroom's responsibilities

☐He draws up an invitation list with his parents; he chooses his best man and the ushers; he pays for the wedding ring and all fees and expenses at the church except for the flowers and the music (organist and choir); he buys presents for the bridesmaids and pays for their bouquets and that of the bride, not forgetting a button-hole for himself; he organizes and pays for transport for himself and the best man to the church and for himself and his bride to the reception; he arranges and pays for the honeymoon.

The bride's parents' responsibilities

☐They draw up the guest list in collaboration with the bride and bridegroom and his parents; they arrange to have the invitations engraved and the order of service (chosen by the bride and bridegroom) printed for the ushers to hand out to guests in church (it is also their duty to pay for these); they pay for the flowers in church and the music, also the carpeting up the nave and the awning outside the church (if these are provided); they order, plan and pay for the reception including flower decorations, the drink, the wedding cake and food; the photographer and toastmaster; also the conveyance of the bride, the family and guests staying in the house to and from the church; they arrange for the display of wedding gifts (if done) and guards for these if considered necessary; they pay for the bride's dress, her trousseau and her going-away outfit (See also 'Reception costs', page 54).

Summary ☐Weddings do not run themselves; the success of such an occasion is in exact proportion to the amount of thought and hard work that goes into its planning. Details can go wrong, of course, through no fault of the organizers. But a wedding run with effortless ease and efficiency leaves less chance for untoward happenings: the bride arrives on time, the service is well rehearsed, the guests are not obliged to hang about in long queues or in the rain, the speeches are to the point and the wedding is meticulously timed to end at a certain moment—on these points hang the happiness of all concerned.

Church preparations ☐There are certain practical matters that must be discussed with the clergyman at an early stage. First and foremost, the wedding ceremony must be planned. The bride and bridegroom will have their own ideas on the subject, and the clergyman will outline what is and what is not permissible in his church. Together, the three will discuss and agree upon the form of the service and choose the hymns and the prayers. (For information about the types of services that may be held, see 'The wedding ceremony', which is described further on.)

Friends in Holy Orders

☐The bride or the bridegroom may have a relation or a close friend in Holy Orders whom they wish to officiate at the ceremony, or their parents may wish to ask a bishop to do so. The clergyman of the parish should be consulted before anyone else is invited to participate.

☐Generally speaking, the two will conduct the ceremony together with the bishop or the visiting priest marrying the couple and giving the address and the blessing.

☐Fees are paid to the parish clergyman and not to the visitor, but it is customary to give the latter a small gift (a book, perhaps), from the bridegroom if the contact is his, from the bride if hers, or from both the bridegroom and bride together if this is more appropriate.

Music

☐The clergyman will provide the names of the parish organist and choirmaster (if not already known) and perhaps give an idea of their capabilities. This is useful information; it may be worth importing an organist for the occasion particularly in a country parish. However, this may give great offence; so a tactful approach at an early stage is advisable. Certainly, the music must be discussed with the organist before any steps are taken to print the order of service. If both the bride and bridegroom are unmusical and the organist is unhelpful, the advice of a musical friend should be sought wherever possible. Music plays an important part in a wedding ceremony and a little time expended in the selection of music and musician should be rewarded by the appreciation of many in the congregation.

Service sheets

☐As soon as the order of service has been finalized, the text is sent to a printer. The Christian names or the initials of the bride and bridegroom, the name of the church and the date of the wedding are printed on the cover.

Flowers

☐The bride's ideas on the flower decorations

should also be discussed with the clergyman as he may well have views on their colour and positioning. □If more than one wedding is to take place in the church on the day (and this frequently happens in London), it is essential to liaise with the other bride about the flowers. It may even be possible to share them (see also page 54).

Photography and recordings

□The clergyman's views on the use of photographic and recording equipment in the church should be sought before any orders are given.

Design of church

□On one of their visits to the clergyman, the bride and bridegroom should examine the church in detail. The clergyman will know the seating capacity.
□It is worthwhile drawing a rough sketch plan of the seating arrangements and estimate how many members of the family can be seated in the front pews with a reasonable view of the ceremony. This plan can be passed on in due course to the ushers.
□The bride should note the width of the centre aisle as this will affect her procession and also the width of the chancel. She should check that there is a space in which the bridesmaids and pages can assemble to await her arrival.
□The bridegroom should plan where he is to wait with his best man before the ceremony and note the whereabouts of the vestry.
□Some churches, particularly grand London churches, provide a red carpet which can be laid from the altar to the street and an awning outside the church; these are available on payment of a fee and should be ordered well in advance.

Fees

□The bridegroom should check with the clergyman about the payment of fees. These may be paid by him in advance or by the best man immediately before the wedding ceremony.

Invitations

□The wedding guest list is drawn up by the bride's mother and father. They will have an idea of the number of people they wish to invite bearing in mind financial considerations, the capacity of the church and reception room if they have been chosen, and the wishes of the bride and bridegroom.

☐It is customary for the bride's parents to invite the bridegroom and his parents to submit half of the names. The guest list for a large wedding generally consists of members of the two families, parents' friends, and friends of the bride and bridegroom, in equal proportions. However small the wedding, the guest list is always divided between the two families. If one family is considerable larger than the other or has a wider circle of friends, an amicable compromise must be reached. But the bridegroom's parents should remember that they are not the final arbiters in this matter.

☐The invitations are sent out six clear weeks before the wedding takes place and are sent from the home of the bride's parents (or sponsors) whether they know the recipients or not. One is sent to the bridegroom's parents as a formality and others to the vicar and his wife, the priest or any other officiating clergyman.

☐If children are not included in the invitation they are not expected at the wedding.

Wording of invitations

☐For the correct format and wording of wedding invitations, see pages 189–191.

Enclosures

☐Sometimes maps, parking details or train timetables are enclosed to assist wedding guests. (For details of these, see 'Transport' below.)

Planning the reception

☐The bride's parents' house is the traditional setting for a wedding reception and many brides are anxious to be married from home rather than the less personal choices available. This is often the most agreeable for the guests too. A village church and a beautiful house and garden on a hot, summer afternoon is a magical setting but not every father

can oblige his daughter in such a way. More
frequently, the reality is acute lack of space and
stormy weather.

☐A marquee in the garden is one solution but this
is suitable only if there are enough bathrooms and
lavatories in the house for the guests, bedrooms in
which to leave coats and in which the bride and
bridegroom and their retinue can change, and
rooms where the catering staff can organize their
various functions. Also, a marquee is unsuitable for
winter weddings.

☐It is not unusual for a friend or relation to lend a
house for the occasion, failing which the choice lies
between an hotel, a club or perhaps an historic
house in the district with rooms available for hire.

☐As hotels, clubs and catering companies are
booked up for months ahead, it is essential to
secure the setting and/or the caterers before any
other arrangements are made.

Drinks ☐A dry champagne, generally non-vintage, is
usually served throughout the reception. Frequently
a dry white wine is offered as the alternative for
those who prefer a still wine, and whisky if the
reception is in the early evening. Soft drinks should
always be provided.

☐The choice of champagne and the quantity served
is a matter for discussion between the bride's father
and the caterer; a reputable wine merchant will
advise on the purchase and serving of champagne if
the bride's parents are making their own
arrangements for the reception.

☐At many weddings, particularly in the summer,
tea is served towards the end of the reception.

Food ☐If the reception takes place in a private house
and there is a good cook in the family, the food is
made at home. This may be impracticable, in which
case caterers are engaged.

☐Savouries, canapés, bouchées, vol-au-vents and so
forth, all small enough to be eaten with fingers,
provide the lightest refreshment and are handed

round by waiters or waitresses.
□If there is enough space, some of the cold food
may be laid out on one or more buffet tables ranged
along the sides of the reception room. The buffets
are covered by white-damask cloths and decorated
with flowers (see 'Buffets' in Chapter Six.)

Wedding-cake □This is traditionally a rich plum-cake elaborately
iced with appropriate decorations. Frequently, two
or more cakes are arranged in tiers. If the cake is
made by a caterer, it should be ordered in good
time and delivered, if necessary, the day before the
reception.
□Wedding-cakes are often home-made by the bride
herself or by her mother. If they feel that the iced
decoration is beyond their capabilities, the cake can
be taken to a professional to decorate—large
bakeries will advise on this point.
□If a bride or bridegroom is particularly fond of
some other variety of cake—chocolate cake, for
instance—and wishes to have this instead of plum-
cake, there is no reason why this whim should not
be indulged. There is one draw-back: chocolate
cake is not easy to eat and the thought of guests
with sticky fingers will probably deter many who are
initially attracted by the idea.
□The wedding-cake sits in the place of honour on
the buffet throughout the reception, or if there is no
buffet, on a small table awaiting the ceremonial
cutting by the bride and bridegroom.

Staff required □The following staff are required: a man or woman
to open the front door (if the reception is held at a
private house in a city or town); one or more women
to care for the coats (depending on the number of
guests); a toast-master to announce the guests and
introduce the speakers and to act as a master of
ceremonies; waiters or waitresses to hand round
the food and pour the drinks; car park attendants
(for country weddings); policemen to direct traffic
(for country weddings); a guard for the display of
wedding presents.

Reception costs	☐The cost of a wedding reception on any scale is considerable; although the tradition that the bride's parents pay is an ancient one, the bride herself or the bridegroom and his parents frequently do make a contribution. ☐If the bride's mother is a widow or her parents obviously lack the worldly means of the bridegroom's family, such an offer should be freely made and accepted without embarrassment. This matter is probably best discussed when the invitation list is drawn up, this being the only occasion when the bridegroom's parents have a hand in the arrangements.
Flowers	☐The creation of bouquets for a bride and her bridesmaids is such a specialized art that the bridegroom (whose gifts these are) is best advised to order them from an experienced florist. The bouquets provide the theme for the flower decorations in the church and at the reception.
Choice of bridal flowers	☐Flowers are chosen to harmonize with the dresses of the bride and her attendants. White or cream flowers are the most beautiful, reflecting the colours of the silk or the lace of the bride's wedding dress. Lilies, orchids, roses, stephanotis and lilies-of-the-valley are favourite choices, but pink or red roses or other brightly coloured flowers provide a stronger colour scheme if that is desired. ☐The bride's headdress is sometimes held in place by a circlet of flowers including, by ancient tradition, orange blossom, white heather and myrtle.
Church flowers	☐The flowers in church can present a glorious spectacle when they are imaginatively arranged, and as the congregation is able to sit and admire them for some length of time, the efforts of the flower arrangers will not be wasted. ☐The focal points for decoration are the chancel steps and the altar. The window sills provide further space for smaller arrangements. In summer, when flowers are plentiful, a small posy attached to

the ends of each pew gives an enchanting effect as the bride proceeds up the nave to the altar and helps create the impression that the church is filled with flowers.

Reception flowers ☐At the reception, an arrangement is placed at the entrance which guests will see when they arrive. Arrangements in the room in which the reception is held should be placed high enough to be seen above the heads' of the crowd. Flowers decorate the buffets and surround the wedding cake.

Dress ☐A formal wedding invitation indicates that the dress worn by all guests is expected to be formal too. A wedding provides a good excuse to dress up. Some people enjoy wearing elaborate or formal clothes but others find this tiresome. The effort involved should be made whenever possible as a compliment to the bride.

The bride ☐Wedding dresses bear little relationship to current fashion; each age evolves its own style which tends to draw deeply on inspiration from the past.
☐For almost 200 years, white—the symbol of purity—has been the traditional colour, and lace and silk the traditional materials, for wedding dresses. From time to time within this period other colours have been used, such as the shell-pink and pale blue fashionable in the 1920s; and lengths have varied over the years from the ankle to the knee— and above. But a long white dress has retained its favoured position over the years and shows every sign of continuing to do so.
☐Today, cream and ivory with gold and silver accessories are as popular as the traditional white. Dresses are of lace or silk with veils of lace or tulle held in place by a circlet of pearls or flowers, by hairpins concealed by tiny bunches of flowers, or by a diamond tiara.
☐Lace veils and tiaras are treasured by many families, and some brides wear the dresses of their

grandmothers or great-grandmothers in keeping with the present nostalgia for late Victorian and Edwardian times.

☐Lace and jewels are lent to some brides by the bridegroom's family, but these are by tradition the only adornments the bridegroom or his family provide for the bride on the wedding day, apart from her bouquet. (See also 'Going away clothes' below.)

Bridesmaids and pages

☐The bride chooses the design, the material and the colour of the bridesmaids' and pages' clothes to complement her own. It is the responsibility of the bridesmaids, or their parents, to have the clothes made at their own expense. These are generally designed so that they may be worn at subsequent parties or other festivities.

☐Pages' uniforms are obtainable from dress-hire shops or theatrical costumiers.

☐The bride may suggest the name of a suitable dressmaker who will undertake to make all the dresses or provide the patterns for the bridesmaids or their mothers to arrange this themselves.

☐The bridesmaids carry bouquets or posies of flowers provided by the bridegroom.

Bridegroom, best man, ushers and male guests

☐At all formal weddings, men wear morning dress. (for details of morning dress see Chapter 16).

☐The bridegroom, the best man and the ushers wear a button-hole—usually a carnation or a rose-bud.

☐See also 'Jewish weddings' and 'Going away clothes' below.

Women guests

☐Dresses and hats for summer weddings are often more elaborate than at other times of the year as the season lends itself to soft, light materials and exotic colours.

☐Fur coats or similar warm garments are worn in the winter over dresses or coats and skirts.

☐Hats are invariably worn at weddings together with jewellery, gloves and other smart accessories.

☐See also 'Jewish weddings' below.

Dress at Jewish weddings	☐Jewish weddings frequently take place late in the afternoon and are followed by a formal dinner and dance. The invitation will indicate whether dinner jackets are to be worn by the men. If so, the guests will attend both the wedding ceremony and the party afterwards in formal evening dress.
Register office weddings	☐Dress is entirely optional but formal or very elaborate clothes are rarely worn. The bride may decide on a long or short dress, with or without a hat; many brides carry a bouquet (the flowers in the register office are artificial). ☐The bridegroom wears a lounge suit with a buttonhole. ☐Witnesses and guests dress according to taste, bearing in mind the style of the bride and bridegroom and the nature of the event.
'Going-away' clothes	☐The bride chooses her clothes for the honeymoon and must have these in order and packed in suitcases the day before the wedding. One set of clothes is left in readiness for her to change into as soon as she leaves the reception. The choice of clothes depends much on the time of year and the couple's destination. ☐Most brides attempt to choose going-away clothes that look elegant as they say goodbye to family and friends and yet have some positive use on the honeymoon and on their return. At town weddings, going-away clothes tend to be smarter than at country weddings, in fact, only a little less formal than the dress of the wedding guests; at country weddings, informal going-away clothes are generally chosen. ☐Men change from their formal wedding attire into lounge suits.
Transport	☐Transport for the bridal party to and from the service will be needed, and if the wedding is in the country special arrangements may be necessary to meet trains and make sure that motorists know the way.

The bridal party ☐A spacious car is required to transport the bride and her father from their home to the church and, after the ceremony, the bride and bridegroom to the reception. The car and the driver are booked through a car-hire company unless the bride's father has a suitable car of his own.
☐Arrangements are made for the transport of other members of the family: the bride's mother, the chief bridesmaid or friend assisting the bride to dress, and the other bridesmaids and pages. This will entail the provision of two further cars and drivers, one of which will return the bride's parents from the church to the reception and the other the bridesmaids and the pages, all of whom must arrive before the main body of guests for the wedding photographs.
☐The best man accompanies the bridesmaids unless he has his own car available in which he drove the bridegroom to the church.

Country wedding transport ☐Country weddings require more organization than town weddings as far as transport is concerned, particularly if the setting is far off the beaten track.
☐The bride's parents are not responsible at a town wedding for the guests either before they arrive at the church or after they leave the reception; at a country wedding, however, the bride's parents usually offer their guests some assistance with travel arrangements. Details are printed on a sheet of paper or a postcard and sent with the wedding invitations.

Motorists ☐For the convenience of motorists, a map should be included showing the precise location of the church and the reception with the mileage from London or a nearby town noted so that a rough estimate can be made of the length of the journey. Much time is wasted by frantic motorists combing country lanes for sign-posts to village churches as the minutes tick towards 2.30pm.
☐Parking arrangements can also be shown on the map.

Travelling by train   ☐For train passengers, it is helpful to include a printed list of convenient train times to and from the nearest station. The bride's parents ask those intending to travel by train to indicate in their replies to the invitation whether or not they wish to be met.
☐The guest pays for his own train ticket but the cost of the car that meets him is customarily borne by the host (less so as the years go by—the guest should be prepared to pay if a taxi is sent). Guests assemble at a stated time to return to the station after the reception is over.
☐Buses are laid on at some large country weddings for guests who have come by rail.

Accommodation   ☐As soon as the wedding is announced, friends in the neighbourhood may offer to have guests to stay for one or two nights, particularly if distances are great.
☐Accomodation must be offered to the bridegroom's parents, the bridegroom and best man, the bridesmaids, and possibly the ushers and close friends assisting the bride.
☐The bridegroom's parents and the bridegroom and best man may prefer to stay in an hotel in which case they make their own arrangements.

ATTENDANTS   ☐The bride is escorted from her home, or from wherever she is staying, to the altar by her nearest male relation and 'given away' to the bridegroom at the marriage ceremony.
☐Bridesmaids and pages add character to the occasion and have a practical purpose too but are by no means essential. Many brides dispense with the retinue of children in favour of one adult bridesmaid, or prefer to be unattended.
☐However, the bride usually calls upon a sister or close friend or both (who do not necessarily play any part in the ceremony) to help her dress for the wedding and for her going-away. Her mother assists as far as the many claims on her attention allow.
☐See also 'Responsibilities of the participants',

described earlier on in this chapter.

Giving away the bride

☐This is an important role with a definite place in the wedding ritual and is performed by the bride's father.
☐If her father is dead, she is escorted to the chancel steps by a male relation—a brother or an uncle perhaps—and given away either by this relation or by her mother. It is a well established tradition for a widow to give away her daughter; she does not escort her up the nave but instead steps out of the front pew to join her as she approaches, the escort stepping aside into a seat reserved for him in the front left-hand pew.

The best man

☐The best man is chosen carefully from among the bridegroom's inner circle of relations and friends, perhaps a brother or a brother officer. He is generally a bachelor but not necessarily so. He plays a vital part in the arrangements so it is well worth while choosing someone who is reliable and who has some organizational ability. He should be invited as soon as possible.

Best man's duties before the day

☐The best man keeps in close touch with the wedding plans as they progress.
☐He is in charge of the ushers who hand out the service sheets and show the guests to their seats in church; he hands them the seating plan for the family pews and makes certain that the service sheets arrive at the church. The best man liaises with the toast-master about the timing of the speeches, the cake-cutting ceremony and the departure of the bride and bridegroom. If a toast-master is not engaged, his duties devolve on the best man. The best man will have a hand in the arrangements for the bridegroom's bachelor party.

Best man's duties on the wedding day

☐The best man makes certain that the bridegroom's clothes for the ceremony are laid out and in order, that he has his own ready and that the wedding ring is in a safe place in his possession. He makes provision for the payment of fees on the bridegroom's behalf to the clergyman before the ceremony.

☐He takes charge of the clothes into which the bridegroom changes after the reception, the luggage (of both bride and bridegroom) for the honeymoon, the car and the tickets, passports, travellers' cheques and other items.

☐He encourages the bridegroom to have a good lunch before the ceremony however nervous he is feeling and ensures that they are both changed in good time.

☐He drives the bridegroom to the church and they enter through a side entrance (if there is one); and he pays the fees to the clergyman in the vestry.

Best man's performance at the ceremony

☐The bridegroom and best man wait in the vestry or seat themselves in the choir stalls or the front right-hand pew. As the time for the arrival of the bride approaches, they take up their positions before the chancel steps, the best man standing to the right of the bridegroom.

☐He accompanies the chief bridesmaid to the signing of the register in the vestry and after the ceremony he escorts one of the ladies in the procession down the nave. He sees the bride and bridegroom into their car.

Best man's duties after the ceremony

☐The best man gathers together the various people who appear in the wedding photographs.

☐If the best man acts as master-of-ceremonies at the reception, he is responsible for the timing, he calls for silence for the speeches, he introduces the speakers and replies to the toast of 'the bridesmaids'; he also announces the start of the cake-cutting ceremony.

☐He makes certain that the bride and bridegroom leave the reception to change at the appointed time and that their car is brought to the front of the house or hotel for their departure.

☐If the reception takes place at a hotel, he takes

charge of the bridegroom's wedding clothes.

Bridesmaids and pages
□The bridesmaids and pages are chosen by the bride in consultation with the bridegroom. Their number depends on the size of the wedding—eight or more would be inappropriate at all but the largest weddings.
□A chief bridesmaid of the bride's own age with two child attendants, two older bridesmaids without child attendants or a collection of four to six children are popular combinations. Bridesmaids are always unmarried girls; the chief bridesmaid is usually a sister or close friend of the bride; the child bridesmaids and the pages are nieces, nephews, godchildren or the children of friends of both bride and bridegroom.
□The children look best when they are matched in height; their ages will vary but the bridesmaids or pages who carry the bride's train in the procession should be over five years old.

The chief bridesmaid
□The chief bridesmaid waits in the back of the church for the bride to arrive and keeps an eye on the children; she helps the bride adjust her veil and train. At the chancel steps, she takes care of the bride's bouquet for the wedding service and returns it to the bride for the procession down the nave.

Ushers
□Three or four ushers are needed to hand out the service sheets and to guide the guests to their seats in church. (The best man gives them an idea of the lay-out of the church in advance; he also hands them family seating plans and the service sheets.)

Where to seat guests
□The ushers direct friends of the bride to seats on the left-hand side of the nave and friends of the bridegroom to those on the right-hand side. Members of both families are similarly directed to reserved seats in the front pews.
□All unaccompanied ladies are escorted to a seat by an usher.
□After the wedding ceremony, the ushers help the

best man to organize transport for the guests from the church to the reception.

WEDDING PRESENTS
☐Wedding presents are a time-honoured way for friends and relations to help a new couple to set up house, but gifts are also exchanged between the bride and groom and presented as compliments by the groom to the bridesmaids, and to the pages by the bride. Most important is of course the wedding ring for its symbolic nature as a pledge increases enormously its value as a gift.

Wedding rings
☐The wedding ring is made of gold or platinum and fashioned as a circle, the symbol of eternity. This is worn on the fourth finger of the left hand. The custom of wearing a wedding ring continuously is of modern origin and some brides in the past were bequeathed their rings by their mothers or mothers-in-law. There was strong prejudice against wedding rings for centuries; the Church of Scotland did not make provision for wedding rings in its early days and the Puritans in Cromwell's time thought of them as popish relics and attempted to abolish their use.
☐In England, only the bride receives a wedding ring unless the bridegroom comes from a country in which it is customary for him to receive one too (most of continental Europe, for instance).
☐A bride wears her engagement ring on her right hand before and during the wedding service and transfers it to her left hand in the car on the way to the reception.

Family gifts
☐The bride and bridegroom exchange presents. The bridegroom's parents make some gift to the bride (usually jewellery) and similarly, her parents give a present to their future son-in-law.

Gifts for the attendants
☐The bridegroom makes each of the bridesmaids a small gift; this usually takes the form of a small brooch or bracelet that is worn at the wedding. The bride gives a memento of the occasion to the pages.

Presents from wedding guests

□As soon as the engagement is announced, friends and relations will ask the bride and bridegroom for their ideas on wedding presents.
□Donors vary in their attitudes to presents. Some prefer to choose the present themselves without consulting anyone, others ask if the couple would like a book or a piece of glass or a lamp and send whatever comes to hand most easily, regardless of the couple's tastes. There are, of course, people who take infinite pains to search for the perfect gift—and find it too—but they are not in a majority on any bride's guest list. Many friends will ask for and expect to receive a specific suggestion; this saves time, spares effort and enables the bride and bridegroom to get just what they want.

The bride's list

□The easiest way to ensure this is for a bride to make use of a service run by stores throughout the country. The bride and bridegroom compile a list of their needs from the stock held by a store: china, glass, silver and linen form the main categories. This list is retained by the store and produced for anyone directed to it by the bride.
□Any number and variety of objects may be listed in a wide price range; thus one friend has the opportunity of buying two cups and saucers of a specified design and another, the matching plates. The list is compiled a week or so before the wedding invitations are dispatched and kept up to date as purchases are made from it. Many brides have lists in two or three stores.

Who sends presents

□It is customary for relations, close friends and anyone who accepts a wedding invitation to send a present; acquaintances who decline the invitation have no need to do so.

Wording on cards

□Wedding gifts are usually sent with a card from the shop at which they are bought. The wording on the card may be formal or informal. Examples are: 'With all good wishes from'; 'With much love and best wishes for your happiness'.

Where to send presents

☐Wedding presents are sent to the bride at her home before the wedding takes place and afterwards to the couple at their new address. The card is normally addressed to both.
☐There is a growing tendency for guests to take their presents to the wedding rather than to send them. This is acceptable if the reception is in a private house but inevitable delays in the acknowledgement of the gift must be expected.

Acknowledgement and thanks

☐All presents are carefully listed by the bride as they arrive and acknowledged with thanks by her as soon as possible before or after the wedding. (See 'Thank you letters', Chapter Eight.)

Display of presents

☐In the past, the display of presents was an important element in the wedding reception. Brides' mothers sent extensive lists of presents and donors' names for publication in *The Times* and the local newspapers. The lists no longer appear but from time to time the displays are seen at country weddings. Distinguished precedents do not lessen the aura of ostentation that invariably surrounds these shows.
☐If the presents *are* placed on view, the services of a security guard may be necessary.

THE WEDDING CEREMONY

☐The last two or three days before a wedding are bound to be hectic no matter how carefully plans are laid, and the few hours before the bride leaves for the church are filled with all the activities that she must leave until last. However early in the morning she begins, she is invariably rushed, but the presence of an unflappable chief bridesmaid, sister or friend will help to steady her nerves and ensure that she makes her entrance, not one minute late, looking serene and unhurried on her father's arm.

Arrivals at the church

☐The ushers arrive 40 minutes before the wedding begins with the service sheets given to them by the best man.
☐The bells peal for the half-hour before the

ceremony begins while the organist plays introductory music as the bridegroom and the best man arrive and the guests appear.

☐ The guests are met at the church porch by the photographer; the ushers must ensure that the combination of guests having their photographs taken and old friends greeting one another does not cause too much of a crush at the church door.

Seating ☐ The ushers direct members of both families to seats reserved for them in the front pews, the bridegroom's family on the right-hand side with his friends ranged behind, and the bride's family and friends on the left.

☐ The seating of parents who have been divorced and have remarried can cause difficulties if relationships between the former spouses are strained. But parents and step-parents must not allow past animosity to obtrude upon the present and spoil the atmosphere of what is, after all, the bride and bridegroom's day.

☐ A space is left for the best man in the front right-hand pew.

☐ The bride's mother is the last person to take her seat; her arrival five or ten minutes ahead of the bride is the signal that the ceremony is about to start. She is usually accompanied by a member of her family and together they are escorted to their seats by the head usher. She leaves a space for her husband who joins her after he has given away the bride.

The procession ☐ The bridesmaids and pages assemble near the main door of the church with the chief bridesmaid and a mother or a nanny to place them in order five minutes before the bride arrives. The pages or train-bearers stand nearest to the door and together with the bridesmaids they form two columns through which the bride and her father pass.

☐ If the choristers and the priest form part of the procession, they assemble at this point ready to precede the bride and her father up the nave. (If

the choristers do not process, the priest waits on the chancel steps to welcome the bride.)
☐The bride arrives with her father and they pose for photographs. The chief bridesmaid or a friend helps her to adjust her veil and spreads out her train. The signal is given and the organist begins to play the entrance music which is usually rather solemn; at some weddings a hymn is sung at this point.
☐The bridegroom and best man take up their positions.
☐The bride's father steps out with his daughter on his right arm and they proceed slowly up the nave followed by the pages and the bridesmaids in pairs. Father and daughter stand to the left of the bridegroom, and the bride lets fall her arm.

At the altar   ☐Their order as they stand facing the altar is: bride's father, bride, bridegroom and best man.
☐The pages or bridesmaids lay down the train and the chief bridesmaid steps forward to help the bride remove the veil from her face and receive her bouquet, which she holds until she returns it during the signing of the register. (If there is no chief bridesmaid, the bride removes the veil herself and hands the bouquet to her father. He passes it to his wife and she carries it with her to the vestry to return it to the bride.)

Church of England service   ☐The marriage service begins with an introductory passage on the meaning and purpose of Christian marriage read by the clergyman to the congregation. The older versions of the Prayer Book (1662, and the revision of 1928 now entitled *Alternative Services Series 1*) list three purposes: to have children, to avoid immorality and to give each other 'mutual society, help, and comfort'. This order of precedence is altered in *Series 3* (the modern language version found in *The Alternative Service Book*, 1980) so that comfort and help are listed first, 'to know each other in love, united in body, heart and life' second, and children third.

'Wilt thou have this woman...?

☐The clergyman asks the bride and bridegroom if there is any reason why the marriage should not take place and, satisfied on this point, he proceeds with the ceremony. He turns to the bridegroom first and asks him 'Wilt thou have this woman to thy wedded wife...?'. He then questions the bride about her intentions towards her bridegroom; the liturgy of 1662 includes the controversial sentence 'Wilt thou obey him, and serve him?'. The objections of generations of women to these concepts have encouraged the church to provide in *Alternative Services Series 1* and in one of the versions of *Series 3* an alternative form, which omits the passage. There is an option in *Series 3* which makes it possible for the bride to promise to obey.

'Who giveth this woman...?'

☐The clergyman continues by asking 'Who giveth this women to be married to this man?', at which point the bride's father takes the bride's right hand and passes it, palm downwards to the clergyman. (The bride's father then retires to his place in the front pew beside his wife.)
☐The clergyman places the bride's right hand in the bridegroom's and the bridegroom recites his vows. They then loose their hands, the bride takes the bridegroom's hand and she in turn recites her vows.

Presentation of the ring

☐They loose hands again.
☐The best man produces the wedding ring and places it on the open prayer book held by the clergyman. He blesses it and gives it to the bridegroom who puts it on the fourth finger of the bride's left hand repeating his promises as he holds the ring in place.
☐This is followed by a prayer, a blessing and a psalm.
☐The clergyman then goes to the altar, followed by the bride and the bridegroom but leaving the best man and the bridesmaids at the chancel steps. An address may be delivered by the clergyman to the couple at this point.

Prayers for children □After the psalm, the congregation kneel for the Lord's Prayer, followed by a prayer to bestow on the couple 'the heritage and gift of children'. This is omitted when the couple are past child-bearing age and can be replaced by a prayer for the unborn child if one is expected.
□There is no set prayer for an unborn child and those that are heard at weddings tend to be composed for the occasion by the clergyman in collaboration with the couple.
□Further prayers and a hymn are followed by the address and the blessing.

The signing of the register □The signing of the register concludes the wedding ceremony.
□The bridegroom gives his left arm to the bride (for the first time) and they walk towards the vestry followed by certain members of their families. The bridegroom's father conducts the bride's mother but does not take her arm; similarly, the bride's father follows with the bridegroom's mother, the best man with the chief bridesmaid and anyone else who has been invited to act as a witness.
□As the pages and bridesmaids remain standing throughout the ceremony, it may be prudent if they are very small children to allow them to join the procession to the vestry. If they are unable to keep still they remain in their places in the nave.
□Meanwhile, the congregation listens to an anthem or sings a hymn which allows time for some relaxation in the vestry and for greetings and congratulations.
□The bride signs the register in her maiden name.

The recessional □A signal from the vestry warns the organist that the signing is concluded and he begins to play the recessional music—usually a jubilant piece such as a march.
□The pages and bridesmaids separate into two columns as soon as they see the bride and bridegroom emerge from the vestry. The bridegroom gives his left arm to the bride and they

proceed at a measured pace down the nave, smiling at the congregation, followed by bridesmaids and pages who fall in behind them, the chief bridesmaid and the best man. After them, the mother of the bride is escorted by the bridegroom's father, and the mother of the bridegroom by the bride's father.
□The clergy and choir do not form part of the recessional.

Leaving the church

□The photographer is waiting for the couple as they process down the nave and as they emerge from the church the bells begin to peal. They are seen into their car by the best man as soon as possible to avoid the throng of well-wishers leaving the church, and set off for the reception.
□The best man follows in another car with the bridesmaids and pages.
□There is no order of precedence among members of the congregation leaving the church but it is customary to allow members of both families to go first.

Church of Scotland service

□The form of service will generally follow that laid down in the *Book of Common Order* (see above) but there is much scope for improvisation in a wedding ceremony in the Church of Scotland. The minister will advise and offer suggestions.

The Roman Catholic service

□The bride and her father may be met at the church door by the priest who leads them to the altar.
□There are two rites of marriage now in general use in the church. The first is the Rite of Marriage during Mass at which the bride and bridegroom (who will, generally speaking, both be Catholics) and many members of the congregation receive communion. The second is the Rite of Marriage outside of Mass used in the case of 'mixed marriages' and whenever a shortened version is thought desirable.

The Rite of Marriage during Mass

☐The Rite of Marriage during Mass consists of an entrance rite, the Liturgy of the Word (the first reading usually from the Old Testament or the Epistles and the second from the Gospels, and the marriage rite; this is followed immediately by the Mass which includes the Nuptial Blessing, and the concluding rite which contains the blessing and the dismissal. Those who wish to receive communion (this is not at present given to non-Catholics) make an orderly procession to the altar and afterwards return to their seats.

The Rite of Marriage outside Mass

☐This begins with the entrance rite and the Liturgy of the Word (the first reading and the gospel). This is followed by a homily, the marriage rite and the Nuptial Blessing. The conclusion of the celebration consists of the thanksgiving, the final blessing and the dismissal.

Religious Society of Friends (Quaker) ceremony

☐A Quaker wedding is unlike any other. It consists of a simple declaration on the part of both the bride and bridegroom in front of witnesses; there is no ceremonial or pre-arranged service, no elaborate dress or attendants. A wedding ring plays no part in the marriage (although it is customary for the bridegroom to give one to his bride at some point).
☐The marriage takes place at one of the usual meetings of Friends who gather together for worship based on silence. One of the Friends will explain the nature of a Quaker wedding, and a prayer may be spoken or someone may give utterance to their thoughts.

The vows

☐At some point the bride and bridegroom stand up and declare in turn: 'Friends, I take this my friend (name) to be my wife/husband, promising, through divine assistance, to be unto her/him a loving and faithful husband/wife, so long as we both on earth shall live.'

The wedding certificate

☐Afterwards, the wedding certificate is signed by the bride and bridegroom and two witnesses, and read aloud by the registering officer.

Jewish service
□ Jewish weddings are solemnized by a rabbi in the presence of at least a *minyan* (a group of ten male adult Jews).
□ It is customary for the bride to wear white with a headdress and veil; she is escorted by her father, followed by bridesmaids, her mother with an escort, and the bridegroom's parents.

The marriage contract
□ The bridegroom must first attend to the writing of the *ketubbah,* or marriage contract. He undertakes to honour the obligations outlined in this by a symbolic act: he takes an item of clothing (a handkerchief, for instance) from the officiating rabbi, lifts it and returns it. The *ketubbah* is signed by the bridegroom and witnesses.

The betrothal
□ The betrothal ceremony takes place under the *huppah,* a ceremonial nuptial canopy. The bridegroom takes up his position with his best man standing to the left a pace behind him; the latter has the ring in his possession.
□ The bride stands on the bridegroom's right. Both sets of parents stand with them under the *huppah.*
□ The betrothal begins with the rabbi's recital of the benediction over a glass of wine. This is followed by the betrothal blessing.
□ The bridegroom places the ring on the bride's right index finger and recites the following words after the rabbi: 'Behold, you are consecrated unto me by this ring, according to the law of Moses and Israel.'

□ The bride's acceptance of the ring signifies consent to the marriage. This part of the ceremony must be witnessed by two individuals who are related neither to the participants nor to each other.
□ The *ketubbah* is then read out and handed to the bride.

The benedictions
□ The ceremony ends with the recital of the seven benedictions, the drinking of wine by the bride and

bridegroom, and the ceremonial breaking of a glass by the bridegroom.

☐The couple sign the marriage documents and process with their attendants out of the synagogue.

REGISTER OFFICE WEDDINGS

☐Many people choose to marry before a superintendent registrar; the ceremony is of the simplest nature and consists of a straightforward exchange of vows before witnesses.

Witnesses

☐The couple must ensure that two witnesses are present to sign the register; the witnesses may be members of the family or friends.

Guests

☐Some register offices can accomodate a few guests in addition to the witnesses but the couple should clarify this point with the registrar on their first visit as offices vary greatly in size. The ceremony itself is brief and is probably sandwiched between two others. The restrictions on time and space makes participation by the guests awkward and hurried. Six or eight is probably the maximum number thus allowing for the presence of members of both families.

Photographs

☐The bride and bridegroom must make the arrangements with a photographer if they wish one to be present. Permission to take photographs after the ceremony must be obtained beforehand from the superintendent registrar.

The ceremony

☐The bride, the bridegroom and the two witnesses are required to arrive five minutes before the ceremony is timed to begin.

☐The bride and bridegroom stand before the superintendent registrar and exchange the following vows: 'I do solemnly declare that I know not of any lawful impediment why I (name) may not be joined in matrimony to (name).' And to one another in turn: 'I call upon these persons here present to witness that I (name) do take thee, (name) to be my lawful wedded husband/wife.'

Presentation of the ring	☐It is customary for the bridegroom to give the bride a ring at this point but it has no legal significance under civil law.
Signing of the register	☐The marriage register is then signed by the bride, bridegroom and witnesses.
Entertaining afterwards	☐A register office wedding may be followed, if this is desired, by a reception similar in all respects to one following a church wedding (see below). However, as the majority of guests do not attend the ceremony, it is usual for this to take place for practical reasons some hours before the reception. As most register offices close at noon on a Saturday, this is essential if that day is chosen for the wedding. ☐Many couples who choose to marry in a register office prefer not to have a formal reception but hold instead a small lunch party after the event for the participants, or a party in the evening.
Costs	☐The costs of many register office weddings are paid by the bride and bridegroom. ☐The costs of the entertainments, a lunch perhaps for the participants between the marriage and the reception, and the reception itself, may be paid for by the bride's father but this is not invariably the case, particularly if the bride is marrying for a second time.
THE RECEPTION	☐Following a wedding in the traditional style, the bride and bridegroom return with all possible speed to the scene of the reception. They will wish to tidy themselves in readiness for the photographer, and then await the best man, bridesmaids, pages and both sets of parents, all of whom appear by custom in the wedding photographs. ☐There is little time between their arrival and the appearance of the first guests so it is important that someone is there to direct the guests to cloakrooms, to take their coats and subsequently to direct them into an informal line to await the bride and

bridegroom and their families from the
photographic session.

The receiving line ☐As soon as the photographs are taken, the
receiving line is formed. The full receiving line is
composed as follows: bride's mother, bride's father,
bridegroom's mother, bridegroom's father, bride,
bridegroom.
☐The guests form a queue in the order in which
they arrive. The toast-master (or butler or whoever
assumes this duty) asks each guest their name and
announces it in stentorian tones as they approach
the receiving line. (For conventions of giving names
to be announced, see page 165.) Guests shake hands
with each person, ending with the bride and
bridegroom.
☐Brief introductions are made if necessary by the
bride to the bridegroom and vice-versa if the guest
is a member of the family or a very old family
friend. But guests must keep moving.
☐As soon as the last guest has passed along the
receiving line, the bride and bridegroom circulate;
no one should monopolize them for too long.

Informal receiving   ☐Many people find a full receiving line impractical
line   as the inevitable delays are frustrating for guests.
For this reason, at many weddings only the bride
and bridegroom receive, while the parents mingle
from the start with their guests. The names of the
guests need not be announced to the bride and
bridegroom unless they particularly wish it.

The bride's mother   ☐The receiving line is a recent innovation. Before
receives   the Second World War, the bride's mother, as
hostess, received the guests alone standing in the
hall, or at the top of the stairs. Guests were
announced to her by the butler and they then
passed on to greet the bride and bridegroom who
stood in the drawing room or reception room—a
custom worth reviving.

Food and drink   ☐Beyond the bride and bridegroom, at the

entrance to the reception, a waiter is ready with a tray of drinks to offer each guest champagne, white wine or a soft drink as desired.
☐The waiters and waitresses pass round the food and ensure that guests' glasses are filled. As the host and hostess are unable to make any but the briefest introductions, it is the duty of all guests to approach each other, particularly if some appear lost.

Speeches and toasts
☐After an hour, the bride and bridegroom are shepherded by the best man to a position near the wedding cake and the toast-master (or best man) requests silence for the speeches.
☐It is essential to keep the speeches as short as possible and whoever is chosen to propose the toast of the health and happiness of the bride and bridegroom must be chosen with care. Sometimes the bride's father undertakes this himself although it is in order for him to call upon a family friend who has known the bride for many years.

The bridegroom replies
☐The bridegroom thanks the bride's parents for the reception and for their daughter, and the guests for their presents. He then proposes a toast to the bridesmaids on whose behalf the best man replies.

Telegrams
☐This flurry of speechmaking will have exhausted the patience of the guests; the reading of telegrams which sometimes follows at this point is unpopular and unnecessary.

Cutting the cake
☐The bride and bridegroom move towards the wedding cake. Conversation will have broken out again among the guests so the toast-master (or best man) must request silence for the cutting of the cake.
☐The bride cuts it with a knife or sword, the bridegroom placing his hand over hers to help her force the blade through the cake.
☐The cake is then removed by the caterers and swiftly cut and divided into segments; the waiters or

waitresses distribute these to the guests helped by the bridesmaids.

Departure ☐A quarter of an hour after the cake cutting ceremony, the best man, with his eye on his watch, urges the bride and bridesmaid to leave. The temptation to stay and talk to guests at the reception for a while longer is considerable but must be resisted.
☐The bride and bridegroom leave to change into their going-away clothes, the bride accompanied by her chief bridesmaid. The best man checks that their car is standing outside the building and joins the bridegroom. As soon as he can, he removes their luggage and packs the car.

Departure of the bride and groom ☐The toast-master (or best man) announces to the guests that the bride and bridegroom are about to leave and guests crowd into the hall. They depart with fond farewells, thanks and good wishes, the bride turning as she goes to throw her bouquet into the throng.

Departure of the guests ☐The guests say goodbye to their host and hostess, gather their belongings and leave.

WEDDING ANNOUNCE-MENTS ☐Weddings may be announced briefly in the Personal columns of *The Times, The Independent, The Daily Telegraph, The Guardian, Scotsman, Yorkshire Post* and many local newspapers.

Example ☐**Williams: Johnson**—On October 9th, 1980, at St John's Church, Knebworth, John Robert Williams to Jane Mary Johnson.

☐Weddings are described in greater detail on the court and social pages of *The Times* and *The Daily Telegraph*. The text must be submitted in writing to the social editor and the costs are paid by the bride's father.

Example | **Mr Robert Smith and Miss H.M. Jones**
The marriage took place on Saturday at Holy Trinity Church, Amberley, between Mr Robert Smith, younger son of the late Major R.E. Smith and of Mrs R.E. Smith, of 30 Lennox Road, London SW1, and Miss Hazel Jones, of The Cottage, Amberley. The Rev Arthur Edwards officiated.
The bride, who was given in marriage by her father, wore a gown of embroidered ivory silk, and a lace veil held in place by a circlet of flowers. She carried a bouquet of white roses, stephanotis and lilies-of-the-valley. Mary Webb, Laura Richardson, Christopher Jones and Robert Ellis attended her. Mr John Russell was best man. A reception was held at the home of the bride and the honeymoon will be spent in Italy.

Register office weddings

□Announcements are made in the newspapers in a similar fashion to church weddings. However, the register office is rarely specified, the announcement reading: 'The wedding took place 'in London' or 'in Oxford' or 'in Edinburgh'.

Reporters and press photographers

□Many newspapers in the country will send a reporter and a photographer to a local wedding.

The editor should be sent a note to inform him of the event well in advance. In the case of magazines, wedding photographs are submitted to the editors together with full details of the wedding.

Postponed weddings

☐The marriage ceremony may have to be postponed because of illness, or the death of a parent or brother or sister. In the event of a death or similar tragedy a card should be sent to all the guests, worded on these lines:

Example

It is much regretted
that because of the
death of Mrs Richard Burnett,
the marriage between
her daughter Sarah and
Mr Peter Porchester
on the 18th May will
be postponed.

☐As soon as a day can be planned for the wedding, completely new invitations must be sent out.
☐If the circumstances of postponement are less sombre and there is time to fix another date before informing the guests that the wedding has been postponed, a printed card giving the revised details is sent to every person on the guest list.

Example

Mr and Mrs Robert
Smith regret that owing
to the sudden illness of
their son they are
obliged to postpone
their daughter's wedding
on Saturday 9th May
until Saturday 14th
July at 2.30pm

Cancellation of wedding

☐If the wedding is cancelled by the bride and bridegroom, printed cards are sent if time permits.

Example

Mr and Mrs Robert

Smith regret to announce that the marriage of their daughter Mary with Mr Charles Edwards on Saturday 14th May will not take place.

☐There may not be time to print and send the cards to the guests in which case each one must be contacted by telephone or telegram.

☐An announcement in the newspapers is not adequate notification of the cancellation of a wedding if the invitations have already been sent to guests.

Wedding presents ☐As soon as possible after the wedding plans are cancelled, all wedding presents are returned by the bride or bridegroom. There is no need to include any details of the circumstances that led to the calling off of the wedding.

SECOND WEDDINGS ☐Second weddings fall into two categories: the remarriage of a widow or a widower or the remarriage of a divorced person.

☐Widows and widowers may remarry in a church or synagogue but the question of the remarriage of the divorced is more complicated. Anyone who is free to marry may do so at a civil ceremony in a register office (see pages 43 and 73).

Widow's remarriage ☐The invitations are sent out by the parents of a young widow. If she is an orphan, the invitations are sent out in the name of a married sister, an aunt or a cousin and the relationship is stated on the invitation thus: 'Mr and Mrs Robert Evans request the pleasure of your company at the marriage of their niece...'.

☐A widow may if she prefers send out the invitations in her own name.

Ceremony in church ☐The giving-away ceremony is optional for a widow

but if she dispenses with this she will need a male relation or friend to escort her up the nave. There is no procession but she may be attended by a *dame d'honneur*, married or unmarried, who awaits her before the chancel steps and takes care of her bouquet.
□The bridegroom is attended by a best man.

Dress
□Gone are the 'grey or tender shades of mauve' once thought appropriate to the marriage of widows. Today, a smart dress, long or short, with a hat are usually considered suitable; a white dress and veil, orange blossoms and bridesmaids are all the prerogatives of the unmarried and do not reappear.
□The bridegroom wears formal dress.

Wedding rings
□A widow removes the wedding ring of her first marriage shortly before the ceremony.

Reception
□The guests are received by the bride and bridegroom.
□The reception follows the pattern of a reception for a first marriage with speeches and a wedding cake.

Costs
□A widow bears the costs of a second marriage herself unless her parents or some friend offers to do so.

Widower's remarriage
□There are fewer constraints in the case of a widower's remarriage; he wears formal clothes and the bride, if she is marrying for the first time, wears a white dress and veil, is given away by her father and is attended by bridesmaids.

Divorced person's remarriage
□Religions differ in their views on the subject of divorce and remarriage:

Church of England
□The official position of the Church of England at the present time is that the use of the marriage service is not permitted in the case of anyone who

has a former partner still living. There is no appeal against this ruling.

☐However, it is possible to hold what is known as a Service of Prayer and Dedication in church. This is, in fact, a service of blessing and follows the civil ceremony at register offices.

Invitations ☐The social nature of the service of blessing depends entirely on the views of the clergyman. If he agrees, there is no reason why friends should not be invited to attend the service, which can take place before a wedding reception. However, he may object to this and suggest instead that a few friends only attend the service of blessing.

Dress ☐For the bride's dress see opposite.
☐If the service and the reception are formal occasions and the clergyman agrees, the bridegroom wears morning dress to the service of blessing; if less formal, a lounge suit is worn.
☐The style of invitation will indicate to the guests the appropriate dress for the occasion.

Church of Scotland ☐A minister of the Church of Scotland is unlikely to refuse to remarry a divorced person. He would use the full marriage service.

Roman Catholic Church ☐The Roman Catholic Church believes that marriage is indissoluble. If a person has contracted a marriage valid in the eyes of the Church, that person cannot contract another marriage in a Catholic church as long as both are alive. A subsequent marriage is not recognized.
☐This is true, however, only of a marriage that is a true marriage within the concept of the church. A marriage might be declared null by the church authorities.
☐The Roman Catholic Church in this country will only consider a request for a decree of nullity once the marriage has been dissolved in the civil courts.
☐The normal approach to the marriage court is through a parish priest who will arrange for an

appointment with a member of the diocesan tribunal.

☐If a marriage is declared null, the partner who wishes to remarry may do so in a full marriage ceremony except that the Nuptial Blessing (which is bestowed once only in a lifetime) is not repeated.

The Religious Society of Friends (Quakers)

☐The Quakers are prepared to consider the question of the remarriage of a divorced member of the Society, but this would not take place until the Monthly Meeting had examined the circumstances in detail and was convinced of the sincerity and good faith of the applicants.

Jewish

☐A Jew will first receive a civil divorce and then apply for a religious bill of divorce known as a *get*. This is written, signed and delivered by the husband to the wife.

☐A subsequent remarriage with another Jew almost invariably takes place in a synagogue.

Presents

☐Presents are sent by guests to second marriages as in the case of a first marriage; a wedding present list is drawn up by the bride and bridegroom if desired (see page 63).

WEDDING ANNIVERSARIES

☐Many couples faithfully observe their wedding anniversaries as they occur and celebrate with a dinner or a visit to the opera or the theatre; it is an opportunity, too, for the exchange of presents.

☐These are private occasions although parents and brothers and sisters may remember and perhaps send a card or flowers.

Special anniversaries

☐There are four wedding anniversaries that are family celebrations and, to give them their traditional names, these are: *25th* Silver wedding, *40th* Ruby wedding, *50th* Golden wedding, *60th* Diamond wedding.

Public announcements

☐Many couples make an announcement in a newspaper.

Example   **Radcliffe: Martin.** On
20th March 1925 at St
George's Church, Bristol,
John Radcliffe to Anne
Martin. Present address:
15 Rochester Street,
London SW1.

Entertainment   □The choice of a suitable entertainment to
celebrate the event is dependent on family
circumstances and the state of the couple's health.
Children generally make themselves responsible for
arranging a party—a dinner party, a drinks party or
an afternoon reception if their parents have a wide
circle of friends. Many couples, however, prefer to
organize the commemoration themselves.
□Members of the family and friends gather
together, many of whom will have attended the
wedding years before. Toasts are proposed by a
son, or by the best man if he is present, and a
wedding cake is cut ceremonially by the couple.

Presents   □Presents are given, although these tend to be
tokens of affection rather than elaborate
silverware and precious objects reminiscent of
similar celebrations in the past. To avoid
embarrassment, it is possible to make clear in the
invitation that presents are not expected and ask
instead that each guest write their name during the
course of the party in a special book to
commemorate the occasion.

4 DIVORCE

□'Love is absolute, while it lasts.' Nothing in human nature has altered since Stendhal made this remark in 1822, but the erosion of marriage as a durable social institution has proceeded at an ever quickening rate.
□The law reflects this devaluation: a marriage can be terminated in Britain in six to eight weeks provided that both parties agree, a time-scale that bears no relationship to the traditional evaluation of marriage and family life. The fact that more people petition for divorces than are granted them indicates that reconciliations do occur. But too often divorce presents itself as a relatively effortless alternative to the responsibilities that marriage entails.

SEPARATION

□No one likes to admit that they have failed in a matter as important as marriage, and thus any announcement of a separation is difficult to make. However, most friends who are in contact with an unhappy couple will be aware that separation is a possibility and confirmation of the fact may well come as less of a surprise than expected.

Announcing a separation

□Once the separation has taken place, friends should be told for uncertainty breeds all manner of speculation. Friends may be told informally, and news of what has happened will soon spread in a small social circle. However, there are certain to be members of the family who ought to be told before they hear the news from a third party, and friends living at a distance who will not hear on the grapevine. A brief letter is all that is required, a lengthy explanation is unnecessary.
□Above all, recriminations must be avoided; the sympathy of relations and friends will soon evaporate in an atmosphere of self-justification and allegations of wrong-doing, to say nothing of the likely effect on any children who are caught in the cross-fire. The support of a family and friends at such a critical moment in life is vital.

Children

□Many people who decide first in favour of

separation and then become reconciled after a period of time do so because they place the well-being of the children above their own differences. This is commendable, and preferable for the children. But a reconciliation is a dubious advantage to everybody concerned if warfare continues. The decision to reconcile must be accompanied by a firm commitment to peace, however difficult this may prove in practice.

Telling children

☐If a separation is planned and no reconciliation is in sight, and the children are of an age to understand, they should be told as soon as possible. This should be done gently and without accusations by one party against another. However bitter the wrangle between husband and wife, the temptation to encourage the children to take sides must be avoided. An atmosphere of uncertainty and insecurity will undermine any child's relationship with the world, without the added burden of being forced to partake in the demolition of the character of one parent by the other.

Attitudes of family and friends

☐The attitudes of third parties are largely dependent on the behaviour of the estranged couple. The urge to take sides can be very strong. The immediate reaction of most friends to the news of a separation and subsequent divorce will be one of sadness but this is easily transformed into condemnation of one partner or the other if the couple engage in open recriminations.
☐Fortunately the moral condemnation familiar in the past has largely disappeared and the days when a divorce would estrange two families and split a circle of friends are over. But judgements are still made, however misplaced these may be. No outsider can fathom the depths of a broken marriage, and the roots of the problems that wrecked it are rarely visible. Friends can do no more than offer sympathy and support to one or both parties and avoid the temptation to encourage further strife.

Invitations to estranged couples

☐After the separation, friends must use their own discretion about invitations to estranged or divorced couples. Generally speaking, it is diplomatic not to invite them to the same social gatherings although this may be difficult to avoid among a small circle of friends.

☐To some couples, subsequent meetings present no emotional problems, whereas others may be horrified at the prospect of a meeting, particularly in the early stages of a separation.

☐If in doubt, it is better not to invite both parties or to give one or the other the option of refusing the invitation, rather than leave matters to chance.

☐Whatever the circumstances, two people who are on bad terms have no excuse for showing their bitterness towards each other in public if by chance they do meet at a social gathering.

MONEY AND POSSESSIONS

☐The divorce laws date from 1969 when the Divorce Reform Act made the sole ground for divorce the irretrievable break-down of the marriage. This is established to the court's satisfaction by means of evidence of adultery or intolerable behaviour and the new element of separation—two years if both parties agree, and five years if one party disputes the divorce.

☐Orders for maintenance and provisions for any children are made before the decree is granted.

☐The Act of 1969 was supposed to remove the allegations of wrong-doing levelled by one party against the other, but the concept is still very much alive. The bitterness overflows into a contest for the human and the material possessions of the marriage.

☐A minute proportion of divorces are contested and yet the most virulent wrangles take place over the custody of children, access, maintenance, and the division of family property. This is a tragedy for all concerned, children in particular, but it is one that is enacted relentlessly by one couple after another as they face the watershed in their married lives.

Separating possessions

□People vary greatly in their attitudes to material possessions; some acquire the minimum necessary to sustain their way of life whereas others are acquisitors at heart, developing emotional attachments to objects which can prove as strong as any human tie.

□Material objects are made precious through associations with a person or a place, or by a financial value which gives an added dimension— again emotive—of security. These are all powerful forces which contrive to make discussion of the division of property a potential minefield. The element of guilt added on one side or the other in more cases than not adds to this danger. One person may walk out of a marriage with a suitcase of belongings, while another may insist on a division of every object in the house.

□An estranged couple may be lucky and find themselves in complete agreement, but until the matter is settled battles can flare over the fate of the most unimportant household items.

□This is an area that falls within the jurisdiction of the courts and a decision will be forced upon a couple who cannot agree. A civilized division is infinitely preferable to a legal wrangle.

Presents

□It is considered correct to return presents exchanged during the marriage. A woman generally offers to return her engagement ring but this is seldom accepted; she keeps it, gives it to a daughter or sells it.

□The return of presents depends on the nature of the divorce rather than any other factor. If it is amicable, both parties may decide to retain the presents they have given each other, despite conventional practice. A compromise is sometimes reached by making over an object, a valuable painting perhaps or a diamond bracelet, to the children of the marriage.

Wedding presents

□Wedding presents probably fall into natural divisions or they can be divided by reference to the wedding present list—the wife retaining the presents given by her family and friends, and the husband retaining those given by his.

Possessions acquired before and during the marriage

☐Possessions acquired before marriage are retained by the original owner.
☐If a man is an avid collector of postage stamps and his wife of Indian miniatures, it seems fair for each party to retain his or her own collection even if it was made during the course of the marriage. A collection formed together can probably be split.
☐However, the longer the marriage has lasted, the more blurred are the dividing lines of ownership. And the less money available to maintain two homes instead of one, the greater the possibility that objects may have to be sold.

Household furniture

☐Common sense should indicate that if there are children, it is sensible to leave the necessary household furniture and kitchen equipment with whoever gains custody.

Family heirlooms

☐Broadly speaking, possessions such as family heirlooms remain with the person in whose family they originated. This includes jewellery from the man's family worn by his wife during their marriage.

REMARRIAGE OF ONE PARTNER

☐If one party decides to remarry, it is kind and courteous to inform the other well in advance. This is essential where children are involved so that they are not presented with a sudden and possibly alarming *fait accompli*. They should be encouraged to attend the wedding and to feel from the start an integral part of what will become a second family to them.

5 DEATHS, FUNERALS AND MEMORIAL SERVICES

☐The Victorians shrouded grief in elaborate and complex rituals. The depth of the band on a man's hat and the width of the black border of a piece of writing paper indicated to the world the precise stage that mourning had reached. Whether this made sorrow any easier to bear is debatable. Perhaps all that can be said in favour of these fashions in mourning is that their intricacy kept people occupied when they most needed to be and provided an elaborate facade behind which to conceal their sorrow.

☐But this facade, maintained with such extravagant care until the outbreak of war in 1914, crumbled as the fighting dragged on and the death toll mounted. There was no call then for hired mourners.

☐The ritual surrounding death and burial today is confined to religious observances and much of this has been simplified in recent years. Although the network of conventions through which family and friends expressed their sympathy in the past has disappeared, this is no excuse to hold back for fear of intruding on private grief. It is a time for friends to act, for love and understanding can go far to alleviate sorrow; time alone eases the pain.

AFTER A DEATH

☐There are several official contacts that must be made immediately after a death; these are the family doctor, the registrar of births and deaths *or* the coroner, a local undertaker, the family solicitor and relevant minister of religion.

Legal points

☐Every death in England and Wales must be registered by the registrar of births and deaths for the district in which the death occurs or the body is found. This also applies to Scotland with the added provision that there a death may be registered in the office of the district in which the deceased lived before his death. This registration cannot take place until the cause of death has been ascertained and a certificate issued by either a doctor or a coroner. A doctor will issue a medical certificate if he has attended the deceased within 14 days prior to the death, or examines the body immediately after death.

The coroner

☐Deaths are reported to the coroner by the doctor if there is any uncertainty about the cause of death, by the police if a death is violent, sudden or unnatural, by a hospital if a patient dies in the course of an operation, by the registrar if he lacks adequate information to grant a certificate or by a member of the public unhappy about the circumstances of a death.

☐The coroner's principal function is to investigate any death reported to him. He will examine the evidence and decide whether to order a post-mortem or to hold an inquest. The majority of deaths reported to a coroner result in a post-mortem but only a small proportion lead to an inquest. The coroner is legally obliged to hold an inquest if a death occurs in violent circumstances such as a motor, rail or air accident.

☐The procurator fiscal undertakes similar duties in Scotland.

Registering a death

☐A death should be registered as soon as possible. The law in England and Wales requires that the details should be reported within five days but a period of 14 days is allowed for full registration to take place.

☐In Scotland, eight days are allotted.

☐If a death has been referred to the coroner, it cannot be registered unless the registrar receives authority to do so from the coroner.

☐Registration is a task that can be delegated. However, there is a list of people who are entitled to act as informants and some registrars are strict in enforcing the order of priority. Generally speaking, the informant should be the widow, widower or child of the deceased; but a person who was either present at the death or found the body is also acceptable.

☐The visit to the registrar is an occasion when a companion can be a great support and a help too, for the paper work is considerable.

What is required ☐The information required by the registrar is as follows:

The date and place of death and the deceased's usual address (and in Scotland, the exact time of death).

The full names and surname (and the maiden name if the deceased was a woman who had married).

The deceased's occupation (and the name and occupation of her husband if the dead person was a married woman or a widow).

If the deceased was married, the date of birth of the surviving widow or widower.

A child under the age of fifteen is described as 'son of' or 'daughter of' followed by the name and occupation of the father.

Informing family and friends ☐There are certain members of the family, close friends, colleagues or business associates who must be informed immediately. The telephone is the best means but in certain cases a brief letter is more appropriate. This is an onerous duty but one that is possible to delegate to members of the family or to close friends. It is essential to ensure that those who knew the deceased well receive the announcement of death directly and not through a third party.

Responding to the news ☐All those contacted by the bereaved should send letters of sympathy without delay and indicate whether they intend to be at the funeral or not. Those in a position to help in one way or another should make this clear.

Giving assistance ☐It is invaluable to have one person take charge of all the arrangements for the funeral. This task may fall to a son or daughter, a brother or sister, or perhaps to the family solicitor. If there is no obvious candidate, any friend who feels close enough to the bereaved to offer should do so without fail.

Public announcements

☐An announcement in the national morning newspapers, *The Times, The Independent, The Daily Telegraph*, or *Scotsman*, is one of the best means of informing friends and acquaintances outside the immediate family circle. Announcements may be made also in *The Guardian*, the *Yorkshire Post* and many local papers. The newspapers accept these notices by telephone and advice is given if needed on their wording. The funeral arrangements may be given at the same time. If these are not finalized at the time of the first announcement, a second may be made within a matter of days.

Examples

SMITH—On 28th July 1980, in London, Mary, wife of the late George Smith and mother of Richard, aged 84 years. Funeral service at St Peter's Church, Ripley, on 1st August at 2.30pm followed by private cremation. Family flowers only.

ROBERTS—On May 5th 1980, peacefully in hospital, Charles Edward Roberts of Gretton. Dearly loved husband of Pamela. Funeral service at Stone Parish Church on Wednesday May 12th at 3pm. No flowers. Donations, if desired, to the National

93

Trust, 42 Queen Anne's
Gate, London SW1.
Memorial service to be
announced later.

Mourning dress

☐Dress is entirely a matter for individual taste.
Sombre colours are generally worn at funerals but
are by no means obligatory; jewellery should be
unostentatious. It is unfair to stipulate that
mourning dress should not be worn; widows may
wish to wear black and others may feel more
appropriately dressed in dark colours.
☐Mourning writing paper is no longer used.

Letters of sympathy

☐If there is no request to the contrary in the
newspaper announcement (and such a request
should be honoured most scrupulously), letters of
sympathy should be written and dispatched *without
delay*. The thoughts prompted by their contents will
give support on the harrowing day of the funeral
and in the bleak days that follow.
☐For suggestions on writing letters of sympathy,
see Chapter Eight.

Addressing letters

☐There is a convention that the deceased is not
'the late' until after the funeral. For example, letters
to the son of the deceased Earl of Charmington
would still be addressed to Viscount Dalsany until
after the funeral.

Answering letters of
sympathy

☐Letters should be answered as soon as possible
after the funeral. The task is formidable if one
person tackles it alone and may take months rather
than weeks to accomplish. But there is no
substitute for a personal reply and if this is
attempted the delay is immaterial.
☐It is probably easiest to formulate a short
paragraph that can be used to acknowledge the
majority of letters. There is no reason why other
members of the family should not help with the
replies. If the deceased was a public figure, the
number of letters may be enormous and if the

bereaved is elderly, replies to everyone may be impossible without assistance.

Interim notices ☐Interim notices may be placed in the court pages or personal columns of the newspapers.

Example Mrs Robert Smith
wishes to thank all
those who have sent
letters of sympathy and
flowers on the death of
her husband, Captain
Robert Smith. She
hopes to write personally
to all at a later date.

☐Although these notices were commonly placed in the past, not everyone today has the time or inclination to scan the newspapers in such detail. To ensure that each individual item does receive an acknowledgement, a custom has grown up of sending notices of this kind as printed letters or cards. These may be worded formally in the manner of the newspaper notices, or informally if this is preferred.

☐If the circumstances are such that it is impossible to write to all the sympathizers—in the case of a famous public figure for instance—then an acknowledgement in the press may be the only solution but a good compromise is to print a circular letter of acknowledgement and gratitude with space left for some member of the family to write a few words when appropriate.

Sending flowers ☐The public announcement of a funeral generally indicates whether flowers are desired or not, eg 'No flowers', 'No flowers by request' (generally of the deceased), 'Family flowers only'. If flowers are expected, they are sent to the undertakers or the house of the chief mourners the afternoon before the funeral takes place. A card bearing the name of the sender of the flowers and some appropriate words is attached.

☐If flowers are sent to a distant funeral, this can be done by telephoning the order to a local florist who will write the message and deliver the flowers to the funeral.

Funeral flowers

☐Flowers are sent as a tribute to the dead not as a gesture to the living, thus the words 'In loving memory' are suitable, but 'With deepest sympathy' are not. The flowers are addressed to the deceased: eg. 'Captain Robert Smith', 'Mrs Walsh'. The cards are collected by the family or, if asked, by the undertakers, so that the flowers can be acknowledged.

☐Family flowers are placed on the coffin.

Flowers sent to the bereaved

☐Close friends may wish to give or send flowers to the bereaved and enclose a card expressing sympathy. The announcement in the newspaper regarding flowers concerns only the funeral arrangements.

Donations

☐Increasingly, donations to charities are requested in lieu of funeral flowers. Medical charities are most appropriate but the choice may reflect the deceased's interest in such causes as the preservation of historic buildings and the countryside, or the welfare of children and old people.

FUNERALS

☐Many people indicate in the course of their lives where they wish to be buried. Directions may be left informally in a letter or more formally in a will and although there is no legal obligation to carry these out, such requests should be respected where practicable. Other people rely on the good sense of those left behind to choose an appropriate farewell. This will depend on the religious persuasion of the deceased and the choice that is made between burial and cremation.

☐Those in close contact with a priest, or who are members of a parish or a particular religious organization, should inform the appropriate person immediately. Others uncertain or undecided can discuss the alternatives with an undertaker.

Undertakers ☐In the past, coffins were provided by the local builder but the demand for more elaborate funerals in Victorian times gave rise to specialized firms who would 'undertake' all the necessary arrangements. ☐In recent years, certain undertakers have banded together to form The National Association of Funeral Directors whose headquarters are in London. Members of this organization will be found throughout England, Wales and Scotland and their strict code of practice should ensure that anyone approaching a member firm is offered fair and comprehensive advice.

Services available ☐The funeral director, or undertaker, selected (the majority run a 24-hour service) will care for the body, make all the arrangements for the funeral service and pay the participants. He will offer a wide range of assistance beyond the provision of what is termed 'a basic, simple funeral', much of which is optional.

Arrangements for funerals ☐The undertaker will help to decide where the body will await burial. It was customary in the past to lay out the body and place it in a coffin, leaving this in the house until the funeral. This is a much less widespread custom than it used to be but the undertaker can make the appropriate arrangements if this is desired. In the case of Roman Catholics and some Anglicans, the coffin rests in a chapel or church. Alternatively, the undertaker will retain the coffin on his premises.

Place of burial ☐The place of burial must be decided with the undertaker and the person officiating at the ceremony. These arrangements cannot be made until the registrar or the coroner has issued a certificate for the disposal of the body. (In Scotland, the certificate of registration of death is adequate for the purpose.)

☐Anyone who lives in a parish of the Church of England, whatever his religion and wherever he dies, has the right in theory to be buried in the parish churchyard. Permission to be buried in a parish in which an individual does not live may be granted by the incumbent and the Parochial Church Council.

☐If the deceased has been granted a grave space in a churchyard, a document called a *faculty* should be found among his papers; if in a cemetery, there will be a *deed of grant.* Otherwise a grave space must be bought.

☐Most cemeteries are now non-denominational. As soon as the place and the time of the funeral have been arranged, a decision must be taken about the participation of relations and friends so that a full announcement may be made in the newspapers.

Time of ceremony ☐This depends largely upon the priest and the undertaker but the distance that friends may have to travel should be taken into account. A service in the early afternoon is probably the best time for funerals in the country. This enables family and friends who have come from afar to assemble for lunch before the ceremony and for tea to be given afterwards to local friends.

☐If arrangements are not made to meet those travelling by train, local taxis should be warned so that transport to the house or church is available with the minimum of delay.

The ceremony ☐If the coffin is in the house, family mourners assemble there for prayers before moving to the church whether by car or on foot. The prayers are said by a member of the family, occasionally by a priest although it is more usual for him to await the coffin at the church gates. The coffin is transported in a hearse manned by the undertaker's bearers.

☐The other mourners wait in the church, and ample room should be left in the front pews for the family. There may be a verger to help marshal the mourners; if not, someone should be deputed to see that the pews are filled in orderly fashion.

□The principal mourners enter the church either before the coffin is brought in by the bearers or after it—a choice dictated by considerations of space as much as sentiment. If there is no initial ceremony at the house and no procession, the coffin is generally put in place before the mourners assemble. In certain cases, the coffin remains in the church overnight. It is placed on trestles in front of the chancel steps.

□These practices vary from parish to parish and most priests will have decided views on the subject. In High Anglican and Roman Catholic churches, a velvet pall covers the coffin; in certain circumstances, a Union Flag is draped over it.

Church of England

□Recent liturgical revision in the Church of England has resulted in a much greater degree of flexibility in the form of the funeral service. Until 1966, the burial services from the revised Prayer Book of 1928 were in general use. There is a version for adult burial and one for a child.

□These are now incorporated in *Alternative Services Series 1* and are available in booklet form for as long as they remain authorized for use.

□A second burial service, known as *Series 3*, has been introduced in recent years. This is written in contemporary language and is incorporated in the *Alternative Service Book* of 1980.

□Observances vary from parish to parish, but the parish priest will take into account the private nature of a funeral service. The family may help select the lessons and psalms and choose the hymns, the readers of the lessons and the giver of the address.

Burial

□If burial takes place in the churchyard or in the cemetery immediately after the service, this is attended by the chief mourners only. In the past, women did not attend the ceremony at the graveside but this custom is no longer observed and occasionally the entire service takes place there.

99

Cremation

☐If a service in church is followed by cremation, the chief mourners leave for the crematorium as soon as the church service is over. They form a procession of cars behind the hearse. However, many people today prefer to have the ceremony in the crematorium chapel (See 'Cremation').

Church of Scotland

☐The funeral service may be said in a house, church or crematorium chapel. The minister may use one of the forms of service in the *Book of Common Order* or arrange the service with the family. There is no formal address although a few words are said about the deceased.

Roman Catholic

☐The Funeral Mass for the Dead may be celebrated on any day except a Holiday of Obligation and a Sunday in Advent, Lent or Eastertide.

☐The variable parts of the Mass, the prayers, readings and Bidding Prayer, may be chosen by the priest in consultation with the family of the deceased. If the Funeral Mass is followed at once by burial, the concluding rites are omitted and the Final Commendation and Farewell take place either in church immediately after the Postcommunion or at the graveside.

☐Catholics in England and Wales who wish to celebrate a requiem Mass according to the old Latin liturgy may obtain permission to do so from the local Ordinary under an indult granted to Cardinal Heenan by Pope Paul VI in 1971.

The Religious Society of Friends (Quakers)

☐Most Monthly Meetings will appoint at least one member who will help in the planning of funerals, offer advice to the family and liaise with the undertaker. He will also alert other Friends in the area so that they can attend the funeral if they wish.

☐Cremation is acceptable to the Society but burials take place in the old Quaker burial grounds if space is available, and in cemeteries.

☐A Meeting for worship based on silence may take place in the cemetery or crematorium chapel.

Alternatively, the death may be commemorated at a Memorial Meeting on another occasion such as the burial or the scattering of the ashes.

□The simplest cut flowers are acceptable although charitable donations are more usual.

Jewish

□Jewish funerals take place with the minimum of delay but they are not permitted on the Sabbath, the Day of Atonement or on festivals. The observances vary according to the congregation. The law of *sitting shivah* (week of mourning) is observed by all Orthodox and many Reform and Liberal Jews. This takes place for a week in the house of the bereaved and is attended by close relations and other members of the family. Each evening the rabbi conducts prayers in memory of the dead and as a consolation to the living. On leaving it is customary to say to each mourner, 'I wish you long life'.

Secular

□Most cemeteries allow a non-religious ceremony to be held at the graveside. This will probably take the form of an address. Various organizations offer advice on this point and both the British Humanist Association and the National Secular Society, whose headquarters are in London will provide someone to officiate and to give an address.

Cremation

□The Cremation Society of Great Britain was founded in 1874 and the first crematorium was built a few years later at Woking. From the start, the Church of England was unenthusiastic. Cremation was considered pagan and many people found the practice of burning a body difficult to reconcile with belief in its subsequent resurrection. Thus, the trappings of cremation remained secular, both architecturally and symbolically, which is disturbing and distasteful to many Christians today. However, a recent statistic demonstrates its popularity: some 67% of those who die in the United Kingdom are cremated.

□The Cremation Society is a registered charity and

invites members of the public to join and demonstrate their support for the concept of cremation; forms are supplied on which the living can express 'an earnest desire to be cremated'. The Society runs an information service for both members and non-members.

Arrangements ☐No one can be cremated until the exact cause of death is known and the forms that must be completed before cremation are more elaborate than those for burial. They are:

An application form signed by the next of kin or the executor.

Two cremation certificates, signed by the family doctor and another doctor.

A third certificate signed by the medical referee at the crematorium. He has power to refuse cremation, require a post-mortem examination to be made or refer the matter to the coroner.

If the death is referred to the coroner, the two doctors' certificates are not needed. The coroner will grant a certificate for cremation.

Religious restrictions ☐The Roman Catholic Church permits cremation to take place with the appropriate funeral rites but does not conceal a preference for the custom of burying the dead in a grave.
☐Orthodox Jews do not permit cremation of their dead but it is allowed in Reform and Liberal congregations.

Service ☐The crematorium authorities place no restrictions on the form of service in the chapel provided that they are informed beforehand. The chapel is non-denominational and non-religious ceremonies are permitted. The services provided by crematoria vary widely; in some, a roster of clergymen is maintained and an organist is available on request;

but in others, the family or the undertaker will have to obtain their own local vicar's services and the only music available will be pre-recorded.
□The Cremation Society publishes a booklet which contains both the funeral rites for use in crematorium chapels by the Roman Catholic Church as authorized by the Liturgical Commission and by the Anglican Church as approved by the Archbishops of Canterbury and York.

Ashes □The crematorium authorities will wish to know what arrangements will be made for the collection of the cremated remains. There is no law relating to these although there are certain places where permission to scatter ashes will not be granted—the Royal Parks for instance. The owner of the land should always be approached first.
□Ashes may be scattered in a favourite place chosen by or associated with the dead person, buried in a churchyard or cemetery, scattered at sea or kept in an urn.

MEMORIAL SERVICES □A memorial service or requiem Mass is held as a tribute to someone who was prominent in public or in social life. In the past, the funeral ceremony and the memorial service often took place simultaneously, the funeral in the country and the memorial service in a nearby town or city, or in London. Today, the two events are more likely to be separated by some weeks.
□A memorial service is a public occasion in a way that a funeral service is not. Many people prefer to retain the private character of a funeral and announce a memorial service or requiem Mass to indicate this preference. There may also be practical reasons. A funeral service may take place in a small church in an inaccessible village, far from the centre of the professional or social life of the deceased.

Arrangements □The arrangements for a memorial service are made and announced well in advance so giving ample notice to those wishing to attend. It is possible to give much greater attention to the planning of the ceremony and to find a setting worthy of the occasion.

☐Those who decide for one reason or another to cremate their dead and long to counteract in the memorial service the tastelessness of the average crematorium chapel may do so with all the riches of English ecclesiastical architecture to choose from. Permission rests with the relevant clergyman; there are no residential or other qualifications. In London, certain churches are favourite settings for memorial services: St Martin-in-the-Fields, St Margaret's, Westminster (near the Houses of Parliament), St Paul's, Covent Garden (often used by the theatrical profession), St George's, Hanover Square, St James's, Piccadilly, and the Brompton Oratory.

Announcement ☐As soon as the date and the time are arranged, an announcement is made in the press. *The Times, The Independent* and *The Daily Telegraph* accept these for inclusion either on the court and social pages or in a section for memorial services on the back page. Announcements may be made in *The Guardian, Scotsman,* the *Yorkshire Post* and many local newspapers.

☐Personal notes may be sent to friends and acquaintances informing them of the date, time and place; but if the deceased had a wide social or professional acquaintance, then printed tickets giving details of the service are usually sent out in addition to the press announcement. The wording is the same for both (see examples below). If the deceased was a person of national importance, only a limited number of tickets may be made available to the public and, if so, this will be announced in the press, together with details about obtaining them. It is not unusual for applicants who write in to be asked why they wish to attend, so that priority can be given to those more directly linked with the deceased.

☐Normally, memorial services take place at around noon or, occasionally, at about 5 pm, always on a weekday. Drinks and sometimes a light lunch may be served afterwards at a nearby location. If everyone present is invited, this invitation can be issued at the service. However, it may not be possible to include everyone, and in such circumstances it is advisable to enclose a separate card with the admission ticket, giving details of the reception afterwards.

Examples

A memorial service for Mr John Smith will be held in Chichester Cathedral on Tuesday May 30th at noon.

A service of thanksgiving for the life of Mrs James Russell will be held at Holy Trinity Church, Brompton Road, London, on Wednesday February 14th at 11.30 am.

A requiem Mass for Mr John Smith will be celebrated at St James's Church, Spanish Place, London W1 on Friday May 16th at 11 am.

Anglican service

☐The Anglican church emphasises the celebratory nature of a memorial service and this is reflected in the title now widely used 'a Service of Thanksgiving'.
☐The service will be arranged by the parish priest and the family together. There is no memorial service in the *Book of Common Prayer*. Generally speaking, hymns and prayers alternate with readings from the Bible and works of literature and an address is given by an appropriate person.

105

☐It is customary to distribute printed service sheets with the name of the person commemorated on the cover. These are handed out at the door by ushers.

Jewish ☐The Jews may hold a memorial service in the synagogue and a memorial gathering at the consecration of the tombstone which takes place in the graveyard some months after the funeral.

Roman Catholic ☐In the Roman Catholic Church a memorial requiem Mass is celebrated. The emphasis lies on prayers for the repose of the soul of the departed rather than on thanksgiving for life.
☐An address may be given after the Mass but the homily after the reading of the Gospel will be of a religious nature.

Reporting ☐If the memorial service or Mass is given for someone of particular public importance, *The Times*, *The Independent* and *The Daily Telegraph* may print on their court and social pages an account of the service and a list of some of those present. The newspapers will send their own reporters to gather the names and the notice will appear in print free of charge.

Alternatively, these announcements may be inserted by the family for a fee, in which case one or two people must be deputed to gather the names of those present as they enter the church or synagogue. A visitor's book may also be used for this purpose.

Dress ☐A memorial service or memorial requiem Mass is a formal occasion. In the past, men wore formal dress: a morning coat, dark trousers and top hat of black silk, but this is seldom seen today. A black tie is probably the only visible sign of mourning. Women wear dark clothes and, more often than not, hats. Jewellery should be unostentatious.

6 TABLE MANNERS

☐Sharing food has always been the fundamental expression of friendship, and the reasons for it—dating from times when many did live by bread alone—are easy to understand. The word companion literally means 'sharer of bread' and few deeds throughout history have been deemed more terrible than to turn on a fellow eater. The host who has harmed his guest or the guest who has harmed his host are, among men, the most treacherous. Macbeth's real crime was the former; the massacre at Glencoe scarred history because it involved the latter.

☐In the early 19th century, when the French gastronome Brillat-Savarin observed that 'to receive any one as our guest is to become responsible for his happiness during the whole of the time he is under our roof', he was stating a law that had been sacred for many hundreds of years.

☐Shorn, happily, of its starker implications, that law holds today and whether host and guest are sharing a meal of gastronomic splendour or beaming at each other across a hotpot, the relationship between them remains the same. The host honours his guest by putting his needs above all else; the guest, through his behaviour, strives to show himself worthy of such honour. At its simplest, the exchange can be summed up in those two most basic expressions of courtesy, 'Please' and 'Thank you'. In these words lies the essential etiquette of the dinner table; but due to ancient tradition, connotations of binding social ties and the fact that all activities need orderly procedure, dinner parties are not as simple as that. They are, however, simpler than they have probably ever been and, where rules are concerned, the functional has triumphed over the vainglorious.

Background ☐In the 15th century, feudal households had no forks and more than one person ate off the same plate (were messmates), but strict rules of precedence (which are only just dying out) governed the seating arrangements and there was an elaborate ritual of bringing in the food by special escort while

everyone stood up and took off their hats. This was
followed by token washing, tasting, announcing the
already obvious arrival of the food to the lord, then
bowing and kissing—by which time dinner must have
been very cold indeed.

□It is hardly surprising that the lord eventually left
the hall to his servants and created a 'dinner room'
for himself and his friends where he could relax,
enjoy his meal and get away from all the formalities
needed to impress his minions. In time, functional
improvements like the fork arrived and then special
forks, spoons and knives for different courses—with
plates and glasses to go with them—and more
courses. To avoid confusion and guide people
smoothly through these new intricacies of eating and
drinking, a set of instructions became necessary and,
to be on the safe side, they were eventually
extended to include dress and topics of conversation.
The Edwardian dinner party had arrived, and as a
highpoint of elegance, impeccable service and
refined display it has probably never been equalled.
But the rules of precedence, the protocol, the sheer
refinement made it all rather exhausting on a regular
basis; just as its feudal antecedent had been. The
reaction was bound to come and two wars
contributed to it. The result is that nowadays, as like
as not, the lord is to be found enjoying good food,
wine and relaxing talk with his friends, at the head of
the kitchen table—though lack of servants more than
a craving for informality may be at the root of it.

Be that as it may, the fact remains that the dinner
table today, wherever it is located, has its
accompanying conventions reduced to a useful few.
Self importance and 'appearances' count for little or
nothing and there is flexibility in almost all aspects
and on almost all occasions. The emphasis is on good
food, good wine, relaxation and conviviality. But
even though the form is relaxed, the need to know
the ground rules remains, for only when people know
what is expected of them can things proceed
smoothly and everybody feel 'at home' and at their
best.

SEATED DINNERS ☐Dinner parties may of course vary greatly in degree of formality, number of guests, ways of serving and design of the meal. There may be a host and hostess or only one of these, and dinner can be served in a dining-room, at a table in a sitting-room or in the kitchen. But whether it is an elaborate or simple affair, the seated dinner party is probably the most satisfying form of domestic entertaining. It appeals to all senses and, if it is a success, produces that glowing spirit of goodwill which is the true aim of social gatherings.

Timing ☐Dinner is usually served between 8pm and 9pm but guests are invited to arrive up to half an hour beforehand. Some invitations make this interval clear by giving the time dinner will be served as well as the time guests are invited to arrive: 8pm for 8.30pm for example. There can be no misunderstanding if this formula is used and it is all right to arrive up to eight or ten minutes before dinner is served. If guests are invited for a specific time, 8pm for instance, they may safely allow some 15 to 20 minutes leeway. While it is of course a mistake to arrive *before* the stated time, it is most improper to be late. To keep others waiting is not only inconsiderate, but dinners must be carefully-timed events and delay can cause misfortunes in the kitchen. If there is some unavoidable delay, the hostess should be warned by telephone so that she may plan accordingly. Sometimes the happier solution for all concerned is to start dinner rather than wait.

Numbers ☐The maximum number of guests depends, of course, on the size of the table, but there are other considerations to be borne in mind. If there are more than four or five around the table, general conversation becomes difficult unless the table is round and so it is important to have even numbers in order that everybody may have a partner to converse with. It is also useful to keep in mind the fact that with eight or 12 people the host and hostess cannot keep their traditional places at ends of the table and at the same time divide the sexes evenly. But this may not matter.

Invitations

☐Invitations to dinner are issued by written notes, printed cards or by telephone. If the invitation is by telephone it is often wise to send a reminder by post. (Invitation cards and examples of replies appear in Chapter Eight). Printed invitations usually imply a relatively formal occasion but if 'black tie' is required it will be stated on the card. If an invitation is made by telephone it is helpful to indicate how formal the party will be so that guests may dress accordingly. At a few houses in the country a dinner jacket is still a matter of course, but this fact should be made known to a guest who has never dined there before.

☐All invitations to dinner should be answered immediately and no dinner engagement should ever be broken without serious reason. Although good friends can be invited at short notice, people should be invited to a sizeable party between 10 days and three weeks before the event. The greater the notice, the more likely it is that all the guests will be able to accept and every hostess knows how a well-planned party can go wrong if gaps have to be filled at the last minute. If stop-gap guests do have to be found it is wise to look for them among good friends and perhaps to be honest about the purpose in inviting them; also to take care to invite them to another dinner party in the future for their own sakes.

The menu

☐The composition of a meal depends on several things: the skills of the cook, the help available, the budget, the equipment in hand, the time of year and the degree of formality aimed at. But nowadays on even the most formal occasions, three courses are considered adequate—a first course, a main course and a pudding, or cheese and fruit (dessert). Often pudding *and* cheese and fruit are served, and sometimes these are replaced by a savoury. But if working on a very restricted budget, there is nothing wrong with compressing the menu into a main course and perhaps a salad, followed by a pudding. See also, 'Order of courses'.

☐In planning a menu three main rules ought to be followed. First, it should be balanced: a menu consisting of mussels, jugged hare and chocolate mousse would be unbearably rich. A strongly-seasoned dish should be balanced by one or more that are less demanding on the palate and digestion, while light dishes should be balanced by sustaining ones.

☐Second, the food should be varied. A main course of fish would not be preceded by scallops, nor a soup finished with cream followed by chicken in a cream sauce.

☐Third, do not attempt too much. An elaborate menu requiring last-minute attention will not present difficulties if there is competent domestic help, but a hostess without such aid is strongly advised to plan a menu that can largely be prepared earlier in the day. One of the greatest failings of modern dinner parties is the prolonged and continual absence of the hostess whose attention to food must take precedence over her attention to guests.

Special diets ☐When planning a menu it is obviously important to consider guests' likes and dislikes insofar as these are known. Some foods may be barred on religious or medical grounds and vegetarians are becoming ubiquitous. A vegetarian guest at dinner does not mean that the rest of the party must put up with the same diet, only that he must be well-fed too (sometimes fish is a happy compromise).

Equipment ☐The equipment needed to give a dinner party can be divided into five categories: silver, china, glass, serving dishes and kitchen utensils.

Silver ☐The silver (it may not be silver, of course) should comprise large knives and forks, small knives and forks; spoons for soup, pudding and coffee (fig 1 over-leaf). These should all match with the possible

1. Forks for 1) pudding or first course, 2) main course, 3) fish; knives for 1) meat, 2) butter, 3) fish; there is a pudding spoon, two styles for soup, teaspoon, coffee spoon.

exception of the knives which are often bone-handled. A selection of serving spoons and a good carving knife are also essential.

☐ Our forebears appear to have invented a spoon or a fork for every contingency, from spearing a pickle to removing the stuffing from a turkey, and while these are as unnecessary today as they were then, anyone who has them will be the better prepared for all eventualities.

2a. Shown above: a dinner plate, pudding plate, intermediate size for cheese/salad, and butter plate.

2b. Soup plate, bouillon bowl and crescent salad plate.

China ☐With the exception of the dessert plates, all the china used at a formal dinner party ought to match. At a very informal dinner this does not matter so much but the dishes used for each course should match *each other*, because, quite simply, it looks nicer. Large, medium and small plates will be needed, together with soup plates or bouillon bowls, if soup is to be served. A fourth plate of intermediate size is useful for cheese (or salad). Fig. 2 a. and b. shows the full range of plates.

☐Another essential is a coffee service: the coffee pot, cream jug and sugar basin may be silver or china; the cups and saucers should be demi-tasse (fig. 3).

3. A coffee service can be china or silver.

Serving dishes ☐Most of the serving dishes used for dinner parties may form part of the hostess's dinner service. The minimum requirement for anyone who entertains on a regular basis is two vegetable dishes, several flat serving dishes of different sizes, a gravy boat, one or more large glass bowls for puddings and a wooden cheese board. Trays are equally important, and a salad bowl is a great asset.

Glass ☐A separate glass is needed for each wine served and fig. 4 overleaf, shows the full complement. This includes a water goblet and a glass for port (sometimes brought in later). Details for setting the table and serving wine are given further on.

☐Glass finger-bowls are brought in on the dessert

4. Glasses used for: a, liqueur; b, port; c, sherry; d, white wine; e, red wine; f, water; g, champagne.

plates at many formal dinners (see page 117) or they may be used after any course which is eaten with fingers, such as asparagus. If the table does not have a cloth then a small mat should be placed under the bowl.

Kitchen utensils □Everyone has favourite pots and pans and if they are used behind the scene then their condition does not matter in the least, but if the kitchen and dining-room are one, then their appearance ought to be considered, as should that of kitchen dishes such as casseroles or soufflé dishes which are brought to the table.

Laying the table □A dining-table may be covered with a cloth but if the table has a beautiful surface, place mats are often preferred. If a cloth is used, it should hang about half way down to the floor and it must of course be spotlessly clean. Traditionally, the cloth used for a dinner party was white and the practice is still widely observed, but it is a matter of personal taste and a hostess need not be dissuaded from developing her own colour scheme if she has the style to bring it off.

Silver □The position of the silver at each place is governed by two basic rules. The first one is that the forks go on the left and the knives and spoons on the right. The second is that the diner starts with the implements on the outside and, course by course, works inwards to the centre. Fig. 5 shows different settings for different menus. The setting illustrated in fig. 5a is for a meal consisting of soup, meat,

5a. Table setting with glasses for sherry, red wine, champagne.

5b. Glasses (left to right) for water, white wine, red wine, port.

5c. Informal table setting for soup, main course, pudding.

pudding and cheese. On the diner's right, working inwards, are the bread knife, soup spoon, the knife for meat and the spoon for pudding. On the left are the forks for meat and pudding. If the pudding is ice cream, and to be eaten with a small spoon, the spoon still goes on the right, inside the knives. If the first course is to be eaten with a fork then the soup spoon on the right is replaced by a small fork on the left, as in fig. 5b. Note that the tines of the forks always point upwards and the blades of the knives inward.
☐The practice of putting the spoon and fork above the setting as shown in fig. 5c is perfectly correct, but slightly less formal. It does save space.
☐At a formal dinner, if there is any dessert, the dessert knife and fork are brought in on the dessert plate with the finger-bowl, if used (fig. 6).

Glasses   ☐At the vast majority of dinner parties only one wine is served and the glass for it is put just above the blade of the dinner knife. When more than two wines are served, it is customary to position the glasses in the order in which they will be used, working from right to left, or from left to right, or in a triangular pattern.
☐It should be noted, however, that there is no hard and fast rule dictating the way glasses are set out. Two arrangements are shown here (figs. 5a,b). The types of glasses used for each wine are also shown (see fig. 4). It is worth knowing what shape means what wine; for example, white wine glasses are usually smaller than ones for red; hock glasses are taller.
☐If water is served, then the water goblet is put on the table and a jug of water as well. Glasses are filled by request.
☐If port is served, the glasses for it may be put on the table when it is laid or when the port is served. (Information about serving wines is given further on.)

Plates   ☐Normally a butter plate is put on the left of the forks and, at informal dinners, this often doubles as a cheese plate which you put in front of you when the cheese is served.

Napkins   ☐Napkins may be folded into shapes such as 'mitres' and erected in the centre of the place setting (see fig. 5c), or folded into nothing more complicated than triangles or quarters, and laid across the butter plate (see figs. 5a,b). Napkins for dinners should be large: paper ones are perfectly acceptable at very informal gatherings and their use is bound to become more widespread, but where possible, linen napkins are strongly recommended.

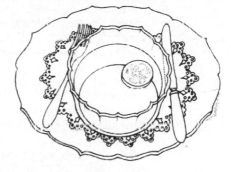

6. Finger bowl on mat, dessert fork and knife.

Candles   ☐Candlelight is indispensible both for setting the mood and making the table—and the people round it—look their best. Its softness cannot be duplicated by electricity. Whether candelabra or candlesticks are used is up to the hostess but, as a rule, the shorter the candlestick the taller the candle.
☐At a formal dinner party the candles are normally white and at all dinner parties there must be enough light, either from candles or from the candles plus electric light, for people to see what they are doing. The mood of a too subtly-lit dinner table is gloom.

Flowers   ☐Flowers on the dining table should be short-stemmed, as a tall centrepiece will screen diners from the people sitting opposite them.

Miscellaneous   ☐Salt cellars and pepper shakers are placed at regular intervals round the table when it is laid.

Ideally, there should be one set for every two diners, but this is very unnecessary. Pepper mills do not traditionally appear on dinner party tables but the superior quality of freshly-ground pepper has rightly caused the culinary-minded to waive this rule.
☐If mustard is to be used, it too is put on the table when it is laid, in a little silver pot or a dish; also butter. Sometimes small ashtrays are put round.

Wines and liqueurs ☐Many books exist about types of wine and how to serve them but, very briefly, wines can be categorized as follows: by colour—red, white and rosé; by character—light and heavy; dry, medium and sweet; still and sparkling. A good wine merchant will guide the prospective host or hostess (by custom wines are a male preserve) through the maze of possibilities, but as a rule of thumb
*the traditional accompaniment of soup is sherry
*shellfish and fish should be accompanied by dry white wines
*rich or highly-seasoned red meat and game are served with a full-bodied red wine, typically a burgundy
*other red meat goes well with lighter red wines such as bordeaux
*white meat can be accompanied by light red wines, medium dry white wines, or rosé
*cheese can be eaten with red wine and is, of course, the ideal background for any sort of port
*a sweet white wine, or champagne is served with puddings
☐See also 'Service of wine'.

Temperature ☐The temperature at which wines taste best varies according to their type. Red wines are normally served at room temperature, as are port and madeira. (Beaujolais is sometimes chilled, also very dry sherry.) Champagne should be served cold, but not frozen, and the same applies to white wines and rosé. Wines can of course be chilled in an ice bucket, but in no circumstances should glasses contain lumps of ice.

Decanting ☐Wines are transferred—via a wine strainer—to a decanter if they are of an age or type that is marked by the collection of sediment at the bottom of the bottle. In practice, this means that vintage port and old red wines are always decanted; that other red wines may be; and that white wines—including of course champagne—are served from the bottle. A wine that is being decanted should be poured through the strainer slowly, and the process should stop while there are still a couple of inches left in the bottle.

Opening ☐Red wines should be uncorked and allowed to stand for a while before being served. The younger the wine, the longer it needs to breathe: a young red wine should stand for several hours, while an older one needs only an hour—or less.

Seating ☐A hostess once needed to be mistress of the exquisitely precise science of equating the various ranks of her dinner guests with the places they occupied at table. Armed with the fruits of considerable research, she would arrange matters so that her husband took the highest ranking woman in to dinner and seated her on his right; she herself was taken in by the highest-ranking man and seated him on her right; the second most important man was seated on her left; and any male left without a partner in the procession to the dining-room was young, outranked by his fellows, or both.
☐In private houses today, people just 'go' into dinner and the intricate conventions of precedence are no longer rigorously obeyed in the seating plan. Since a dinner party is a social occasion, its prime purpose is that it should be a social success and, with this in mind, private hostesses are tending to concentrate on seating arrangements that make for good fellowship and easy conversation. It is now guests' personalities rather than their rank that govern seating plans. But the modern hostesses who choose to disregard precedence completely in favour of sociability, should keep in mind the fact that an

older person may be offended by this treatment because he or she misunderstands what is behind it. ☐Some of the old rules still apply in many households, and in them all, if there is a guest of honour. If no guest has an outstanding claim to importance by reason of rank or occupation, places of honour go to the oldest people present.

Seating plans and place cards ☐The hostess must work out the seating plan beforehand, and keep a note of it. If the party is a large or formal one, she will probably use place cards. On these, the guest's names are always handwritten and, if the party is small and informal, the first name is enough. Cards at a formal dinner should give the full name: Miss Margaret Dalloway, Mrs Richard Dalloway, Mr Peter Walsh, Lady Bruton. (See also charts, pages 208–233.)

Before dinner ☐If there is a servant, guests' coats will be taken at the front door; if not, the hostess should say where to leave them. When the host and hostess have greeted a guest, one of them (usually the host) offers him a drink. Sherry is the most usual drink, and sometimes the only one, but alternatives include whisky, gin or some other spirit.
☐If there is someone to pass the drinks, he will either hand round a tray or ask each guest what he would like to have. If there is no domestic help, and if several guests arrive at once, the host or hostess may ask the new arrivals to help themselves from a drinks tray; alternatively, they could ask a close friend to lend a hand. A guest may begin to drink as soon as he is given a glass. (Late arrivals should refuse the polite offer of a drink.)
☐As soon as the guest has a drink (or before), he should be introduced to everybody, and this must be gone through with each new arrival. For information about introductions, see Chapter Eight.

Announcing dinner ☐Dinner is announced by a servant saying simply 'Dinner is served', or, if there is no help, the hostess will ask her guests to come to dinner and lead the

120

way. Everyone finds their places either by reading their place cards, or at a word from the hostess. (There is no reason why the hostess should not produce her note of the seating plan to help her remember where everyone is to go.) The hostess should sit down as soon as she can and so should all the other women. The men should pull out the women's chairs for them before sitting down themselves.

Serving dinner □Part of the secret of a successful dinner party is that it should run smoothly, with minimal interruption to the flow of conversation. But without servants this presents considerable difficulty: somehow the food has got to be passed round, the plates removed after each course, new ones put down and the wine poured. The poor host and hostess on whom this burden falls find, more often than not, that they are continually joining conversations half way through, have no control over their party and are spending the evening as mere drudges, fetching and carrying. In the back of their minds they may be finding compensation in the thought that turn about is indeed fair play and, in the foreseeable future, those who are now merrily seated round the table will be slaving for them while they in turn sit happily eating, drinking and chattering away. □The truth is that there is no absolute way round this problem since nothing can beat a dinner that is served by professionals and enables the host and hostess to appear to blend into the company as though their responsibilities were as few as those of their guests. One solution is of course to hire temporary help to wait on the table, or to get someone to come in and do both the cooking and serving (a job popular with the young). But few people can or wish to undertake this expense every time they give a dinner party. The best solution, therefore, is to find ways of organizing the service of the meal so that it is both efficient and suits the facilities on hand; and, of course, by planning a menu that can be served easily and needs little last-minute

121

preparation. But whatever the mode of service, certain conventions still govern it.

Order of courses ☐The courses of a meal are served in the following order, but only very rarely would all the courses given in the list be served.
Soup (or other first course)
Fish (rarely served as a second course preceding the main one)
Sorbet (very rare)
Meat and vegetables (the main course)
Salad (sometimes served as a course, sometimes with the main course, often not at all)
Pudding
Savoury (rare)
Cheese (a fairly recent addition to the dinner party table)
Fruit (dessert)

Options ☐A variation in the above is the service of pudding and cheese. This is sometimes reversed. In France, the cheese always precedes the pudding and many British hostesses prefer to follow the French example if the cheese is to be eaten with the red wine served with the main course, instead of with port. Very often, too, the cheese and fruit appear at the same time and this makes service easier.

How to serve ☐Food is *always* served to each person on his left, while plates are normally removed from the right. No plates are removed until everyone has finished the course, then they are taken up and new ones put round. When taking away plates, no more than two should be removed at a time, one in each hand.
☐Anything that is served in a bowl, such as soup, should really have a plate, or saucer, beneath it and this is removed in one gesture along with the bowl.
☐If salad is served with the main course, it ought to have a plate of its own; crescent-shaped plates are sometimes used and these are put on when the table is laid. If the salad is served after the main course, a medium-sized plate should, correctly speaking, be

used, though admittedly an increasing number of
hostesses ask guests to use their dinner plates for
this. (Some people prefer not to serve salad at very
formal dinner parties, because the vinegar in the
dressing adversely affects the taste of good red
wine.)

☐Strictly speaking, separate plates ought also to be
brought in for cheese, but the servantless household
is likely to combine the service of fruit and cheese
and expect guests to use their butter plates to eat it
from.

Order of service
☐Traditionally, the woman on the host's right is
served first and the food is then passed round the
table clockwise (to the left), the host being served
second. If the party is large and two people are
serving, one of them begins as described, but
finishes with the person on the hostess's right. The
second begins by serving the hostess, then the
person on her left and, lastly, serves the person next
to where the other began (fig. 7).

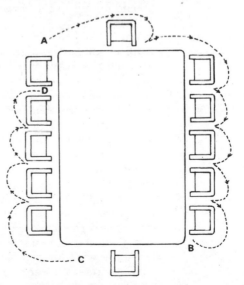

7. *A to B is one service, C to D another.*

□If there is only a hostess, she may either deputize someone to be 'host', so that service can begin with the woman on his right, or she may choose to implement the 'second servant' service described above, thereby being served first herself, the service proceeding clockwise round the table. She might also start with the person on her right.

When host and hostess serve

□If host and hostess are both serving, each taking round a different dish, it makes sense to start with the woman on the host's right as usual and to help their own plates as they go round.

The hostess serves

□If the hostess is doing her own serving, the best solution is often to have guests pass the food among themselves. In this case, the service must proceed to the *right, anti-clockwise,* so that each dish will be presented to the diner on his left side. The easiest thing to do usually is to hand each dish to the man on her right and let it continue on round the table. But if the hostess wishes to take a dish round herself, she should pass it *anti-clockwise* also.

Service of wine

□Wine, like food, is passed to the left but the glass is filled, unlike the plate, from the right (it is easier to reach that way). Each glass is filled only to about two thirds of its capacity. At most dinner parties only one wine is served and whether it appears at the beginning of the meal or with the main course is a matter of personal judgment. If it is quite an ordinary wine and does not conflict with the first course, then the more usual thing is to serve it throughout the meal.

□The order of wines appears under 'Wines and liqueurs' above. If there is a servant the wine will be passed round as required; if there is not, the host often takes the wine round (at least to begin with) and if there is only a hostess she might ask a man to serve the wine for her. Traditionally wine bottles or wine decanters never appeared on the table and if there are servants there is no need for them to do so today. But at dinner parties without extra help, the now well-established convention is either to leave the bottle on the table after the host has taken it round once, or to put it on the table to begin with and ask the guests to help themselves and pass it on. The empty bottle is removed of course when a new one is brought in and a half-filled bottle of one type of wine would not be left on the table after the wine for another course arrives (except by request).

Clearing the table ☐It is customary to clear away all plates, used glasses, salt and pepper pots, and any unused silver from the table before the pudding (or cheese) is served. At a formal meal this would certainly be done; at an informal one it is up to the hostess to decide how much she wants to comply with tradition. Many, understandably, regard it as a waste of time.

Dessert ☐At a very formal dinner, finger-bowls are brought in on the dessert plates, as well as a fruit knife and fork, which are placed on either side. If the table has no cloth, then small lace or linen mats are put underneath each bowl so that it can be set on the table safely (see fig. 6).

Port ☐Port is brought to the table at the same time as cheese and/or dessert, and put in front of the host. As has been said, glasses for it are either put on the table at the same time or set out when the table is laid. The host, still sitting, serves the person on his right, helps himself and then passes the decanter to the *left*. Port is always passed clockwise and each person helps himself. It is the responsibility of those present to see that the decanter keeps moving at a leisurely pace.

DIY dinner parties ☐Dinner parties given without servants must improvise on established convention and this has been going on long enough for a few improvisations to have become established customs in their own right. Most of them work fairly well, but one or two, though rising out of good intentions, are not really conducive to the pleasures of the dinner table, for example, the habit of passing plates down to the hostess, and stacking them on the way. It is, of course, meant to save her time and effort, but it is both ugly to look at and disruptive.

☐In addition to the modifications of tradition already mentioned in this chapter, there are others which also contribute to the successful service of dinner without help. For instance, if the first course is cold it may be put on the table before people sit down, saving one trip. If plates are stacked on the sideboard and taken to the kitchen when convenient, the hostess is less likely to lose track of the conversation by being out of the room so often. Reducing the number of courses is an obvious simplification, but perhaps the most useful practices involve how the food is served. Three systems are given here and each hostess should choose the method that best suits her facilities.

Method one
☐The hostess or host (or both) can take the food round. There are two disadvantages to this: being waited on by their hosts can embarrass some guests, and the system removes host and/or hostess from their places at table for too long a time.

Method two
☐The main course (with plates) can be put on the sideboard, and guests help themselves. This improvised buffet is an old tradition and works well, provided the main dish has already been cut up into servings, and there are adequate arrangements for keeping plates and food hot, but it means everybody has to get up and down.

Method three
☐A further method is to serve and pass the meat along on plates—or take it round—and let guests pass the rest (or everything) among themselves. This is a modified version of one of the oldest systems of serving food and it involves less bustle and movement than either of the other systems described.

Behaviour at table
☐Paradoxically, a guest at table should try and

make others forget that he is eating. He eats and drinks quietly and without fuss, does not, of course, talk with his mouth full, avoids looking greedy, and also avoids eating so slowly that the progress of the meal is held up. The actual techniques of eating and drinking are described in detail further on.

□Faced with something you do not know how to eat, there are two ways out of the difficulty—watch what everyone else does, or confess ignorance. Few people will think less of anyone for admitted inexperience; on the contrary, you will probably be showered with advice from all quarters.

Being served □Food is presented to the diner on his left. He picks up the serving implement(s)—one in each hand if there are two implements—helps himself to as much as he wants, then replaces the implements side by side on the serving dish. When being served by a servant it is polite to say 'thank you' when offered something, but this is unnecessary when things are removed. If the host or hostess is serving, the same applies, except that additional remarks relevant to the current conversation or the delicious appearance of the food are normal, but to engage either in conversation when they are trying to get round the table with the food would obviously be thoughtless.

□If food is being passed along by the seated guests, often the man will offer it to the woman on his right, holding the dish while she helps herself. If the dish is cumbersome, a woman may also offer to hold it for a man and, if so, he should accept (as should she). But it is equally acceptable just to pass things round the table from person to person, if they can be managed alone.

Offering to help □Although the polite offer of help, particularly to a hostess giving a dinner party on her own, is a courteous gesture, such an offer should never be pressed. If members of the party are bobbing up and down throughout the meal then conversation is going to be sporadic and dinner partners stranded with no one to talk to—and perhaps feeling guilty about not being on their feet too. As a rule, it is far better if guests allow themselves to be waited upon and refrain from gallant gestures of assistance unless there is reason to believe it is really needed.

The chief reponsibility of guests is to be agreeable, charming, attentive to partners at dinner and to contribute as much as possible to the conversation and spirit of conviviality. They are there to enjoy themselves, not to man a production line, and any hostess who has a system of service worked out (as she should have) is more likely to find well-meant assistance a hindrance rather than a help.

When to begin ☐It is correct to begin to eat as soon as you are served, even if others have not been. This is the established custom and it has practical advantages; first, the food is more likely to be hot, and second, the hostess is spared boringly repetitive remarks of encouragement like 'Please don't wait...' or 'Please begin'—a familiar litany at so many dinner parties. Waiting for everyone to be served—though clearly instinctively polite—serves no useful purpose at a modern dinner table where there is no doubt that everyone *will* be served.

Conversation ☐See also Chapter Eight. At any dinner party— large or small, formal or informal—everybody has a duty to talk to the person sitting on either side. However shy a guest may be feeling, he can still follow the conversation round him and he should make a contribution where he can. It is not polite to sit through the meal in meek silence, and a good guest will always pull his own weight.

☐Conversation should be divided between the partners on either side and it would be extremely rude to spend most of the meal with your back turned to one of your companions at the table.

Topics ☐In earlier years, there were four topics of conversation that were discouraged in society that was both polite and mixed; servants, illness, religion and politics. There was a strict taboo in most circles on sex. While there has been a sharp decline in the popularity of discussing servant problems, the others are, with the exception of illness, some of the greatest subjects for conversation that have ever existed, and nowadays they are fair game, *as long as no one present is upset by what is said.*

□A hostess should constantly be on the watch for danger signals. If, say, one of her guests is rather straitlaced and the conversation starts moving from films in general to pornographic films in particular, she should divert the talk. In an emergency, a way of doing this is to say, 'Going back to what you were saying just now . . .', pulling the talk back to its earlier general ground, and keeping it there until someone else steps in. She should be even more watchful if religion is being discussed. If the talk drifts close to the religion practised—unknown to the rest of the party—by one of the guests, it is safest to head the conversation off at once. The guest may of course forestall this move by stating his own convictions and inviting discussion; even so, the hostess should be ready to intervene if this discussion becomes argumentative or painful.

□Politics are a slightly less delicate subject, but the hostess should be aware that they are as boring to some people as they are fascinating to others. It is her aim that everybody round the table—not merely the politically-minded—should enjoy themselves, and it is her duty to guide the talk so that they do.

□A conversational gambit which is always taboo is malicious, ill-natured or ill-worded gossip about someone who is not present. If three people are talking in a group, it is also impolite for two of them to spend long discussing people or places unknown to the third.

□It used to be the custom that a guest never expressed appreciation of the food or drink served at a dinner but this reticence is now completely out of fashion. Indeed, a modern guest who did not find something pleasant to say about his dinner or his surroundings would be considered almost rude.

Refusing food	☐While it is generally impolite to refuse a course, you may do so if the reason is a very important one: if, for instance, you are allergic to the food offered. In some cases, however, it is more unobtrusive to take a very small amount and simply leave it on the plate.
Drink	☐Wine may always be refused simply by saying, 'No thank you', or putting a hand briefly over the glass when you are offered wine. If you would like water to drink and there is no jug on the table, or water goblet, it is perfectly correct to ask if you may have some.
Second helpings	☐It used to be the rule that second helpings of food were not offered at dinner parties. This, however, has changed and, depending on the nature and quantity of the food left, the vast majority of hostesses offer second helpings. When offered a second helping, there is no need to feel ashamed of saying 'Yes'; your enjoyment is a compliment to your hostess (especially if she has also been the cook). But everyone is free to refuse.
Accidents	☐In case of accidents, the guiding rule is, 'Don't disrupt the party'. A guest who, for example, has dropped the gravy-boat should apologise, but he should not make loud and continuous protestations of remorse. And the hostess, if there is no servant present, should mop up the mess as quickly and as deftly as she can. In a servantless household, the guest should certainly offer to help with the mopping up. But, if the hostess refuses, he should not press the point. With all accidents, commonsense should take precedence over gentility and nowhere has this been better expressed than by Dr Johnson who, having taken a mouthful of scorching soup, spat it out again, exclaiming, 'Now a fool would have swallowed that!'
Smoking	☐It is very discourteous to smoke at table unless the hosts in some way give the lead, by offering cigarettes or by lighting their own. No smoking

should take place until all eating has finished.

After dinner   □After the meal is finished the hostess will rise and ask the guests to follow her into the drawing-room (or to more comfortable chairs, if the dining-room and drawing-room are one); or she may ask only the ladies to go with her, leaving the men to port and cigars. If the last is the case, the men should stand up when the ladies leave and the man nearest the door opens it for them.

Departure of ladies   □This ancient custom of separation of the sexes has fallen into some disrepute of late, but before it is relegated to the dustbin it deserves reconsideration, as there are several things to recommend it. First of all, women do have *toilettes* to put right and this is an excellent opportunity to do so. Secondly, it gives women a chance to make friendly connections with their own sex which is harder to do in a drawing-room where the sexes are supposed to mingle. The objection appears to lie in the implication that the ladies are being got rid of, but this is an illogical attitude and women are wrong to feel disadvantaged simply because the men remain congregated in the dining room.
□If a hostess chooses to divide her guests after dinner, it is very impolite not to comply willingly. It is also impolite for either party to remain away from the drawing-room for more than about 20 minutes.

Coffee   □While it is the more usual practice to leave the table for coffee (and liqueurs), many people prefer to have coffee at the table.

□When serving coffee, the coffee-tray is taken into the drawing-room or to the dining table, if preferred. If coffee is served at table, all remnants of the meal are first removed.

□In a well-staffed house a servant takes the coffee round, pouring it for each guest and allowing him to help himself to cream and sugar from the tray. A simpler alternative is to put the tray by the hostess and leave; she then pours the coffee herself. (The correct service of coffee differs from that of tea in that the guest, rather than the hostess, puts in the cream and sugar.)

Liqueurs

☐Brandy and liqueurs—if any—are offered immediately after the coffee is served. If the coffee is served in the drawing-room, liqueurs and liqueur glasses can already be in place on a side-table; if the guests are to remain round the dining-table, glasses and liqueurs will have to be brought in on a tray. In the absence of domestic help the host normally attends to the liqueurs. After each guest is given coffee, the host asks him to make his choice among the drinks available and pours it out for him. Well-known liqueurs include Cointreau, Drambuie, Chartreuse and Grand Marnier.

Remaining at table

☐If, owing to personal inclination, or lack of space, no move is made to leave the dining table after the service of coffee, guests should feel free to get up from the table, move their chairs, or swap seats, provided nobody's feelings are hurt. The safest way to avoid this is for the host and hostess to initiate the swapping.

Departure

☐People generally leave dinner parties between 11pm and midnight but of course there are many exceptions to this. Certainly anyone staying later should gauge their hosts' states of mind, and, if in doubt, go unless pressed to stay.
☐The hosts should always go to the front door with departing guests who will naturally thank them for their hospitality before leaving.

Thanking

☐In addition to thanking the hosts at the end of the evening, you must write a letter of thanks, preferably the next day (although a week's grace is permitted). In it, you should again express appreciation of the hospitality and—very important—mention one or two aspects of the party that you found particularly pleasant. Traditionally, such letters are addressed to the hostess only, but if both host and hostess are good friends, and particularly if both have assisted in serving the dinner, then it makes sense to write addressing them both. Details of writing thank you notes appear in Chapter Eight.

☐If the hostess is a close friend, it is normal to telephone her the next day instead of writing. This gives her an opportunity to have a chat about the party and to assess it with the help of another pair of eyes and ears.

☐There is no need for both husband and wife to write thank you notes. Usually it is the wife who does so on behalf of them both. It is worth noting, however, that a hostess who gets a letter of thanks from both partners is likely to remember it as a special mark of courtesy.

EATING AND DRINKING

☐At a dinner party, food and wine really form the background of the occasion, even though they are very important. The central occupation is of course conversation and the desired effect from this combination of ingredients is goodwill. Good table manners therefore mean keeping the mechanics of eating and drinking from drawing attention and keeping the evening's priorities in the right order.

Holding a knife

☐When using a knife, hold it with the end of the handle tucked down into the palm of your hand. The thumb extends down one side of the handle and the index finger points down the back: this finger *never* touches the back of the blade. The other three fingers are curled round the handle to hold it in place, as shown in fig. 8.

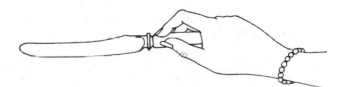

8. The proper way to hold a knife.

Holding a fork □When a fork is used *without* a knife, it is held with the tines pointing up, as in fig. 9. Always hold a fork as near the tip of the handle as possible, not clutched at the base. The fork rests on the middle finger which is supported by the outer two fingers.

□Left-handers come into their own with forks. Since these implements were late arrivals at the dinner table the only place left for them was on the left side of the plate, so left-handers can just pick them up and start eating while the right-handed must awkwardly transfer the fork to the right hand. For this reason, using a fork by itself is not correct once the knife (or dessert spoon) have been brought into action too. There would be too much laying down and switching over.

□A fork by itself is used at fork suppers or for any course that does not require a knife or dessert spoon. This applies, for instance, to some first courses, pastries and also to main courses which, needing no cutting up, can be eaten like fork suppers.

Using a knife and fork together □In this case, the knife is held as described above and the fork is held like the knife (fig. 10). The tines point *downward.* The knife and fork are used together normally for the main course, but if there is nothing to cut the fork may be used alone, as has been said. Both methods are correct. Other courses and dishes which need cutting up, such as some melons and savouries, are also eaten with a knife and fork.

□In addition to cutting up food (you eat each piece as you cut it), the knife is used to guide food on to the fork (fig. 11). Some foods such as rice and peas (described in detail further on) can either be loaded on to the back of the fork, or the fork can be turned over momentarily to make a scoop and the food pushed on to it with the knife (fig. 12). If this is done, the knife must guide the food to the *inner* side of the fork, not the outer (fig. 13), which might cause you to poke your neighbours with your elbows.

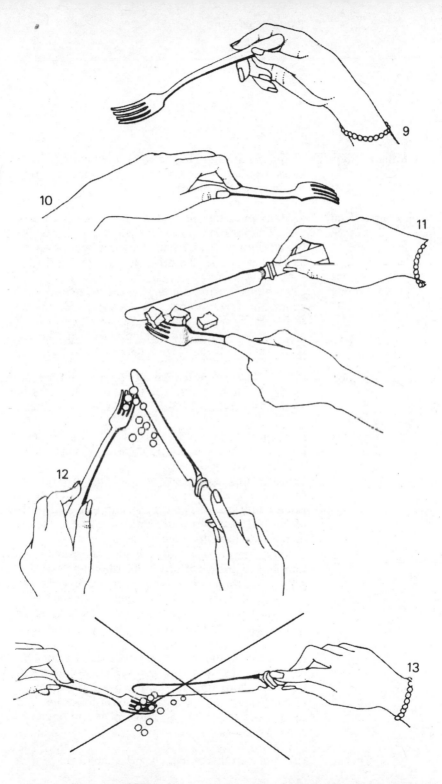

Holding a spoon	☐Spoons are held in the right hand exactly like forks. Remember to hold the spoon near the tip, not the base, of the handle.
Using a spoon and fork	☐Many puddings are eaten with both spoon and fork. The fork is held as it is when used with a knife, tines pointing downwards. One implement operates as the receptacle, the other as a guide (fig. 14).
Stopping	☐To pause during dinner, lay the knife and fork (or spoon and fork) at angles to each other on the plate, as in fig. 15. When you have finished, lay the knife and fork (or spoon and fork) side by side (fig. 16). Note that the tines of the fork point up.
Special techniques	☐Definite techniques have been evolved for eating the following foods. In some cases, more than one method exists; important alternatives are given.
Artichokes	☐Whole artichokes are served hot with melted butter or a hot sauce, or cold with a vinaigrette dressing or a cold sauce. ☐Using fingers, tear off each leaf in turn, dip the broad fleshy end into the sauce and, with a gentle pulling motion, scrape off the sauce-coated portion of the leaf between your teeth. The rest of the leaf is discarded on the edge of the plate. ☐Near the centre of the artichoke the leaves become thin and fleshless; if lifted off, they disclose a whiskery substance or 'choke', which is gently scraped off with a fork. Underneath it lies the choicest bit of the vegetable, the artichoke heart. This is eaten with a knife and fork.
Asparagus	☐Asparagus, like artichokes, is served either hot or cold with accompanying sauce. Pick up a stalk at the base with your fingers, dip the head in the sauce and bite off the tip. Continue eating in this way. If the base is too tough to eat, leave it on the edge of the plate.
Cheese	☐When eating cheese, cut off a small piece at a

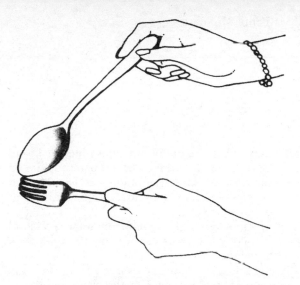

14. *Eating pudding with a fork and spoon.*

15. *This angle of the knife and fork indicates that the diner has not finished eating.*

16. *The position of knife and fork when the diner has finished.*

time. This is usually put on a piece of bread or biscuit, which you may have buttered, and eaten with the fingers. Some people like to eat the rind of soft cheese such as Camembert, but this is a matter of personal taste.

☐When serving yourself from a large V-shaped slice, cut along the arms of the V and not across the tip of the slice.

☐Stilton is sometimes served from the round and a spoon is used to extract the crumbly centre.

Corn-on-the-cob ☐This is eaten with the fingers. (Occasionally a 'knob' is driven into each end of the cob.) Pick the cob up by the knobs, or by holding both ends of the cob, and gnaw the corn off. This can be a difficult operation for people who have trouble with their teeth and because it is messy as well, corn-on-the-cob is best reserved for family occasions.

Fish ☐Opinion is divided on whether to fillet a fish before you eat it or to fillet it a little at a time as you eat. The latter is considered somewhat more correct but the former makes it easier to eat, though there is the problem of what to do with the debris. A very thoughtful hostess might provide a side dish for this. If you get a bone in your mouth, take it out with your fingers as inconspicuously as possible and put it on the edge of the plate.

Fruit ☐The best guide to the degree of formality required is the silver you have been given. If there is both a fruit knife and fork at your disposal, you should use both.

Apples and pears ☐The most formal way to eat either of these at a dinner party is to quarter them, peel each quarter and eat them with a fruit knife and fork. This remains a highly practical way of dealing with pears, since the juice makes them very messy to eat; but most people today eat the peeled quarters of either an apple or a pear with their hand. If you like peel, there is no reason why you shouldn't eat it.

Oranges	☐Oranges are rather difficult to eat tidily and are worth refusing at a formal dinner party unless you have mastered the technique. This is to peel the orange with a knife, remove the flesh from the skin with a knife and fork, and eat with a fork. A less formal and much more popular variant is to peel the fruit with a knife, divide it into sections and eat the sections with your fingers.
Fruit with stones and pips	☐Fresh fruit such as cherries and grapes are eaten with the fingers: to get rid of the stones or pips, put your hand to your mouth, let the stone drop into it and discard the stone on the edge of your plate. ☐If a pudding with fruit in it has pips or stones, unobtrusively spit them into your spoon and, again, put them on the side of your plate. In the case of large stoned fruit, such as peaches, cut the stone out while dividing the fruit into quarters.
Meat	☐When eating meat, it is only necessary to use a knife if there is something to cut, but a knife makes a useful pushing device too. Chops, roast beef and steak, for instance, are eaten with both knife and fork while fish pie and beef stroganoff may be eaten with a fork only.
Mussels	☐Mussels are sometimes served in their shells, as in the dish *moules à la marinière*. The British usually pick them up shell by shell and spear the mussel with a fork. The French method, also acceptable in Britain, is to replace the fork with an empty mussel shell: this is used like a scoop to extract each mussel from its shell.
Oysters	☐When they are served on the half shell, hold the shell steady on the plate with one hand and use a fork to lift the oyster out. After eating it you can pick up the shell and drink the juice.
Pasta	☐Pasta is unlikely to figure on a formal dinner party menu as it is both a homely dish and a messy one. But it might well appear at an informal dinner. When

confronted with a mound of pasta noodles, drive your fork into it, and with a lifting motion, partially separate a few strands from the heap. Then hold the tip of the prongs against the edge of the plate and carefully twirl the fork round so that the strands wind themselves on to it. The ideal result is a compact bundle, with few short ends hanging loose. □Some people use a spoon to hold pasta noodles in place while the fork is twirled, but this betrays the novice spaghetti-eater.

Pâté □Pâté is accompanied by toast and butter. Cut off a piece of toast with your butter knife, butter the piece and spread some pâté on it. Continue in this manner, preparing and eating a piece at a time.

Peas □It might well be claimed that it is as possible to tell a princess by the way she eats peas as by the way she sleeps on them. Certainly, eating peas is very tricky. In about 1830 it was done with a spoon; it has never been done with a knife, despite what some people like to think. There are two ways to go about it when eating with a knife and fork. One is to spear a couple if you can and then push a few more on to the back of your fork with your knife, but this is not a very pretty sight. The recommended method is to turn your fork over (do not change hands) and simply scoop the peas up, giving them a push, if necessary, with your knife (see fig. 12). Then, turn the fork back to its original position, tines downward, and continue eating.

Pudding □It is now general practice to eat puddings with either a fork or—if the pudding is difficult to reduce to mouth-sized pieces—with a spoon and fork. Two of the exceptions to this rule are ice cream and sorbet, which are always eaten with a spoon.

Rolls □These are broken open with your fingers, not cut in half with a knife. Tear off a small piece, butter it if you wish, and eat it.

Salad   ☐If necessary, salad can be tackled with both a knife and a fork.

Snails   ☐Snails, or *escargôts*, are rarely encountered in private homes in Britain but they often appear on menus in restaurants. They are served with a special pair of tongs and double-pronged fork. Grip the shell of the snail with the tongs, holding them in your right hand, and pick out the snail with the fork. If there is bread on the table it is perfectly correct, and delicious, to mop up the remaining garlic sauce when you have eaten the snails.

Soup   ☐Soup is drunk from the side of the spoon, never from the end. Dip the spoon sideways into the soup, at the bowl edge nearest you, push the spoon across the bowl, lifting it out at the far side. This way, if there are any drips they will land back in the bowl and not on you. When the bowl is almost empty, tip it away from you slightly and scoop up what is left.
☐If soup is served in large soup plates (bowls), the spoon is left in the bowl when you have finished. If it served in bouillon cups, put the spoon on the saucer.

Finger-bowls   ☐These may be served with any dish that is eaten with fingers. At very formal dinner parties finger-bowls are brought in on the dessert plates: you pick the bowl up (and its mat if there is one) and set it on your left above your fork. Dip the tips of your fingers in the water and gently dab them dry on your napkin in your lap.

Napkins   ☐As soon as you sit down, unfold your napkin and lay it across your lap. Use it with restraint, dabbing your fingers on it lightly and merely touching it to your lips. When you get up to leave the table, put the napkin down on the table without attempting to fold it.

Carving   ☐Carving may be carried out in the kitchen or in the dining-room. Either way a considerable degree of skill is needed and practice *en famille* is essential before

17. *How to carve a topside of beef.*

18. *Ham is carved on alternate sides.*

19. *How to carve a leg of pork.*

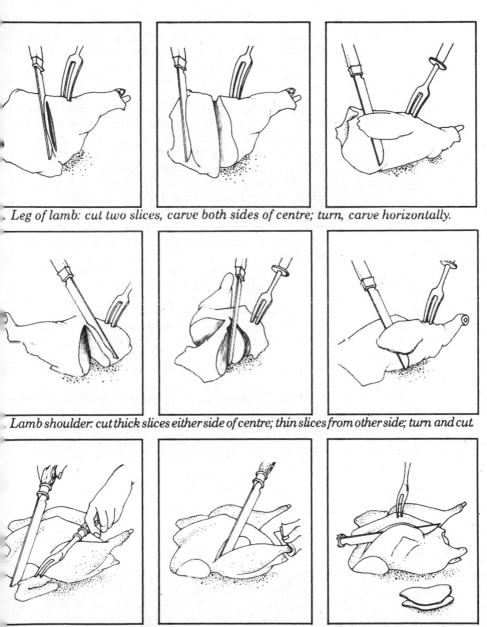

Leg of lamb: cut two slices, carve both sides of centre; turn, carve horizontally.

Lamb shoulder: cut thick slices either side of centre; thin slices from other side; turn and cut.

Chicken: cut off wings and legs at joint; separate thigh and drumstick; carve breast.

any bird or cut of meat is carved in public. Figs 17–22 show the basic methods of carving different types of meat; the pre-requisites are a very sharp knife, a fork with a safety catch, and plenty of space.

Wine etiquette

☐See also 'Wines and liqueurs', and 'Service of wine and port'. If a different wine is being served with each course, aim to finish the wine you have been given before proceeding to the next course and its accompanying wine. Of course this may not be possible, but do not continue drinking the first wine when you have begun to eat the next course.
☐It is perfectly correct to refuse wine at any point during the meal. Simply say 'No thank you' and if you like, put a hand over the glass momentarily for emphasis.
☐Wine is always sipped and the glass put back in its place between each sip.

BUFFETS

☐The word buffet, which means sideboard, has become synonymous with serve-yourself arrange-ments for eating. A buffet supper—or fork supper, as it is sometimes called—at which all the food is laid out at once, has several advantages. The hostess doesn't have to worry about serving each course and can also entertain more people than could be fitted round her dining table. Buffets remove problems of precedence and seating plans (guests simply gravitate towards those they find most congenial). Guests can be added more or less up to the last minute, and since the size of the party is so elastic, there is no difficulty about last-minute cancellations.

Invitations

☐'At Home' cards are usually used and the words 'buffet supper' or 'fork supper' are added. See Invitations, Chapter Eight.

Food and drink

☐People should be able to eat the main dishes with a fork. There should be at least one main dish based on meat or fish and, if the hostess has hot plates, it can be served hot. A cold buffet is perfectly acceptable however. Salads are very popular at buffets; so is cheese. At least one pudding is usually served.

□Pre-dinner drinks followed by wine at dinner is normal but sometimes the wine served at dinner is also served before it; and at very informal buffet suppers and lunches, beer and cider may be options.

Laying the table □The shape of the table will dictate the placing of the dishes. Some buffet tables are approached from one side only (the food being served from behind it, or the table placed against a wall). Other tables allow circulation and some buffets are laid out so that two queues may be formed for service. This is highly recommended for a large party.

□Since buffets dispense with the first course, plates of only two sizes are needed. The plates should be stacked in piles and the cutlery and napkins arranged so that they come easily to hand.

□The table must be covered with a cloth and often this reaches to the floor and has the corners pinned back to prevent accidents.

Service □Guests either help themselves as they move along, or they are served from the opposite side of the table. It is perfectly correct to return for second helpings. The pudding is nearly always collected later and the plates from the main course are either put where the hostess indicates, or they are collected by the staff.

Where to eat □Many people have a habit of eating standing up, bunched near the buffet table. This often means it is difficult for others to be served and is in any case rather awkward since it is almost impossible to hold a plate, balance a wine glass and eat at the same time. To avoid this, the hostess should put round as many chairs as she can and encourage guests to make their way back to the drawing room. Those who are agile enough can sit on the floor. Some hostesses put cushions about—and also stools—and when there is enough space, it is not uncommon to set up card tables—the best solution of all.

LUNCHEONS ☐Like so many kinds of daytime entertaining, the luncheon party given in a private house is by no means as popular as it used to be. Men are rarely available (except at weekends) and women too often have professional or domestic commitments that preclude the devotion of two hours or more to a meal. Nevertheless, when possible, it is a particularly pleasant form of entertaining and a very good way to entertain a few friends of the same sex.

Timing ☐Luncheon is served between 1pm and 1.30pm and the interval between arriving and eating is short—15 to 30 minutes—so it is most important for guests to arrive punctually. In addition, they should not, as a rule delay their departure much beyond 2.30pm.

Invitations ☐Invitations to a private luncheon party are usually made by telephone. A week to 14 days' notice is adequate.

The menu ☐Luncheon menus are lighter than dinner ones, and there is less obligation to serve a number of courses. A total of three is the maximum and two—followed perhaps by fruit or chocolates—is acceptable. In the past, soup was not served at luncheon but this is no longer so now that so many excellent soups can be made quickly in blenders.

Drinks ☐Drinks are normally offered beforehand, and coffee afterwards. To accompany the meal itself, one type of wine is enough, but more can of course be served if it suits the hostess.

Service ☐This is the same as for dinner with the proviso that it needs to be particularly deft and speedy.

Thanking ☐The rule is that guests at a formal luncheon should write and thank their hostess afterwards, but after a lunch among friends this is not necessary and a telephone call is often made instead.

7 PARTIES

☐The parties described in this chapter fall into
four main classes: drinks parties, balls and dances,
afternoon parties such as teas and garden parties,
and children's parties. For dinners and luncheons
see Table Manners, Chapter Six.

☐Many people are frightened of giving parties and
there can be no doubt that they are a big
responsibility—similar in many ways to producing a
theatrical entertainment— and even the most
experienced hostess is on tenterhooks at the
beginning. Will her guests get on together, she
wonders, or will the atmosphere be frosty with
strained politeness? Will there be enough people to
produce an atmosphere? She becomes convinced
her party will flop: oh why did she ever undertake
it in the first place!

☐But if the occasion has been carefully planned
and efforts that show made in the preparation of the
food, the quality of the drink, the visual details such
as flowers, and the arrangements for looking after
people—reassurance will come very soon. The
decibel level suddenly rises from a seemingly
funereal whisper to something like a subdued roar.
This sound—indefinable and unmistakable—is the
best immediate gauge of a party's success. It means
the gathering is no longer just a collection of
people; it has become a social group and the
hostess can forget her worst worries: whatever may
happen later will at least happen at a party that is
worthy of the name.

DRINKS PARTIES

☐Drinks parties fall into two distinct categories—
the pre-dinner, or cocktail party, and the after-
dinner party. The latter may include dancing, and
sometimes supper, and can be quite a formal affair.

Cocktail parties

☐While the cocktail (a mixture of spirits and other
ingredients) is not often served nowadays, it has
given its name to the type of party that starts at
6pm or 6.30pm and continues for about two hours.
Guests may be offered sherry only, champagne only,
red and white wine, a wine cup or a variety of

147

spirits and aperitifs. At least one non-alcoholic drink must also be provided. Food is light, and is presented in such a way that it can be eaten easily with the fingers. A special feature of the cocktail party is that it normally has a definite time limit. This is stated on the invitation card, and guests staying much later are guilty of a breach of manners. In size, cocktail parties range from about a dozen people to well over a hundred.

After-dinner parties

After-dinner parties start after 9pm and there is often no set time of departure. The words 'drinks party' are not used in the invitation, even when it is issued verbally. The occasion is normally referred to simply as 'a party', and 'At Home' cards are the most usual form of printed invitation. If there is dancing, this is sometimes stated on the invitation. Since guests are supposed to have dined already, little food need be served, but if the party is a relatively large or formal affair, there may be a supper later on.
□Recorded music is a popular ingredient of after-dinner parties and space is often reserved for dancing. If the party is large—and dancing is to be an important feature—a disco may be hired.
□The drinks which can be offered are the same as those described for a cocktail party, except that sherry would not be served.

Choosing the type of party

Drinks parties are very adaptable: there is a type to suit every domestic arrangement and financial state. The event can be as simple or as elaborate as its organizer wishes, and it offers considerable opportunity to a hostess who is slightly alarmed at the multi-faceted responsibility involved in giving a seated dinner. But a drinks party should not be seen as a 'next best' to a dinner party. The two forms of entertaining are completely different in their aims and in their style. At a dinner party the efforts of both hostess and guests are concentrated on a small number of people over a fairly long time;

by the end—if the party is a success—all should feel that they have deepened their liking and understanding of each other. At all but the smallest drinks parties the aim is not so much to deepen existing relationships as to make new ones, or to renew acquaintance with people whom it is pleasant to see from time to time. In other words, drinks parties are a useful method of oiling the social wheels of a community.

☐Another of their functions is to provide a time-honoured way of meeting the opposite sex. The high degree of mobility allowed creates a second-to-none arena for the mating game and if this is an aim of the party, then provision for dancing should certainly be considered and a large number of single people invited. If, on the other hand, the point is to welcome old friends back to the area, the guests will be the people who know them and the aim will be to encourage conversation. A small or moderate-sized cocktail party would be a sensible choice, and, afterwards, the guests of honour and a few others could join their hosts at dinner.

☐Many hostesses see drinks parties as golden opportunities to return hospitality in one easy go. As a rule, though, asking someone to drinks is not a proper return for hospitality received on a different scale. If you have dined at someone's home, they should be invited to dine in yours: if, that is, you wish to continue a friendly relationship. If, however, you wish to acknowledge their hospitality but do not wish to develop the relationship, then an invitation to drinks may be the answer.

☐Drinks parties are also good places to develop an acquaintance further. A hostess may have misgivings about inviting someone she hardly knows to dinner, and she might be right. Four hours' concentrated company represents a challenge—though a pleasant one—to any friendly relationship, and this particular relationship may not yet be ripe enough to take the strain. At a drinks party, however, all is well. The new acquaintances—though possibly surprised—will be pleased rather than alarmed to get their invitation and the hostess can relax in the knowledge that there will be a roomful of people to help entertain them. If it emerges that the materials for friendship are there, the invitation will doubtless be returned; the social ice has been broken. But if things do not work out as hoped no one will have cause to remember the evening with embarrassment.

Pitfalls □As well as making sure of the party's aim, it is important to remember that many of the factors that contribute towards its success can, paradoxically, ruin it. A crowded room makes conversation difficult and many people, particularly the elderly, do not enjoy standing for hours at a time. Inviting guests who know no one to a large party means they will have a miserable time because the hostess cannot look after them properly. The style of party should be in keeping with the character of the guests, and while an 18 year old girl may willingly squeeze into a 'sardine-tin' full of attentive young men, her grandmother's expectations and needs will probably be quite different. Yet there is no reason why both guests cannot be successfully accommodated at the same party by a considerate hostess.

Planning □Perhaps greatest enemies of all drinks parties are too much noise and not enough ventilation. Only experience will tell you how many guests can be fitted comfortably into your living quarters. If it is at all possible, however, plan to use (though not fill) any rooms that adjoin the main one where the party is held. This will allow the gathering's density to adjust itself naturally: those who like crowds can stay with the pack, while others can move off in search of space and air.
□A further advantage of this plan concerns atmosphere; a party atmosphere always takes a little while to establish itself, but it will establish itself much more quickly if the party starts off in a fairly small room. Using more than one will allow you to capitalize on this fact and still give the party a chance to expand to its full size.

150

Service □Professional help can always be hired and a good barman is a tremendous asset, but it is perfectly possible for a host and hostess to give a medium-sized party without extra help. If the party is large (or is being given by one person), some assistance is advisable. Without a bar-steward, much of a single-handed organizer's time will be spent serving drinks and there will be no one to answer the door, make introductions, control trouble and run the party generally. One solution is to ask a friend or two to help perform these duties. Most people will be delighted to assist in this way and their services will be invaluable. So, too, will be the moral support which their presence gives to the hostess who is on her own.

Drink □Suitable kinds of drink have been described but whatever you choose to serve, it is vitally important that there is enough of it. It is best to order more than you think you will need and many wine merchants will sell on a drink-or-return basis (though check first). Many also hire glasses and other bar equipment.
□When calculating the amount of drink needed, it is useful to bear in mind that a bottle of sherry holds about 12 glasses; a bottle of whisky, 20; and a standard (70cl) bottle of wine, six. A litre bottle of wine holds nine.
□If only one alcoholic drink is served—as at, for example, a sherry party—it is both correct and practical to fill a number of glasses beforehand and take them round on a tray. If the choice is much wider, drinks can be served more efficiently from a bar. (At very large parties, there may be more than one bar and waiters may be employed to pass drinks as well). The bar need be no more than an ordinary table covered with felt and a thick linen cloth, but whatever its nature, it should be sited where the maximum number of people can get to it. A generous space should also be left behind it for the host or bar steward.
□At all good parties, some non-alcoholic drinks

must be available: fruit juices, ginger ale, mineral waters. Some of these will, in any case, be needed as mixers for alcoholic drinks, so lay in a good supply. A good supply of ice will also be needed, as will plain water for those who like it in their drinks.

Food

□At even the smallest cocktail party, it would be both mean and imprudent not to offer guests something to nibble. Not only are they likely to be hungry, but they will otherwise probably be drinking on dangerously empty stomachs. For these reasons also, food at a cocktail party should be available from the beginning.

□It is not absolutely essential to serve food at an after-dinner party but it is far nicer to do so. The food should not appear however until later in the evening, for guests will presumably have just dined and will not enjoy the sight of yet more food at this point. (For serving suppers, see 'Buffets', Chapter Six).

□The food should be easy to eat and look as appetizing as possible. Suitable food for a cocktail party includes the whole range of nuts and cocktail biscuits, crisps, cocktail pickles (onions, gherkins, olives) canapés, sandwiches (quartered), cheese dips and hot sausages, all of which can be picked up with fingers or eaten off toothpicks.

□Food such as nuts and biscuits should be served in bowls and placed at strategic intervals round the room. Food may also be passed round on trays or laid out on a buffet table where guests can help themselves. Ideally the buffet table should be in a different room from the party and plates and cutlery are unnecessary.

Seating

□Chairs are often removed to make standing room for guests but a balance must be struck between comfort and space, and provision made for a guest who wants to sit down. It will appear unsociable if he sits alone, yet he may fear that if he sits down next to one or two other people he will not be able to get up again without appearing rude. Chairs should therefore be arranged to accommodate quite a large group so that this becomes less of a problem. If there is a buffet table, it is a good idea also to put some chairs near it.

Cloakroom arrangements
☐The correct practice is to segregate the sexes: men put their belongings in the hall or a downstairs room, while women are directed to a bedroom.

Cigarettes
☐Cigarettes should be made available. They can be placed either in cigarette boxes or stood upright in suitable containers (wine glasses will do).

Ashtrays
☐Ashtrays should be large, deep and ubiquitous. A layer of sand at the bottom of a deep ashtray will prevent cigarette ends smouldering and reduce smell.

Neighbours
☐Parties cannot help but cause some commotion. It is courteous, therefore, to warn neighbours that a party is going to take place. (This is particularly important if you live in a flat.) You do not have to invite them but it would be sociable to do so if you think they will fit in and will enjoy themselves.

Invitations
☐Invitations are normally issued by printed 'At Home' cards or by telephone. Specially printed invitations imply that the party will be large, or relatively formal, or both. Invitation cards and examples of replies appear in Chapter Eight.
☐For a small party of, say, 15 guests a telephoned invitation is adequate. The words 'cocktail party' are, incidentally, not used when issuing verbal invitations. Instead, you say something in the order of: 'Some friends are coming for a drink on Friday. Can you ...?'.
☐Except in the case of very small parties, invitations should be sent out about three weeks ahead of the event and guests should, of course, reply at once.
☐No hostess enjoys a last-minute hunt for stopgap guests. So, if you plan to hold a party for 40 people,

invite about 50. If by some miracle they all come, a party that is slightly too big is preferable to one that is too small.

Procedure   ☐Where drinks parties are concerned, punctuality matters considerably less than at a dinner party or luncheon. On the other hand, it is embarrassing for the hostess if many people are late and the party is slow to start. A wise hostess will make sure she can rely on a few good friends to be on time and help get things under way. If the party is a large one, it is a good idea to ask a few friends to help introduce people.
☐If there is staff, a guest's coat will be taken at the front door. If not, the host or hostess should say where to leave it and, when the guest is ready, welcome him into the party and see that he has a drink and someone to talk to.

Hostess's duties   ☐At anything but the smallest party, the hostess will not be able to introduce all the guests to each other, but she should try to pay particular attention throughout the party to any guests who risk feeling out of things by reason of their age, occupation or personality. And of course she should make sure that no guest ends up in a corner alone. (Making introductions is described in Chapter Eight.)
☐A hostess must keep her eye on the conditions of ashtrays, supplies at the bar and availability of food. She should position herself near the door at the beginning of the party, if it is a large one, and should make a point of returning to this position at the end so that guests will be able to find and thank her. If there is a host as well, this rule applies to both.
☐A hostess should also try to have a few words with all the guests during the evening. Abandoning the many for an extended conversation with the few is not, of course, good manners: the hostess is on duty and she must stay on duty for most of the evening, putting the needs of her guests before her own and getting her pleasure from theirs.

Guests' duties □The ideal guest is the one who can look after himself and will circulate freely. In the early stages of a party, at least, circulation is a guest's main duty. If he has the self-possession to introduce himself to others, he should do so. If the hostess indicates she wants him to meet someone, he should obey with good grace and, when talking to a fellow-guest, he should allow his partner in conversation a chance to move on if he or she wishes. At the same time, he should not seem anxious to get away himself. A guest who, during a conversation, scans the assembled throng over a partner's shoulder is behaving badly. He is, in effect, saying: 'You'll do for the moment but as soon as I see someone more important—or interesting or attractive—I'll be off.'

□If a woman's glass becomes empty it is polite for a man to offer to fill it. If they are not part of a group and there is no waiter, he should ask her to accompany him to the bar or make other arrangements so that she is not left standing alone.

□As the party proceeds, the need to circulate diminishes, but a good guest will continue to pay attention to the general plans of the hostess.

Departure □A guest at a cocktail party should leave by the time stated on the invitation. If the invitation was a verbal one (and no time was therefore given), it should be assumed that the party will last two hours. If a guest does stay late and the hostess has a dinner engagement, then it is quite in order for her to make this known. Indeed she has no alternative. She could perhaps say in a friendly way: 'I am going to leave with you, as I have to be at . . .'.

□The time of departure at after-dinner parties is dictated by common sense. If the party is held during the week, a departure between 11 pm and midnight is indicated; at weekends there is considerably more latitude. Unless a guest is a close friend of the hosts, he should avoid forming part of the small group that settles down comfortably when the party is in its final stages.

☐At all but the largest parties it is polite to find and thank the hostess before leaving. But this should be done unobtrusively if you have to leave early, so that other guests will not think it is time to go too.

Thanking

☐It is not absolutely necessary to write a letter of thanks to a hostess who has given a cocktail party or an informal after-dinner party, but such efforts are always appreciated—the more so for being unnecessary. If the hostess is a good friend then a telephone call the following morning will both congratulate her on her success and reassure her if she is in need of it. It is also a splendid opportunity for a cosy chat with plenty of subject matter to sustain it.

Difficulties and emergencies

☐Almost every party has its difficulties at one stage or another and keeping calm and using common sense are the best policy. It may also be necessary to grin and bear it.

'Can I bring a friend?'

☐Few parties are given without the hostess being asked this question by at least one guest. It is quite in order to do this and, in theory, the hostess is free to refuse. In practice, however, many hostesses feel uncomfortable about saying 'No' and for this reason a guest should only ask for an extra invitation if there is reason to believe it will not be inconvenient. Since hostesses usually like to see as many men as possible at a party, extra men are almost always welcomed. But a man who wants to bring a woman should think carefully before putting his request; he may have been invited precisely because he is an unattached male, and his hostess will not be happy at having her plans set awry. By the same token, a woman should think very carefully before asking if she may bring another female as the hostess may already have asked all the unattached females she wants.

☐If there is the least likelihood that the hostess

may object to the **extra guest** on personal grounds, the sponsor should jettison the idea entirely.
□It is not polite—even at a very large and informal party—to bring a friend or friends without consulting the hostess in advance.

Getting stuck □This is the most common hazard at drinks parties. If the stranded guest is in a group, then it is relatively easy to head for the bar. No one is insulted by a failure to return in such circumstances: even a well-intentioned guest can get side-tracked on such a journey. A couple who are stranded have considerably greater difficulty: either one—or indeed both—may wish to separate, yet they remain marooned on their island, searching in vain for rescue. If one of them sees someone whom he or she knows, then a suggestion for both to go over and see him is one way of solving the problem. If the pair are brave enough they can even form a conspiracy, deciding to launch themselves into a nearby group and to introduce themselves.

Spilling food and drink □If there is a major accident with a glass or plate, unobtrusively enlist the help of the host or hostess. Also offer to help clean up, even though the offer will probably be refused. A wise hostess will always have cleaning equipment stowed behind the bar in readiness for emergencies; a supply of newspaper will also be helpful for wrapping up broken glass. (Salt by the way is said to help remove wine stains from a carpet.)

Drunkenness □Drunkenness, leading to unruly behaviour, may become a problem at a party, especially one that continues for any length of time. The best solution is of course a preventive one: do not, if at all possible, invite guests whose inability to behave themselves when drinking is well-known.
□If a guest does become unruly and is making a nuisance of himself, the party-givers might possibly cut off his supply of drink and keep a watchful eye on him. A further stratagem—and an essential one

for a hostess operating on her own—is to secure the help of a guest who knows the culprit well. The helper thus enlisted is asked to watch over the drunken guest, to sober him up (if possible), and to try to contain his worst excesses. The helper should, of course, also be a close friend of the party organizer, since the task of watchdog is not an agreeable one. The hostess should be particularly careful to thank him before he leaves, and it would be courteous if she invited him to a problem-free gathering in the near future.

Drugs ☐The social use of drugs such as marijuana, hashish, cocaine and heroin is illegal and hosts who serve them may be putting guests into an awkward position. The same applies to guests who bring drugs to a party. Some people, politicians and public officials, for example, can have their careers ruined by the news that they were at a party where drugs were in evidence. Many other people quite simply are offended to be around any form of drug-taking.

Bottle parties ☐Bottle parties are a form of entertaining at which most of the drink is brought by the guests. Bottle parties are particularly popular among students and young people and the co-operative effort involved means that entertaining can be done more often than would be the case if all the expense was borne by the hosts.
☐A man *must* take some alcoholic drink to a bottle party. If a man and a woman are attending together, the man's offering may stand for both of them. The obligations of a woman guest attending on her own are somewhat flexible: it will be much appreciated if she presents a bottle but it probably will not be held against her if she does not. (Some women feel embarrassed to be seen on public transport clutching a bottle-shaped parcel.) But if several women attend the party in a group, they should certainly bring some form of alcoholic drink with them.

☐The drink which is most often taken to a bottle party is wine, but spirits—particularly whisky—will normally be welcomed as a special treat. In consideration for everyone's condition the following day, the rock-bottom end of the drinks market should be avoided and home-made wines should not be offered, however proud their maker is of his skill. Beer—preferably in large cans—is also very acceptable.

☐On arriving at a bottle party, each guest's contribution should either be given to the hosts or put on the table which serves as the bar. It is very bad manners indeed for a guest to retain the drink he has brought for his own consumption. Although a bottle party is a joint venture in one respect, it is still *given* by the person or persons who have issued the invitation and the normal courtesies expected between hosts and guests should be exercised.

DANCES AND BALLS

☐Any entertainment that has dancing as its main feature is strictly speaking a 'dance'— even if there is only a record player and some space reserved for dancing. But while this arrangement is similar in many ways to the small, improvised dances held in drawing-rooms of the 18th century, it would not be correct today to *call* it a dance because the word has acquired more elaborate connotations, becoming almost synonymous with a 'ball', while the very informal, often impromptu type of entertainment is designated 'dancing'. Dancing, in this book, is described as a feature of after-dinner drinks parties while the grander style is treated here.

☐Large dances and balls constitute some of the most lavish and expensive entertainment that can be given and for this reason, doubtless, they are rarely given privately nowadays. Perhaps the most usual occasion for a private dance is the coming-of-age or the 'coming-out' of a daughter. Dances are also occasionally held to celebrate young men's 21st birthdays, or other personal events such as anniversaries; but the vast majority are subscription affairs—charity balls, hunt balls, end-of-term balls at universities, or club dances.

☐Both dances and balls demand the services of several groups of professional assistants, and both have guest lists that are counted in hundreds rather than tens. The distinguishing feature of a *ball* seems to be its size: 600 guests is estimated to be the minimum number to qualify.

☐A third form of dance which is increasingly popular as a charity affair (and also given privately) is the dinner-dance. Here dancing may take place between courses or after dinner is over. (If the dinner is not eaten sitting down, however, the proper appellation would be 'dinner and dancing'.)

Hours

☐In the country, dances usually start at about 10pm and continue to any point between 2am and 7am. In London, they start slightly later—at, say, 10.30pm — and end earlier; the last guest has normally departed by 4am. A dinner-dance will start around 8.30pm and guests are served drinks until about 9.30pm, when dinner is served. The event continues until midnight or after. (Normally, invitations indicate the time the function is supposed to end.)

Subscription dances

☐Tickets for charity balls are available from the organizing committee. The main purpose of the event is, of course, to raise money for a particular charity and tickets are made available to the general public as well as to known supporters of the charity and their friends. Details are sometimes announced the press.

☐The normal procedure is to make up a party of friends who will either dine together as a group beforehand, or at the ball itself. Charity balls are not really places to meet other people: each party tends to keep together at its own table and while it is possible, for instance, to dance with someone whom you know in another party, it is not considered particularly polite.

☐Most charity balls indicate the size of the tables

available since, ideally, each party is made up to that size and the table is its base. But a small party can occupy only part of a table, sharing it with another group.

Who pays ☐When making up a party, the hostess must indicate whether she is going to pay for the tickets or whether the guests are expected to buy them. In many invitations the operative word is 'join'. If, for example, a hostess says, 'Will you *join* our party at the Mistletoe Ball?' she means that the guest should buy his or her ticket. If, on the other hand, she says, 'Do come to the Mistletoe Ball as our guest,' the indication is that she will be responsible for the ticket's purchase. It is very important for the hostess to make this point clear but if she fails to do so then it is up to the guest to seek clarification; a continued misunderstanding would be very embarrassing. Any guest in such a fix need only enquire politely, 'How much do I owe you for the tickets?'

What the ticket buys ☐Anyone who has not attended a subscription dance and wishes to buy a ticket should bear in mind that the price which is paid for the ticket does not necessarily include the cost of drinks served at the event. The practice varies: sometimes the wine at dinner is included, up to a point. Aperitifs are nearly always charged separately. A polite enquiry when the ticket is bought is perfectly in order.

Hunt balls ☐Hunt balls involve a similar procedure to charity balls. Again, hostesses make up parties and, again, they must ensure that guests know whether to buy their own tickets or not.

Dress ☐If the dance is to be a formal affair then the words 'black tie' will of course appear on the invitation. It is thought somewhat inconsiderate to specify 'white tie' nowadays since so many people will be put to the trouble and expense of hiring it. (Details of formal dress appear in Chapter 16).

161

☐At a hunt ball, male members of the hunt wear either tails or scarlet. A male member of another hunt wears his own hunt's evening dress.

Planning a dance   ☐Invitations to a dance or ball need to go out much earlier than those to other evening parties, so all initial contacts with sources of professional help need to be made earlier still. This is particularly true if the dance is to be given at the height of the social season: the hostess should book the musicians and the venue the year before.

Invitations   ☐Invitations take the form of specially-engraved cards, with the guest's name written in the upper left-hand corner. (Samples of invitation cards and replies are given in Chapter Eight.) The cards should be sent out at least a month in advance and if the dance is being held in the summer, they need to go out two months or more before the event.

Space   ☐A dance involves three distinct activities—eating, drinking and dancing—and a separate area should be allotted to each. In addition, guests need a place where they can sit, a place where they can leave their coats and somewhere to park their cars. The venue should be arranged so that, upon arrival, guests do not immediately find themselves on the dance floor. Ideally, the first area they enter after being greeted should be the one set aside for drinking. Here the procedure runs along lines similar to a cocktail party: guests can drink, talk, meet established friends and introduce each other to new ones.

Catering   ☐If the dance is to be held in the ballroom of a large hotel, the necessary catering facilities will be provided by the establishment. The hostess or organizer must consult the hotel manager or the head of the banqueting department about the cost, and plan food and drink which will be consistent with the occasion. Flowers can either be provided by the hotel or by a florist of the hostess's choice.

(The importance of the floral arrangements on such occasions should not underestimate). The music must always be organized separately and its quality and style are crucially important.

☐Some premises can be hired independently of catering facilities and in this instance the organization of the event is the same as if the dance was being held in a private house. The hostess will have to hire a caterer or a professional organizer. If she chooses the former, she will need to do a great deal of the work herself: not only must the band and the flowers be organized but—depending on the location and the catering facilities—there may be a marquee, tables and chairs, glasses, linen, china, cutlery and coat-racks to be hired and arranged, as well as the guest-list to be attended to. The co-ordination and attention to detail required in such circumstances are formidable and it is not a task to be undertaken lightly. Producing, directing, stage-managing and appearing as a principal performer at the event is a daunting prospect and demands a wide spectrum of qualities — among which steady nerves and considerable energy are essential.

Food and Drink

☐At a ball given in 1783 at Carlton House, the 600 guests were served a supper at 1.30am that consisted of eight 'removes' (courses). Today a buffet breakfast suffices. It is usually available from midnight onwards and includes such classic breakfast dishes as scrambled eggs, kedgeree, coffee and croissants, along with strawberries (in season) and other fruits.

☐A sensible procedure is to serve additional cocktail party food in the bar area. Guests at a dance are often too energetic or too sociable to bother with serious eating; but hot sausages and other sustaining mouthfuls will help counteract the effects of an evening's drinking.

☐At dinner-dances, guests will of course sit at tables and have dinner served in the usual way (see Chapter Six).

☐The traditional drink at a dance used to be champagne; today though, white wine is often served too and a fully-stocked bar is sometimes on hand, especially at subscription dances where the drinks cost extra.

Staff and service ☐Breakfast can be served in two ways; drink in several. The breakfast can either be presented as a buffet, with staff to serve the guests, or it can be organized on a restaurant system: guests order their food from their tables and wait for it to be brought to them. Of the two, the second method is obviously the more costly and elaborate.
☐If hot cocktail food is served in the drinks area, staff will be needed to hand it round.
☐At a private dance, the first drink of the evening is usually served from a tray. Refills come either from circulating staff or from the bar, or— sometimes—from a supply already placed on guests' tables.
☐The last method can help to cut down on staff numbers considerably.
☐At a subscription dance, if the drinks are on sale, the sources of supply are the bar and the wine waiter who will take a party's order for wine and bring it to the table.
☐In addition to the staff engaged in serving food and drink, it is essential to have someone to open the front door, and the presence of an announcer is also important. (Even when faced with a close friend, a hostess may experience a mental blank as to her guest's identity.) Staff are also needed in the car-park, in the cloakroom and in the ballroom, where small-scale tidying operations such as cleaning ashtrays will go on all the time. Cloakroom attendants should have a supply of tickets and pins.

Music ☐The music must be the best the hostess can afford and it must also be of a type that all age groups present can enjoy. The hostess's professional helpers will be able to suggest names of bands and so, probably, will her friends.

☐A modern dance band is made up of a minimum of four instruments (piano, bass, guitar and drums), and two bands—or a band and a discotheque—will be needed. This is because musicians at a dance work in shifts, one band going off for a drink and a rest while the other plays. It is also acceptable to have a discotheque only.

☐If musicians are present, they must be well looked after. A hostess should make sure that proper supplies of drink and good food are laid on; she should also provide a comfortable room in which the musicians can refresh themselves, along with plenty of coffee, easy access to a lavatory, and someone to see they have all they need.

Procedure ☐On arrival, guests are shown where to put their coats. At a private dance they are then greeted by the hostess, the host and the guest of honour, if there is one. After that, they should find themselves in the drinks area, where they can meet friends and circulate before progressing to the dance floor. As a general rule, this will be surrounded by tables, and guests can sit at any table they please.

☐At a subscription dance, guests are greeted by a reception line that usually includes the chairman and some members of the organizing committee. A name card system indicates which table each party should sit at.

Announcing guests ☐When having herself announced at a dance, a woman gives her full name: Miss Mary Smith, Mrs. John Jones. A husband and wife are announced together: Mr. and Mrs. John Jones. An unmarried couple are also announced together but, in this case, the woman's name is given first: Miss Mary Smith and Mr. David Jackson.

Duties of men ☐A man attending a private dance in a party is allowed to dance with whom he pleases; at the same time, he should not monopolize the company of one female guest for the entire evening. However, this does not apply if he has been invited to bring a partner, or if he attends as the partner of a female guest. In this case, his partner's enjoyment is his main responsibility.

☐At dances given for a girl, it used to be the rule that male guests should ask her for at least one dance, and also dance once with her mother. In addition, a good guest would make a point of dancing with the girls who were on his left and right at dinner, and with his dinner hostess. These rules are now thought old-fashioned, but they are founded on the most basic rules of courtesy. (It is particularly painful for a girl to be short of partners at her own dance) A courteous guest, therefore, will continue to follow the old convention.

Departure ☐When leaving a private dance, guests should try to find their hostess and say good-bye; however, this may not always be possible. They do not seek out the hostess if leaving early.

Thanking ☐A guest at a private dance should write a letter of thanks to the hostess. He should also write and thank a hostess who has given him dinner before either a private or a subscription dance. A hostess who has paid for a guest's ticket at a subscription dance should also receive a letter of thanks.

☐While there is no need to write to a hostess who has invited a guest to join a party at a subscription dance, but who has not paid for the ticket, it is worth remembering a letter expressing appreciation of an enjoyable evening is never out of place.

TEA ☐With one or two notable exceptions, parties are now rarely given during the day. Unless they are given at weekends, there will be few—if any—men present. Many women, too, have full-time jobs and those who do not usually have little time left over from domestic commitments. But some types of daytime entertaining still survive, if in modified form. The hardiest of the perennials is tea: not the grand British tea party of earlier years, but a friendly occasion for eating, drinking and talking.

166

□The modern tea party for three or four friends does have one major thing in common with its Edwardian equivalent, the main aim in both cases is to create happy conditions for conversation. The activities of serving, eating and drinking should interrupt the flow of talk as little as possible, and all preparations should be made with this aim in mind.

Food and drink

□The drink, naturally, is tea: tea made in a warmed pot from water that has just been boiled. China tea is traditionally regarded as superior to Indian. The optional accompaniments to Indian tea are cold milk and white (lump) sugar. Ideally, China tea is drunk without either, but this is a matter of personal preference. The further optional accompaniment to China tea is a slice of lemon; if this is added, milk is not added as well.

□The food served should be light, neatly prepared and—above all—easy to eat. Sandwich fillings should not drip or ooze, and cakes should not be chunky, over-crumbly or squashy. Traditional tea party menus feature such things as hot tea cakes (if the weather is cold), thinly sliced bread-and-butter, cucumber sandwiches, halved and buttered scones, small cakes, shortcake, and large cakes cut into slices before serving. A modern hostess can ring the changes and introduce favourites of her own but she should always remember to present all food in small, easily-managed pieces. If she has the time and skill to do her own baking, she should try to serve at least one home-made item at her tea-table; a home-made cake is evidence that the hostess has taken special trouble to please her guests.

Preparation

□Afternoon tea is, of course, different from a family tea eaten round the dining table. Guests who have come to tea may sit round the fire, or in a window bay, or in the garden. The ideal arrangement is to have two separate tables: one beside the hostess for the tea tray, and one within easy reach of the guests for the food. All guests should have some place near them where they can put their cups and plates; if the circle is to be a large one, a solution is to put small tables between pairs of chairs.

☐The minimum equipment needed on the hostess's tray is the tea-pot, tea strainer and bowl, milk jug, sugar bowl, and a jug for hot water. Each guest will need a tea cup and saucer (with teaspoon), a small plate and a small knife. No forks: if a cake is too difficult to eat with fingers alone, it should not be served.

☐Napkins used to be thought unnecessary at a tea party, but many hostesses include them today. If used, they should be small: paper ones are perfectly acceptable.

☐The tea cups initially go on the tea tray beside the hostess. The plates and knives are placed on the food table, together with the food.

How to serve

☐When all the guests have arrived, the hostess usually absents herself briefly to make the tea. (The cups and saucers may already be in the drawing room.) On coming back with the tea, she sees that each guest has a plate and knife, then turns to the business of pouring. As she pours each cup she asks the guest whether milk, sugar, or both are wanted and then adds them to the cup. (The tea always goes into the tea cup first.) Then she hands the cup and saucer to the guest.

☐Guests help themselves to food, starting with the hot dish (if there is one) and going on to sandwiches and cakes, in that order. The hostess should always be alert to the state of her guests' tea cups, and offer more tea when a cup is empty.

☐When eating, a guest picks up her plate in one hand and then takes the food from it with the other. When drinking, similarly, she holds the saucer in one hand, the cup in the other. She does not, by the way, crook her little finger.

Departure

☐Guests should take care not to overstay their

welcome. A visit of an hour or so is enough. There is no need to write or telephone the hostess and thank her again later.

GARDEN PARTIES

☐The traditional garden party is essentially a buffet tea with alcoholic refreshments. It begins about 3.30pm and usually ends shortly after 6pm (see also 'Royal garden parties', Chapter 10). ☐Because of the extra space at the hostess's disposal, garden parties can be as large as finances and domestic arrangements allow. It is important, though, not to invite more people than can be fitted under a roof if it rains. A hostess giving a really large party might consider hiring a marquee. ☐Invitations to garden parties are sent out on 'At Home' cards about three weeks before the event, and are answered in the normal manner (see 'Invitations', Chapter Eight).

Preparations

☐A garden party hostess has to make preparations on three fronts: the kitchen, the drawing-room (or equivalent) and the garden itself. The garden should look its very best and this will have a bearing on the date of the event. ☐Plenty of garden chairs and small tables should be placed outdoors but the actual service of food and drink is best carried on inside unless it is being passed round. The room used for the buffet should give easily on to the garden and contain some chairs and tables for any who prefer to eat indoors.

Food and drink

☐Garden party food is similar to that served at tea but it is more elaborate and varied. As with tea, all sandwiches and cakes should be presented in manageable form. If they are in season, strawberries and raspberries served with cream are traditionally part of the menu. Suitable garden party drinks are tea, iced coffee, soft drinks and fruit cup.

Procedure

☐If there is staff to answer the front door, the

169

hostess greets her guests either in the drawing-room or in the garden. Otherwise guests are greeted at the front door.

☐The hostess cannot introduce all the guests to one another, but she should make as many introductions as she is able to manage conveniently.

What to wear ☐Clothes at a traditional garden party are rather formal and elegant. Men wear lounge suits and women tend to wear smart afternoon dresses and, if they wish, hats. Women should be practical when deciding what shoes to wear; very narrow heels will sink into a lawn.

CHILDREN'S PARTIES

☐Sooner or later, most parents have to give parties for their children. The occasion is nearly always a birthday; a fact that actually helps the party along since it provides certain fixed points round which the rest of the event can be built.
☐A party for a child of primary school age is essentially a 'tea party' surrounded by a structured programme of entertainment. What the entertainment is depends on your pocket and your children's tastes, but it is crucial that some activity should be planned for every minute.

Guest list ☐Your child will help provide the guest list. It may be single-sex, or it may be mixed: either way, the age-range involved should be a narrow one. Ten year olds and six year olds do not mix.
☐If a child is planning to invite his whole class at school, try to make sure he has left no one out. If he has done so intentionally, ask why. Unless the reason is very serious (in both his eyes and yours), explain the misery of being the odd man out, and insist that the missing name should be included.
☐Naturally, a child should return hospitality to those who have invited him to their parties in the past—even if he doesn't like them.
☐The length of the final guest list will depend on

the space available and on the number of helpers present. However small the party is to be, you will need at least one adult helper. If more than 15 guests are to be present, allow for one further helper for every 10 children.

Invitations   □These should be written (ideally by your child) and posted to the guests' home addresses two or three weeks before the event. Formality of this order is necessary if the guest's parent is to know exactly where and when the party is to be held. The reason for the party should be specified, and so should the time it will end.

Timing   □Children's parties start about 3pm and continue until about 6pm. Parties for very young children should end sooner. The food and drink are served rather early, at 4pm or shortly after. Most of the very active games should be played before tea, with slightly quieter ones afterwards. If you are hiring a professional entertainer, make his performance the last *main* event of the party. The last event of all should be a quiet one. This will help the children's parents to collect them without too much trouble.

Presents   □If your child is going to a birthday party, he should take a present. It should not be so expensive as to outshine the likely offerings of other guests. □It is also usual for guests at all parties to be *given* a small present to take home with them. This makes sure that those who have not won prizes during the games do not go away completely empty-handed. Both prizes and going-home presents normally come from the same large stock of sweets, balloons, crayons and so forth that a sensible mother lays in before the party.

Food and drink   □Very young children like the traditional party fare of sandwiches, jelly, cakes and ice cream. From the age of about six onwards, tastes start tending to the savoury. (Sausages and the whole range of potato crisps are confirmed favourites.) Children

171

also like food to look enticingly 'grown-up'.
□A central part of any birthday party is the cake with its candles. The ceremony of lighting these and blowing them out takes place when the tea is almost over; the lighting should be done by an adult.
□At all parties, soft drinks should be provided in quantity.
□The spread is laid out at a large table, round which the children sit. The use of a name card at each place will prevent shufflings and scufflings as the guests take their places. Breakages are not only expensive but dangerous, so use paper plates and plastic or paper tumblers. Huge supplies of paper napkins should also be on hand, together with more serious cleaning-up equipment for accidents.

Arrival of guests

□Your child should greet each guest as he arrives, help him to put his coat away, and thank him for his present as it is handed over. The adult hostess should stand by in each case to help and to introduce the new arrival to the activities.
□Parents bringing their children should see their offspring absorbed into the household, and *then go*. The hostess will not welcome the unplanned presence of extra adults, and most children hate a too-obvious parental involvement in their affairs. The only exception to this rule occurs in the case of parties for the very young: mothers are invited to these with their children.

Departure

□Split-second punctuality is the order of the day for parents collecting children from a party. If they are early, the already-busy hostess will feel she has to entertain them; if they are late, the party-givers will have another problem on their hands. It is the collecting parent's duty to check that her child leaves with all the possessions he brought.
□Before leaving, a guest should thank both his child host and the hostess. If he looks like forgetting, his parent should quietly remind him. By the same token your own child should be reminded to thank his hosts when he goes to a party.

8 INVITATIONS, LETTERS AND TALK

☐The momentum of life has changed much in the last few years, and often we seem to be speeding through time as if we were travelling by jet. Inevitably our social behaviour has altered. The greatly increased use of the telephone, the unreliability of the postal services and the virtual disappearance of the telegram as a means of communication have transformed many of our social customs, and what was once 'correct form' often seems somewhat archaic. However, a number of classic traditions continue, together with newly established modes, for their charm and courtesy come from consideration and kindness and are unchanged by fashion.

☐The theme of this chapter is, to paraphrase its title, written and spoken communication in the social world today: the conventions of issuing and acknowledging invitations, how and when to introduce guests, the essentials of letter writing. There is a section on conversation (mainly at parties) with a few hints on how to promote it, when to provoke it, when to be tactful and how to mollify. These are not guidelines for the experienced hostess or the popular guest; here rather are suggestions for the young, some advice and reassurance for the inexperienced, and a few words of encouragement for the shy.

INTRODUCTIONS

☐The first duty of a hostess is to introduce her guests. The English are a shy and diffident race, and can sometimes be seen looking lost and lonely at parties because they do not know the other people in the room and are too timorous to introduce themselves.

Conventions of precedence

☐The conventions of introductions are classic. The gentleman is introduced to the lady: 'Mr Newby—Miss Dalsanie'. When introducing two members of the same sex, the junior is introduced to the senior: 'Mr Newby—The Belgian Ambassador,' or 'Mrs Newby—Lady St Edmunds'. Pronunciation is all-important. Never mumble, be audible and clear. It is awkward for guests to have to turn to each other and say, 'I'm afraid I didn't quite hear your name'. ☐If you find you have momentarily forgotten friends' names, you might turn to them with a beseeching smile and say 'I'm sure you know each other'; a tactful woman will say 'Of course, I'm Lily St Edmunds', and the man will reply 'I'm Humphrey Esmond, how do you do?', and a social solecism has been gracefully remedied.

Titles ☐Whether or not one introduces guests by their titles depends much on the formality of the event. When in doubt, do. Ancient families are proud of their historic names (and life peers often prouder of their titles). Christian names could be regarded as *lèse-majesté*. This is especially true when the party includes guests of very different ages. The venerable Duke of Sunborough would not appreciate being introduced as 'Henry Sunborough' to an undergraduate. If the party is informal and most of the guests are friends or likely to become so, then introduction by Christian name and surname is suitable. (A complete list on how to introduce people of title and rank appears at the end of this chapter.)

Married couples ☐They should be introduced individually, even if they are standing side by side, eg 'Henry Newby—Hermione Newby.' People are individuals and a woman's identity does not merge with her husband's on marriage.

Professional women ☐Many women have made a career before they were married and some like to be introduced by their professional names, by which they are best known. Others are deeply offended if not introduced by their married name when the occasion is a social, not a professional one. If in doubt, telephone first and ask.

Introducing children ☐Initial introductions should be formal: 'This is my daughter Rose—Mrs Esmond'. 'This is Rose's friend, who is staying with us, Caroline Hurst—Mrs Esmond.' Should the children's parents be close friends of yours, and if you like children, it is for you to suggest that they call you by your Christian name.

Casual introductions

☐If you encounter a friend by chance—in the street or during an interval at the theatre, for instance—and you are accompanied by another friend, it is polite to introduce them. To fail to do so shows lack of consideration and courtesy. Before the war, photographs in glossy magazines were sometimes captioned 'Miss Cecilia Eccleston and friend'—how nondescript the poor friend must have felt. (See also 'Unexpected meetings' Chapter 11.)

Introductions at dinner parties

☐When inviting guests to dinner, it is sometimes a good idea to tell them who the other guests will be, especially if the party is given for a special guest, for instance a visitor from abroad. If you have a star guest, you should also tell him or her the composition of the party. A little note on some of the other guests will be helpful, eg 'Henry Newby, whose passion is Victorian architecture; Sarah Pagley, who works in the Foreign Office'.
☐If you have not been able to tell your friends about their fellow guests beforehand, you might describe the composition of the party when they arrive and before taking them into the drawing room to be introduced.
☐One hostess, who gives dinner parties for 30 or 40 guests, greets each guest on arrival and takes them round the whole room, introducing them carefully to each person. Though this may seem arduous, it is in fact the correct procedure and it contributes enormously to the success of the party.

Introductions at drinks parties and receptions

☐If the party is small, of course, the hostess will introduce all her guests to each other. Should the party be large, and perhaps noisy, she should try to introduce each new arrival to another guest with a tactful opening remark. (When you make introductions, do not give your guests a potted biography of each other, for example 'Rose is a novelist, and Michael is a barrister'. Michael may never have heard of Rose's books and may not be at all anxious to talk about a very tiring day in court.)

☐Guests can easily feel lost at large cocktail parties, and you are a blessing to the hostess if you can help her by introducing any stray souls. If someone looks lonely, it is perfectly permissible to walk up to them and introduce yourself—and add some innocuous opening gambit which is totally impersonal.

☐Large receptions can be difficult social occasions as there is no hostess to nurture the guests; she is standing at the entrance greeting the new arrivals and rarely has a chance to mix with the throng. It is easy to be isolated, particularly if you know few of the people there. The remarks made previously about taking courage in both hands, and introducing oneself, are applicable here too.

CONVERSATION ☐Conversation is an art, and like all arts, it is improved by experience and practice. Experience is very important for the greatest bar to good conversation is shyness, and the most intelligent people can become tongue-tied when they meet strangers. Letters can be drafted and rewritten till they achieve perfection; conversation must be spontaneous, and mistakes cannot be erased. To paraphrase Charles II, the first art of a good conversationalist is to put people at their ease. Conversation can hardly flourish in a stilted atmosphere. Once we have learned the art of easy conversation, then good conversation can follow. Nothing makes a party so delightful as really good talk. Some people are star performers, some are listeners, but the good listener is one who knows how to inspire the star.

☐Oscar Wilde is said to have found his way to the quietest person at a party and in a few moments made him sparkle. Rare indeed is this genius, but we can all create a pleasant and friendly ambiance which will help to dispel the diffidence of others—timidity freezes not only people's tongues, but their thoughts as well. A warm welcome is a great comfort to the shy, and words alone are not always sufficient; the advice given to actors at the Comédie Française used to be 'the gesture, the look, and then the word', which can be translated into a firm handshake, a smile and a kindly remark. It reassures a newcomer to be greeted by 'I've been looking forward to meeting you for a long time; we have a great mutual friend in Caroline Parr, and she has talked so much about you'. A new neighbour can be delighted by 'I'm so glad you've come to live at Munstead Parva. We always thought that your house was the prettiest in the village'. A quiet compliment goes straight to the heart.

□This chapter discusses conversation among people who are probably meeting one another for the first time and about whom each knows little, if anything at all. (There are of course many other moments in life when one longs for a manual of ready remarks—when meeting one's future parents-in-law, one's children's friends—but at least in these encounters there is the great advantage of knowing something of their lives and interests, and one has a foundation for talk.) Here are a few suggestions on how to skate gracefully on the conversational ice—or how to break it, according to the demands of the social occasion. There are suggestions for beginning a conversation and examples of opening remarks to avoid, for too inquisitive an approach can make the shy withdraw into their shells.

□Conversation can be compared to a dance, and whether it is a *pas de deux* or an eightsome reel, everyone should be encouraged to join in, and enjoy themselves.

Conversation at dinner parties

□See also Table Manners, Chapter Six.
□Good dinner party conversation can be the best conversation of all. Topics may be discussed with

177

profound seriousness or with delightful frivolity, but whatever the mood, the conversation should flow, meandering in its own course like a river, sometimes slipping into a wide estuary of many thoughts and epigrams.

□When the guests are happily chosen, the conversation will develop naturally, but it must be remembered that dinner parties are like small plays, with unexpected situations and actors who may well fluff their lines.

General conversation

□General conversation is the most fun. It is possible with six guests, or with eight if there is a circular table. General conversation is the rule in France and has long been so. Elinor Glyn, writing the souvenirs of an English debutante visiting France in 1900, said, 'They are all so witty, but it is not considered correct to talk to one's neighbour, a conversation à deux. Everything must be general, so it is a continual sharpening of the wits, and one has to shout a great deal, as otherwise, with everyone talking at once, one would not be heard'.

□At French dinners it is usually *les actualités* that are discussed—the latest news, politics and the gossip of the moment—but in Britain general conversation usually has to be directed, and a clever and experienced hostess will know how to orchestrate it. She can lean over the table, ask the guest at the other side their opinion of a subject, invite another guest to comment on it. She will make all her guests provide a positive contribution to the conversation.

Conversation à deux

□This is the general custom in Britain. Of course, at large parties it is the only method possible. It is also dictated by the shape of dining table favoured in England which is an elongated oval. Therefore each guest knows that he or she is going to have to spend the evening entertaining alternately the neighbour on either side. It is a challenge, and it can be very daunting (the wise hostess will, if possible, see that one neighbour is already an

178

acquaintance so one has a smooth start).

☐Sometimes a neighbour talks with ease and charm but if not, one has to make the conversation fluent and agreeable, and find topics on which he or she will speak with interest and enjoyment.

Helpful opening gambits

☐We have to discover what interests our neighbour and do so with as few deft questions as possible.

☐One experienced dinner guest always asks her neighbour, 'What is the nicest thing that happened to you today?' This can be very successful, *if* the neighbour has had a happy day.

☐For the shy, it is recommended before going to the party to make a mental list of possible opening subjects (of course, this will be slanted towards the interest of the other guests who may be there).

☐It is best to begin by topical and neutral subjects.

Examples

☐'What a cold December we are having. If you weren't in England, where would you like to be at this time of year?'

☐'I hear you are off to Greece for three weeks—what books are you packing in your suitcase?'

☐'What beautiful flowers Anne (the hostess) always has—do you like gardening?'

☐'If you were the Queen, what opera/ballet/play would you choose to have performed for your Gala?'

☐'Are you a Wimbledon fan? Have you been watching it?' (Adjust sports seasonally, if you are sufficiently knowledgeable!)

☐'Have you had time to see the Tutankhamen exhibition?' (Substitute whatever is topical.)

☐'What delicious claret—are you a connoisseur of wine?'

☐This has given the neighbour a chance to say if he is interested in travel, art, literature, sport, music, gardening, food ... let us hope he will have responded favourably to a bait.

☐It is unwise to discuss politics with a stranger—he may hold strong views quite opposed to your own.

☐People generally prefer to talk about their

179

hobbies rather than their professions. Your neighbour may be a good amateur pianist or a champion croquet player. He may grow rare roses or be a collector of anything from postage stamps to old gramophone records. If his individual interests are not too recondite for you, you will have an enjoyable and informative conversation.

Opening gambits not recommended

□Avoid asking people questions that might be on a government form or on an application for a visa. One's heart often sinks when asked:
'Do you live in London?'
'What do you do?'
'Have you any children?'
'Have you been abroad this year?'

The receiving end

□If you are asked such questions as the above, you can gauge by the tone of your neighbour's voice if he really does want to know whether you live in Perth or Pimlico, whether you are a botanist or a banker, whether or not you have seen the Mediterranean. If he *is* interested, respond. If he is not then he suffers from conversational poverty and is falling back on tired gambits. The classic move in all these situations is to answer monosyllabically, and then repeat his questions:
□'Yes, I live very near here. And you?'
□'I am a barrister, and I have been trying to guess your profession. Do tell me.'
□'No (children)—but do tell me about yours.'
□'Several times (holidays). Have *you* made fascinating plans for a summer excursion?'
□By thus tossing the ball back into your neighbour's court, he will then talk about himself and what interests him (the architecture of the houses in Islington, his work as a merchant banker, the type of holidays he likes—gastronomic, sightseeing, sporting). But at least now you have some data on which to build.

Conversation à trois

□Often at a large dinner a third person joins the conversation *à deux*, because the chat sounds so interesting. Then one person is left out, sitting alone. Always try to bring him or her into the conversation if you can; lean over and say 'We are talking about the new television serial 'Lily Langtry' (or whatever). Are you watching it?'

Special guests and particular problems

☐Here are a few words of advice on a number of unexpected problems that from time to time arise at dinner tables (and elsewhere). Many potentially awkward situations can be diverted gracefully if one is prepared in advance to cope with them.

The celebrity

☐You may be invited to a dinner where the guest of honour is a celebrity, perhaps a leading politician, a well-known actress or a famous writer. Do not, through diffidence, avoid talking to them about their achievements; most celebrities are delighted to find someone interested in their work (and many are modest, and genuinely pleased to be congratulated on it). They will enjoy talking to an appreciative audience, and equally the listener is lucky to have the opportunity to meet someone who is a renowned, perhaps historic, character. ☐Many hostesses will tell you in advance if someone famous is attending the dinner, so that you may have the chance of doing some homework.

The prima donna

☐It is a golden rule never to ask more than one at a time; prima donnas like to dominate the table and are apt to sulk in the presence of each other. They either remain silent, or they try to score points off their rival, for they are accustomed to being socially spoilt. At one time it was considered fascinating if a famed talker gave a monologue at dinner. Nowadays perhaps we are duller but a more general conversation is preferred to a concert performance.

The disputants

☐Quarrels are unforgivable at dinner parties. Heated discussions, yes, points of view vehemently stated, positions defended and attacked—but always with consideration for the other person's point of view, and without animosity. Should a quarrel erupt, great tact is required. Sometimes it is clever to pretend to be uninformed and with a smile say, 'I wish I understood more. Could you explain to me x, y or z?'. Even if the explanation is a little tedious, the discussion will be slowed down to a speed at which it can be diverted elsewhere—and the disputant will have been mollified by having his knowledge sought by someone who shows a charming and intelligent interest.

The bore □The general rule is never to invite a bore, but sometimes a friend's fiancé, or spouse, though kindness itself, spreads a blanket of boredom over the dinner table.
□Bores come in two categories: those with no conversation and those with too much. Those in the first category blossom if asked the kind of questions that have been forbidden elsewhere, eg 'How are your children?' or 'Have you been abroad this summer?'. Bores in the second category love telling anecdotes, often rather long drawn out ones and often previously recounted. Looking at silver linings, it can be restful for a hostess to sit next to a bore; while listening to a lengthy recital, she can be observing the rest of the table, seeing that all the other guests are happy, and also mentally checking that in 10 minutes time the 'Tarte Tatin' should come out of the oven. Bores, in this respect, can be quite soothing.
□If one really cannot bear the story being told for the third or fourth time, the best solution is to say 'Oh, Henry, I love that story of yours, I've been laughing at it ever since you told it to me when I dined with you'.

The brick dropper □It is inevitable that some bricks are dropped among strangers; the important thing is to see that they do not create a visible gash in the friendly atmosphere of the evening.
□Blunders of a personal nature are of course the worst. A guest may make a reference of a

disparaging nature, quite unwittingly, to one's brother, best friend, former husband. On these occasions, the remedy is to say at once, 'Peter Porter is my brother' or 'Helen Buxton is one of my oldest friends' before various other guests have made the situation worse by concurring with the original speaker that your brother is a bore, your best friend an outrageous gossip. Defend by saying, 'I know Peter is rather quiet, but his opinions are always sound', or 'Most people find Helen very amusing, and her jokes are never malicious.'

☐Some howlers one can do nothing about. If before dinner you say, 'Roses are my favourite flowers, chrysanthemums my least', and then you find the dining room decorated with the blooms you detest, it is a question of least said, soonest mended, unless your hostess has the ready humour to turn it into a joke.

The gossip monger ☐Certain people always seek the limelight and gossip about them is usually fair game; indeed, they would enjoy knowing they were being discussed. Otherwise gossip should be avoided, 'Idle talk, tittle-tattle', says the Oxford Dictionary. The dangers of gossip are: (1) it is often incorrect and will spread quickly; (2) so small is the world that any gossip is almost bound to include a friend of someone present; (3) as a form of conversation it is entirely superficial. There is no excuse at any time for gossip that is malicious. 'Truth travels like a tortoise, rumour like a hare', wrote Ouida most wisely.

When silence reigns ☐There are times when all conversations come to an end simultaneously and total silence comes over the whole room. At such moments one becomes quite dumb and all ideas fly out of the window. However, someone must start the conversation again, and as quickly as possible. Try and think of any question, however trifling, and address it to someone *across* the room or dining table, not your neighbour. Their answer, heard by all, will break the conversational lockjaw.

Conversation at the small drinks party

☐This can be a party with perhaps as many as 30 guests, perhaps only eight or ten. It is a party that is controlled by the hostess, who will have invited people whom she thinks will be interested to meet each other, and she will make all the introductions. Earlier in this chapter (see 'Introductions') it was stated that an introduction should not be followed by a biography but the hostess should open the conversation by a reference to an *interest* shared by her guests, which they can then follow.

Conversation at large parties, private views

☐This is the one occasion at which you should be a social butterfly. When the party is large, one can flit from friend to friend, exchanging pleasantries. Sometimes a smile and a greeting is sufficient, sometimes a brief discussion, but on one topic only and then it is time to move on. A large social gathering provides an excellent opportunity to talk to friends one may not have seen for a long time. This kind of party is a social whirligig—should one be stuck too long with one person, introduce someone else to them, and then move on.
☐After-dinner parties are very pleasant if well arranged. There is none of the stress of an early evening drinks party, when one is rushing off to another engagement. The conversation can therefore be gentle and leisurely. The hostess will, of course, introduce all the guests and see that they circulate.

INVITATION CARDS

☐The busy hostess will find that (with the exception of occasions listed below) all she needs for inviting friends to parties is an 'At Home' card (see example).
☐By tradition, 'At Home' cards measure 4 x 6¾ inches and the heavier the card, the handsomer. 'At Home' cards are exclusively for hostesses; a woman, by tradition is the chatelaine of her household.

Example

Mr and Mrs Peter Stewart

Mrs John Fitzherbert
at Home
Monday, June 1st

R.S.V.P.
v. Hyde Park Gardens,
London, W.1

6.30-8.30 pm

Husband and wife as hosts

□Though the wife is usually the hostess, sometimes husband and wife wish to hold a party together. In this case the invitation would read as follows:

Joint invitations.

Miss Mary Eliot

Sir Derek and Lady Stewart
request the pleasure of your company
at a Dinner to celebrate their
Golden Wedding
on Monday, 18th. October
at Claridge's Hotel (Ballroom Entrance)

R.S.V.P.
Elm Cottage.
Beaulieu.
Hampshire.

7.30 o'clock.

Friends or single man as host

□If the party is given by a single man, or by a number of friends, 'At Home' is not appropriate, and the wording should be 'Mr John Esmond and Mr Oliver Newby request the pleasure of the company of...' or 'request the pleasure of your company'. The name of the person to whose address replies should be sent is printed first on the invitation card.

Peers and honourables	☐A peer or peeress issuing a formal invitation does not normally use 'the'—thus the invitation would read 'Countess of Charmington' or 'Viscountess Dalsany', and on an informal invitation she may simply put 'Lady Charmington' or 'Lady Dalsany'. The name of the recipient is written on the card in matching style, ie an informal invitation from the Countess of Charmington to Viscount and Viscountess Dalsany would be written 'Lord and Lady Dalsany'. ☐In the case of honorables, an invitation card would read 'Mr Michael Wade', except for ultra-formal occasions, eg royalty present, when 'Honble. Michael Wade' might be used.
Addressing invitations	☐When the invitation is to a married couple, the convention is to address the envelope to the wife alone, but the names of both the couple are written on the top left hand of the card, eg 'Mr and Mrs James Evans'. For a single person both the invitation card and the envelope would read 'Miss Ann Aubyn'. But if the invitation is to good friends, prefixes are often dispensed with on the card.
Titles	☐When sending invitations to people of title, the inscription on the envelope and on the card might differ: for example, the envelope would be addressed to 'The Marchioness of Belchamber', but the names written on the card would be those by which the couple would be introduced, 'Lord and Lady Belchamber'. The rule is that dukes and duchesses retain their full title in both instances, but all peers of lesser rank are 'Lord and Lady' in the latter case. (See also 'Peers and honourables as hosts', above.) ☐The charts at the end of the chapter show the correct forms of address in detail.
Prefixes, decorations and degrees	☐When writing names on invitation cards, no prefixes such as 'The Rt. Hon.' or 'His Excellency' are given, nor letters after the name signifying rank or awards (eg. Bart. Q.C., O.B.E.).

186

☐On the envelope it is customary to include all prefixes and any initials or abbreviations signifying rank or decorations, eg 'The Rt. Hon. Sir Arthur Peabody, Bt., O.M., P.C.' (for details about abbreviations of decorations and awards see the Appendix).

Invitations to dinner parties

☐See also 'Table Manners', Chapter Six.
☐It is wisest to use the telephone but once the guest has accepted, it is a good idea to send an 'At Home' card, noting the time of the dinner and if it is black tie. The R.S.V.P. should be crossed through and either P.M. (Pour Memoire) or 'To Remind' substituted. The same remarks apply to luncheon parties.

'At Home' card used as reminder

Mr and Mrs Clive Adams

Mrs John Fitzherbert

at Home

Thursday, June 4th

to remind

1. Hyde Park Gardens.
London W.2

Dinner
8 for 8.30 pm

Invitations to dances

☐Should the hostess be giving the party not in her own house but in a hotel, she may be 'At Home' (see example overleaf), but it is more usual to request the 'pleasure of your company'.

Invitations to drinks parties

☐The time of the party should be clearly marked on the invitation. If the party is for a special event, eg a friend from abroad, the publication of a book or a private view, this should be written on the card (see example overleaf).

Parties at hotels can be 'At Home' or can 'request the pleasure of'.

Mr Alastair Topping

Lady Daulton
Mrs Alexander Charnot
at Home
for Miss Celia Daulton
and Miss Caroline Charnot
Thursday, 12th May,
at the Carlton Tower.

R.S.V.P
Bentham Manor,
Faringdon, Berkshire.

Cocktails
6.30 - 8.30.

A special reason for a party should be stated.

Miss Virginia Jones

Mrs John Fitzherbert
at Home
Friday, May 12th
in honour of the publication of
'Home Truths'

R.S.V.P
1. Hyde Park Gardens,
London. W.2

6.30pm

Invitations to a single woman and 'escort'

□Sometimes when a large reception is being given, the hostess considerately thinks that a single female guest might like to bring an escort. She might then write 'Miss Lily Esmond and Guest' on the invitation. In replying, the name of the escort should be mentioned if possible, so that the hostess will know who is attending her party, eg 'Miss Lily Esmond and Mr Henry Thackeray have great pleasure in accepting . . .'.

Invitations to weddings

☐See also Weddings, Chapter Three.
☐Wedding invitations are different from all others. They are engraved on an upright folded sheet of paper, like old-fashioned writing paper, measuring 5½ x 7 inches.
☐The standard wording is:

Example

> **Mr and Mrs John Allen**
>
> *Mr and Mrs Bertram Scott Grantley*
> *request the pleasure of your company*
> *at the marriage of their daughter*
> *Virginia Elizabeth*
> *to*
> *Mr Roger Clifford Richmond*
> *at St. Margaret's, Westminster*
> *on Saturday the seventeenth of August*
> *at two o'clock*
> *and afterwards at*
> *Grosvenor House*
>
> *R.S.V.P*
> *Dolphin Cottage*
> *St. George's Drive*
> *Plymouth*

Special circumstances

☐There will be variations on the above according to family circumstances. Should a girl be an orphan, her uncle and aunt may well be the hosts at her wedding and the wording will be: 'Mr and Mrs Thomas Eccleston request the pleasure of your company at the marriage of their niece Amanda to Mr Charles Brook'. By tradition Amanda's surname is not given, even though she is Amanda Howard,

the daughter of Mrs Eccleston's sister. But the
bride may care to add her surname as friends may
not know the names of her relations, or of a
mother's remarriage.
☐Sometimes divorced parents reunite and give the
wedding together: 'Mr Nicholas Guthrie and Mrs
Lawrence Palmer request the pleasure of your
company at the marriage of their daughter Virginia'.
☐If only one of the bride's parents is alive, he or
she will give the wedding alone. 'Mrs John
Dickinson requests the pleasure of your company at
the marriage of her daughter Sarah.' If the parent
has remarried, the wording will be, 'Mr and Mrs
Duncan Cassidy request the pleasure of your
company at the marriage of her daughter Sarah'.
(As has been said, Sarah may wish to add her
surname to avoid confusion.)
☐An innovation for a not so young couple is to
issue an invitation jointly on their own behalf: 'Miss
Margaret Emerson and Mr. Harold Patten request the
pleasure of your company at their marriage at the
Brompton Oratory on Monday, 26th June...'.
☐If the bride is a widow her name will appear on
the invitation as 'Jacqueline, widow of Mr Claude
Amory'.

**Invitations to
receptions only**

☐If the marriage is in a register office, or if it is
being held in a very small church, invitations are
issued for a reception after the ceremony. When the
size of the church precludes guests other than the
family and their closest friends, a private note
should be enclosed with the invitation to the
reception, explaining that because of the lack of
accommodation in the church, it is not possible to
invite all the guests to attend the ceremony.

Second weddings

☐Much will depend on the age of the couple,
whether they are widowed or divorced, and what
kind of reception they may wish to give. They may
have a traditional reception, or they may prefer to
give an evening party. (For more details see 'Second
weddings', Chapter Three.)

Service of blessing	□When one or both parties have been widowed, the formula for a second marriage is the same as the first. However, if there has been a divorce, a service of blessing may be held in a church after the civil ceremony. □The couple themselves may be inviting the guests: 'Mrs Jacqueline Amory and Mr Timothy James request the pleasure of your company at a Service of Blessing following their marriage.'
Postponed and cancelled weddings	□See pages 79–80.
Answering invitations	□Always answer quickly. Even if the invitation has been sent out a long time in advance (as perhaps a dance invitation) the hostess will want to know the number of guests as soon as possible; she has complicated plans to make, dinner parties to organize for the dance, possibly even house parties.
Formal replies	□Invitations for weddings and dances should always be answered formally, in the third person (see overleaf) on headed writing paper. If a formal invitation is sent to you for a dinner or a luncheon, without a preliminary telephone call, the third person formula should again be used. 'Mrs Hermione Esmond thanks Their Excellencies The Ambassador for Ruritania and Mme de Bechevet for their most kind invitation to dinner on Tuesday, 28th May, and has the greatest pleasure in accepting.' □If there is more than one host, then all names must be mentioned in replying and put on the envelope, which is posted to the address given on the card.
Informal replies	□With drinks parties less formality applies. Sometimes the RSVP has a telephone number beneath. Otherwise reply in the third person to the address given. □When an old friend is giving a party and puts your Christian name in the top left corner, an informal reply is more friendly: 'Dear Hugh, Thank

30 HOYLAKE GARDENS
MITCHAM · SURREY
CR4 1ET
01-764 3038

Dr and Mrs Thomas Baker thank
Mr and Mrs Grantley for their kind
invitation to the wedding of their
daughter Elizabeth on Wednesday,
26th June and have great pleasure
in accepting.

9 TRAFALGAR TERRACE
BRIGHTON, SUSSEX
BN1 4EG
0273 687974

Mr and Mrs William Morris thank
Mr and Mrs Grantley for their kind
invitation to the wedding of their
daughter Elizabeth on Wednesday,
26th June but regret they are
unable to accept because of a previous
engagement.

you for your invitation for Tuesday 26th. I shall be delighted to come and look forward to the party immensely'.
□ A refusal is often made less disappointing by a charming note:
'Dear Anne, Alas, I cannot manage to join you on the 12th as I shall be away, but I hope your exhibition is a great success. I will certainly come and visit you in the next few days.'
□When refusing invitations, you will of course explain why, eg a previous engagement, absence abroad.

Displaying invitations

□Although this is often done, it does not stand up well to examination as a social custom. It can be hurtful to guests to discover that they have not been invited to a party given by mutual friends, and it is ostentatious to display your own social popularity. If invitation cards are needed as an *aide-memoire*, it is much more tactful therefore to arrange them by your writing desk in a private room.

WRITTEN CORRESPOND- ENCE

□The greatest change in social communication has been the decline of the written word. The vast extension of the telephone service and the introduction of direct dialling to every part of the world have superseded the letter. Furthermore, the delivery of letters is no longer totally reliable and they can take days to arrive. In 1870 Joseph Bowes, staying in Darlington, could write at tea-time to his wife living in Paris, knowing his letter would be on her breakfast tray next morning—alas, such luxuries are no more. Yet receiving a charming letter is one of the pleasures of life. The written word is more eloquent than the spoken, and a letter is a more enduring expression of gratitude, sympathy or friendship than any conversation. Happily there remain many occasions when letters have no substitute.

Left: Two examples of formal replies to a wedding invitation; one acceptance, one refusal.

FOURWINDS,
56 HORSHAM ROAD,
BEXLEYHEATH, KENT.
CRAYFORD 522778.

43 STAFFORD COURT
KENSINGTON HIGH STREET
LONDON, W8 7DN
01 - 937 2951

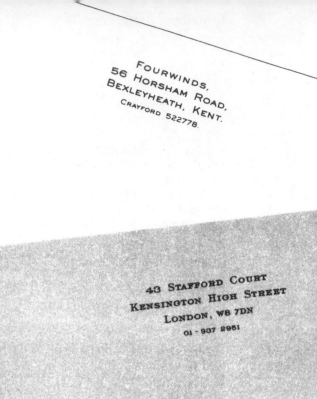

Castle Howard. York

☐While some ideas for the letters we write at various times are shown here, no set example can replace spontaneity of feeling and liveliness of expression.

Writing materials and their uses

☐Below are a few words about the equipment needed for a writing desk. Much of course will be dictated by personal requirements and directed by individual taste. It is surprising how many and how varied are the materials needed by a busy correspondent.

Writing paper

☐One of the pleasures of writing a letter is that of writing on a fresh sheet of paper of one's own choice and perhaps design. There is much latitude in the choice of paper. In colouring, white, cream, grey, and various shades of blue are all equally popular. It is entirely a question of personal preference. Coloured borders are also becoming fashionable and can look very attractive.
☐Writing paper is made in a variety of sizes and weights. There are no rules about this; choose whatever suits your handwriting best. The prolific correspondent has paper in two sizes: one for long letters, and a smaller size for notes.
☐It is acceptable to write on both sides of a sheet of writing paper, if a second sheet is needed it should be on a plain (unheaded) continuation sheet. (Before the Second World War it was customary to write on folded paper, like a wedding invitation. During the war, in a time of great shortage, the supply of folded paper was forbidden by government statute.)

Headings

☐The letter heading can be in script or Roman letters, and is traditionally placed in the centre or on the right-hand side of the paper. Sometimes country dwellers have their address on the right hand side and their telephone number and the nearest railway

Left: Headings on writing paper are either centred or on the right hand side. A famous house speaks for itself.

station on the left. Those entitled to bear them sometimes have their crest or coronet at the head of the paper. (Equally, these can be engraved on the flap of the envelope.)

☐Two innovations have come across the Atlantic in recent years. The first of these (mentioned previously) is writing paper with a coloured border; the second is to print one's name above the address at the top. For a professional or quasi-professional person, this seems a good idea for so many people today run their businesses, however small, from their own homes.

Envelopes ☐The Post Office recommends that your address is printed on the back flap of the envelope, and this is obviously sensible if a letter goes astray; it can be returned to you unopened, and without the embarrassment of a personal letter having been unsealed by the Post Office.

Pen and ink ☐Of course fountain pens are the nicest, but the all-convenient ball point pens have often super-seded them, simply because of convenience and price. Black ink looks best on white paper, or cream or grey; blue ink is best on blue paper.

Correspondence cards ☐Many people use a plain card with their name, address and telephone number printed at the top

Example

from **LADY EGLANTINE** 16 Lancaster Gardens London, S.W.1. 01 - 772 4395

(see example). The use of 'From' is optional.
Correspondence cards are plain on the reverse and
are sent in envelopes.
☐These cards are extremely useful, especially in
any matters concerned with business—ordering
some more claret from the wine merchant, or
enclosed with a cheque for theatre tickets.

Postcards ☐Picture postcards were first printed in the 1890's;
(at that time they were either souvenirs of travel, or
they were collectors' items and pasted in a scrap
book). Apart from pictures of sun-filled beaches
sent home to snow-bound Britons in February, the
sending of picture postcards has become widespread. This has been greatly encouraged by
museums, who find the sale of postcards one of
their most lucrative sources of revenue. Now that
beautiful works of art are reproduced on postcards,
they can be sent as a charming gesture to those who
will appreciate them.
☐Traditionally, postcards and picture postcards,
not being enclosed in envelopes, carry no opening
greeting, no 'Dear Mary', but just bear a message.
At one time it was considered correct to sign a
postcard with initials only, but now most people use
their Christian names.
☐A postcard can certainly be sent to thank the
hostess for a dinner or a cocktail party when she is
a friend; when one is invited for the first time, a
postcard would seem too casual and a hand-written
letter of thanks is appropriate.

Visiting cards ☐Perhaps not many women today have printed
visiting cards, as the days when they were left at a
house to show one had actually called have long
since passed. However, their uses are many—to
send with a bunch of flowers is the first that comes
to mind. One London hostess uses them instead of
'At Home' cards, scribbling 'Cocktails 6.30—8.30'
in the lower right-hand corner.
☐Traditionally, visiting cards for men and women
are in different sizes; the sizes from which women

may make a selection are 2 x 3 in, 2⅛ x 3¼ in, 2⅛ x 3½ in, and 2⅛ x 3⅞ in. The cards will of course be engraved, and the text can either be in script or Roman lettering. It used not to be considered appropriate for a woman to put her telephone number on a card, but now that so many women work from home, eg free lance journalists and Cordon Bleu cooks, a telephone number in such instances is correct.

☐The classic men's sizes are 3 x 1½ ins, or 3 x 1¾ ins; 3 x 2 ins is suitable for both sexes.

Man's visiting card may include his club.

Sir Iain Moncreiffe of that Ilk,

Easter Moncreiffe,
Perthshire.   White's.

Woman's visiting card.

MISS DOROTHY MAYNARD,

ROCKHILL,
HORSHAM.

Typewritten letters   ☐Most people still consider it impolite to send typewritten letters. (Business letters are of course

198

different.) It is a compliment to receive a letter written in a person's own hand and it shows so much of their character—the delicate lacy writing of certain women, the firm vertical hand of an intelligent man; the hand-writing reveals as much, if not more, than the voice. A typewritten letter seems impersonal—and also rather perfunctory—but there are instances when it is permissible to send typewritten letters. The first is when the recipient has poor sight, the second is when one's hand-writing is virtually illegible. If your writing is cryptic, it is acceptable to type social letters, but of course explaining why— either at the beginning, or as a post-script.

☐One's typing must be sufficiently neat for the letter to look pleasing. It is preferable to receive an elegant scrawl to a messily typed letter (and of course 'topping and tailing' are in your own hand).

Beginnings of letters

☐For a younger person, writing to a person he or she knows only slightly, it is always correct to begin formally, 'Dear Mrs Esmond', and sign, 'Yours sincerely'. It is for the older person to reply, 'Dear Mary—please call me Cecilia', and sign more informally, if she wishes. The classic letter opening is 'Dear X', and 'My dear X' indicates a letter to a friend, or a desire to extend the acquaintance. It is worth noting when writing to Americans that the usage 'My dear' is considered somewhat patronising in the United States and should be avoided. (For beginning letters to professional people or those with titles (peers or privy councillors, for example) see the chart at the end of the Chapter.)

Endings of letters

☐In the ending of letters there is a whole spectrum between extreme formality and friendliness. 'Yours sincerely' is correct and dignified. 'Yours' is somewhat cold, dismissive and unimaginative, and not an invitation to friendship. 'Yours ever' is friendlier. 'Yours, as ever', 'Yours, as always' and 'Yours affectionately', although a little old-fashioned, have much charm. We tend to be a shy and tongue-tied race, and sometimes in our letters we can show an amity we are too timid to reveal in conversation.

Business letters ☐When writing business letters in a private capacity, for example, to the bank, or a shop or an official, 'Yours faithfully' is correct.

Royal and diplomatic letters ☐See Chapter Ten.

Correct forms of address ☐A chart at the end of the chapter gives correct forms of address when writing letters.

Letters of thanks ☐Below are given some words of guidance on 'thank you' letters for gifts, parties and various social occasions. Whether you are thanking someone for a wedding present or for an evening at the theatre, always try to make the letter imaginative, and describe the pleasure that the event has given you; a stereotyped note is little better than a printed form. A well-written letter should give your friend as much pleasure to read as you yourself have been made happy by their kindness.

Thank-you letters for presents ☐Probably no advice on this subject could be better than that given by the novelist Scott Fitzgerald to his daughter Scottie, who was then a girl of nineteen at college.

December 1940

'Dearest Scottie,

There has reached you by this time, I hope, a little coat. It was an almost never-worn coat of Sheilah's that she wanted to send you. It seemed very nice to me—it may fill out your rather thin wardrobe. Frances Kroll's father is a furrier and he remade it *without charge*!

So you must *at once please write* the following letters:

(1) To Sheilah, not stressing Mr Kroll's contribution.

(2) To Frances, praising the style.

(3) To me (in the course of things) in such a way that I can show the letter to *Sheilah* who will certainly ask me if you liked the coat.

You make things easier for me if you write these letters promptly. A giver gets no pleasure in a letter acknowledging a gift three weeks' late even though it crawls with apologies—you will have stolen pleasure from one who has tried to give it to you. (Ecclesiastes Fitzgerald)

> with dearest love,
> Daddy'

☐In writing the three letters suggested by her father, Scottie will have pleased her father, gratified Mr Kroll, and delighted Sheilah. It is hoped that Scottie liked the coat, if she really wanted to please Sheilah Graham (who was then Scott Fitzgerald's mistress and who nursed him through his final illness a few months later) she would have told her when she was going to wear the coat, perhaps mentioning a specific occasion, such as a college dance.

☐The ideal thank-you letter will (a) describe one's appreciation of the gift, (b) thank the giver for their generosity, and (c) describe the gift. Remember that the gift may have been sent direct from a shop, who may have delivered as a wedding present two wine glasses instead of six—and the donor would be most upset if this error were not corrected. Therefore recount the qualities of the present, ie if a scarf, how lovely the colour, or if flowers, how glorious the scent. Tell the donor your actual use of the gift, eg 'Your beautiful flowers have filled the drawing-room with colour', or 'I am going to take the book away with me when I go to the country next weekend, and long to read it then'.

Letters after parties

☐The aim of a hostess is that her guests should enjoy the party, and one of her pleasures is to be told how much they have. Any hostess feels that the party is prolonged when she receives letters from friends saying that they had a happy time.

☐Ideally, thank-you letters should be sent promptly. The Latin tag, *Bis dat qui cito dat*—'he gives twice who gives quickly'—is completely true, and a late letter gives an obligatory 'bread and butter letter' impression. It is best if one can write within two or three days of the party. However, should you be extremely busy, it is better to send a good letter a few days late than a prompt but perfunctory note.

☐No letter is given as an example because each party is unique. Two ingredients are necessary: the first is to tell the hostess how much you enjoyed the party; the second, and more important, is to tell her why—and this is a compliment to her gifts as a hostess.

Dinner parties

☐The hostess has carefully chosen the guests, whom she hopes will enjoy each other's company, she has perhaps directed the conversation so that it is amusing and interesting, she has probably taken great trouble with the menu. All this should be incorporated in the letter, and specific guests or good talk recalled. In the past it was considered most incorrect to mention food; this was partly because most English food was dull, and standard dinner party menus were consommé, sole, lamb, game, and an unimaginative pudding, followed by dessert and a savoury; a monotonous succession of predictable dishes. Now the composition of a menu has become a challenge to the imagination rather than a message to the chef, especially when the hostess probably is responsible herself for much of the cooking, and it is always pleasing for her to be told that it was delectable.

House-parties

☐A now obsolete custom was that it was ill-mannered to comment on the decor of a house. One young woman, who had very old-fashioned parents, was invited for the weekend to one of England's loveliest houses. On her return, when asked about the famous collection of paintings, she replied: 'I never looked. My father told me never to notice other people's houses.'. The typical English country house developed in a rambling way, each generation adding a treasure or perhaps a horror, all muddled up together. Nowadays we are all much better informed on works of art and appreciation of them is widespread—and everyone likes to be complimented on the taste shown in their houses.

Letters of sympathy

□See also 'Funerals and Memorial Services', Chapter Five.

□Death strikes several blows to most of us during our lives, and at such sad times one feels singularly desolate and alone. There is no greater comfort for someone who has been bereaved than to know that they have the sympathy and affection of their friends. Many widows and widowers who have been blessed with long and happy marriages say that their sorrow has been alleviated by the letters their friends have sent them.

□Sadly you will also at some time write to sympathize with the death of a friend, or a friend's parent, brother, sister or child.

Example

□A perfect letter of sympathy is that which Henry James sent to Sir Leslie Stephen (the father of Virginia Woolf) on the death of his wife.

London, May 6th, 1895

'My dear Stephen,

I feel unable to approach such a sorrow as yours—and yet I can't forbear to hold out my hand to you. I think of you with inexpressible participation, and only take refuge from this sharp pain of sympathy in trying to call up the image of all the perfect happiness that you drew, and that you gave. I pray for you that there are moments when the sense of that rushes over you like a possession that you still hold. There is no happiness in this horrible world but the happiness we have had—the very present is ever in the jaws of fate. I think in the presence of the loss of so beautiful and noble and generous a friend, of the admirable picture of her perfect union with you, and that for her, at any rate, with all its fatigues and sacrifices, life didn't pass without the deep and clear felicity—the best it can give. She leaves no image but that of the high enjoyment of affection and devotions—the beauty and the good she wrought and the tenderness that came back to her. Unquenchable seems to me such a presence. But why do I presume to say these things to you, my dear Stephen? Only because I want you to hear in them the sound of the voice and feel the pressure of the hand of your affectionate old friend.

Henry James'

☐The great quality of this sublime letter is Henry James's immediate—indeed urgent—conveyal of sympathy, to comfort his old friend. The second impression, which will remain always, and comfort the reader after the agony of his immediate grief has passed, is Henry James's account of how perfect and happy was the marriage, how husband and wife had created an unforgettable happiness that would survive always in the memory of their friends. Death itself could not obscure the joy of their mutual love, and the inspiration that it gave to their many friends. It is as much a letter of exquisite praise as it is of sympathy.

Strangers and acquaintances

☐The above is a letter to a very old and dear friend. Often we read of the death of someone we did not know well, but whose company gave us great pleasure, or perhaps had shown us, at a certain moment, great kindness. It is always comforting for the family to receive an account of treasured memories. Naturally, if you are not an old friend, it is appropriate to write perhaps a week or a fortnight after the death; in the first few days of bereavement family and close friends will be the chosen comforters.

Replying to letters of sympathy

☐See 'Funerals and Memorial Services', Chapter Five.

THE TELEPHONE

☐The telephone is a mixed blessing. A social necessity, it can also be an intrusion into someone's privacy, and its use should be limited and tactful. One can open a letter at leisure but a telephone must be answered at once, and the caller should remember that the friend may be busy writing an article, cooking a soufflé or entertaining friends.

☐Telephone at times that you know will be convenient, and although this will depend on the routines of your acquaintances, before 10am or between 6pm and 7.30pm, as a general rule, is a good time to find people at home. When telephoning abroad, be careful about the difference in time. One can be awoken in the middle of the night by Americans (five to eight hours behind) or at what seems dawn by French friends (an hour in advance).

☐Some people use the telephone almost like a verbal telegram. 'Hello, Anne, this is Sarah. Can you dine with us on July 16th? I'm so pleased, eight for 8.30. I much look forward to seeing you then. Goodbye.'

☐This laconic style has much in favour of it. However, if you want to telephone for a chat, it is always considerate to ask if the other person has time to spare. How convenient would be the invention of a telephone with coloured lights: a red one that glows when the message is important, and a green perhaps for a leisurely gossip, which can then be ignored by the busy.

☐When telephoning a friend at his or her office, always ask if the moment is suitable. Talk briefly, never chat.

Answering the telephone

☐Answer 'Hello'. Do not answer with your telephone number—this practice is for business only (see Chapter 12).

Saying goodbye

☐The caller may have chatted away too long after the reason for the call has been discussed. Tactful goodbyes suggested are: 'It was so enjoyable to have talked to you—but I musn't keep you any longer, as I know how busy you are.'

☐If any meeting has been planned for the near future, this is a very tactful farewell: 'It was such fun talking to you, and I much look forward to seeing you on Friday.'

☐'I wish I could talk a little longer, but I must rush now, as I've got to be at the hairdressers/dentist by four.'

☐To be used *in extremis* only 'Alas, I must go now, as the doorbell is ringing.'

Thanking by telephone

☐The telephone should only be used to thank someone for a party, or perhaps a gift, between friends. Sometimes it is great fun to discuss a party afterwards and, needless to say, you will ask your friend if the time is suitable for a chat.

Telephone answering machines

☐These machines can make the caller feel awkward because one is talking into a void. However, we must learn to use them as they become more popular every day. They are obviously extremely useful for people who work at home and have no office to take messages; for the painter, who does not want to leave the easel to answer the telephone, for writers who have gone to the library to do a few hours research , or perhaps just some shopping.

☐The preliminary rigmarole that most people dictate into recorders is often too verbose, and spoken too slowly. Though few people as yet own telephone answering machines we are all familiar with them. Keep your announcement as brief as possible.

Example 'This is Henry Porter's answering machine. Please leave your name, telephone number, and any message after the signal, and I will telephone you back.'

Leaving a message □After these words comes an unattractive sound, which may be a screech or a deep buzz, and one is left to make an extempore speech. This of course should be brief and to the point. Do not just hang up the telephone either through shyness or boredom; have consideration for your friend who will be playing back the tape.

TELEGRAMS □The speed, the reliability and the expense of the telegraphic service have greatly altered in the last few years. It is no longer dependable, and many of its former uses have been superseded by the telephone. Furthermore telegrams to many people spell bad news. Perhaps it is a war-time memory, when deaths, injuries and soldiers missing or taken captive were announced to their families by telegram from the War Office.
□Do not send a telegram arranging social engagements, except as a last resort, eg you are going to stay with friends in the country, their telephone has broken down and you want to inform them of the time of the train.
□Bad news and sad news should be conveyed by letter or by telephone. Never send a telegram of condolence.

Congratulations □There are certain occasions when telegrams of congratulation are in order, eg marriages, and on certain achievements such as scholarships, winning a parliamentary seat or a literary prize.

The Royal Family	Envelopes	Opening of letter
The Queen	Correspondence should be addressed to 'The Private Secretary to Her Majesty the Queen'	
The Duke of Edinburgh	The same procedure should be followed as with the Queen	
The Queen Mother	The same procedure should be followed as with the Queen	
A Royal Prince	His Royal Highness, The Prince Charles, Prince of Wales	Your Royal Highness
	His Royal Highness, The Prince Edward	Your Royal Highness
A Royal Princess	Her Royal Highness, The Princess of Wales	Your Royal Highness
	Her Royal Highness, The Princess Royal	Your Royal Highness
	Her Royal Highness, The Princess Margaret, The Countess of Snowdon	Your Royal Highness
A Royal Duke	His Royal Highness, The Duke of Gloucester	Your Royal Highness
A Royal Duchess	Her Royal Highness, The Duchess of Gloucester	Your Royal Highness

Peers, Baronets and Knights	NB The social forms of address are given here, For details of formal style etc. see Debrett's 'Peerage and Baronetage' or 'Debrett's Correct Form'.	
Duke	The Duke of Sunborough	Dear Duke of Sunborough or Dear Duke

Introductions and Verbal Address	Place cards
Introduced as 'Her Majesty the Queen'*	
Addressed as 'Your Majesty', subsequently 'Ma'am' (pronounced mam)	
Introduced as 'His Royal Highness', Prince Philip, The Duke of Edinburgh'*	
Addressed as 'Your Royal Highness', subsequently 'Sir'	
Introduced as 'Her Majesty, Queen Elizabeth, The Queen Mother'*	
Addressed as 'Your Majesty', subsequently 'Ma'am'	
Introduced as 'His Royal Highness, Prince Charles, The Prince of Wales'* *Addressed as* 'Your Royal Highness', subsequently 'Sir'	His Royal Highness, The Prince of Wales
Introduced as 'His Royal Highness, The Prince Edward' *Addressed as* 'Your Royal Highness', subsequently 'Sir'	His Royal Highness The Prince Edward
Introduced as 'Her Royal Highness, The Princess of Wales' *Addressed as* 'Your Royal Highness', subsequently 'Ma'am'	Her Royal Highness, The Princess of Wales
Introduced as 'Her Royal Highness, The Princess Royal' *Addressed as* 'Your Royal Highness', subsequently 'Ma'am'	Her Royal Highness, The Princess Royal
Introduced as 'Her Royal Highness, The Princess Margaret, the Countess of Snowdon* *Addressed as* 'Your Royal Highness', subsequently 'Ma'am'	Her Royal Highness, The Princess Margaret, Countess of Snowdon
Introduced as 'His Royal Highness, The Duke of Gloucester'* *Addresssed as* for a royal prince	His Royal Highness, The Duke of Gloucester
Introduced as 'Her Royal Highness, The Duchess of Gloucester'* *Addressed as* for a royal princess	Her Royal Highness, The Duchess of Gloucester
For the Royal Family, a formal introduction is assumed.	
Introduced as 'The Duke of Sunborough' *Addressed as* 'Duke'	The Duke of Sunborough

CORRECT FORMS OF ADDRESS

	Envelopes	Opening of letter
Duchess	The Duchess of Sunborough	Dear Duchess of Sunborough or Dear Duchess
Dowager Duchess	The Dowager Duchess of Sunborough or Heloise, Duchess of Sunborough (both are correct; the usage is a matter of personal choice)	as for 'Duchess'
Eldest son of a Duke	Marquess of Belchamber For our purposes, the Marquess of Belchamber is the eldest son of the Duke of Sunborough, taking as a courtesy title the second title of his father, as is the custom.	
Younger son of a Duke	Lord Charles Pagley	Dear Lord Charles
Wife of younger son of a Duke	Lady Charles Pagley	Dear Lady Charles
Daughter of a Duke	Lady Sarah Pagley	Dear Lady Sarah
Marquess	The Marquess of Belchamber	Dear Lord Belchamber
Marchioness**	The Marchioness of Belchamber	Dear Lady Belchamber
Eldest son of a Marquess (See Earl, below)	The Earl of Charmington	
Younger sons and daughters of a Marquess	Have the same titles and modes of address as children of a Duke (see above)	
Earl	The Earl of Charmington	Dear Lord Charmington
Countess**	The Countess of Charmington	Dear Lady Charmington
Eldest son of Earl (see Viscount below)	Viscount Dalsany	
Younger son of an Earl	The Hon. Thomas Esmond	Dear Mr Esmond
Wife of younger son of an Earl	The Hon. Mrs Thomas Esmond	Dear Mrs Esmond

**See footnote overleaf

210

roductions and Verbal Address	Place cards
oduced as 'The Duchess of Sunborough'	The Duchess of Sunborough
ressed as 'Duchess'	
or 'Duchess'	as for 'Duchess'
	(or 'Heloise, Duchess of Sunborough' if the present Duchess is also present.)
oduced as 'Lord Charles Pagley'	Lord Charles Pagley
ressed as 'Lord Charles'	
oduced as 'Lady Charles Pagley'	Lady Charles Pagley
ressed as 'Lady Charles'	
oduced as 'Lady Sarah Pagley'	Lady Sarah Pagley
ressed as 'Lady Sarah'	
*-d Belchamber'	Lord Belchambei
*-dy Belchamber'	Lady Belchamber
*-d Charmington'	Lord Charmington
*-dy Charmington'	Lady Charmington
Esmond'	Mr Thomas Esmond
*-s Esmond'	Mrs Thomas Esmond

CORRECT FORMS OF ADDRESS

	Envelopes	Opening of letter
Daughter of an Earl	Lady Hermione Esmond	Dear Lady Hermione
Viscount	The Viscount Dalsany	Dear Lord Dalsany
Viscountess**	The Viscountess Dalsany	Dear Lady Dalsany
Son of a Viscount	The Hon. Hugh Trevor	Dear Mr Trevor
Wife of Viscount's son	The Hon. Mrs Hugh Trevor	Dear Mrs Trevor
Daughter of a Viscount	The Hon. Caroline Trevor	Dear Miss Trevor
Baron	The Lord St Edmunds	Dear Lord St Edmunds
Baron's wife**	The Lady St Edmunds	Dear Lady St Edmunds
Children of a Baron	The sons and daughters of barons, and their sons' wives, bear the title of Hon., as for sons of Viscounts above	
Baronet	Sir Arthur Aubyn, Bt.	Dear Sir Arthur
Wife of Baronet**	Lady Aubyn	Dear Lady Aubyn
Children of a Baronet	Baronet's children have no titles	
Life peers***	The Lord Frognal	Dear Lord Frognal
Wives of life peers	The Lady Frognal	Dear Lady Frognal
Life Peer's children	The Hon. Michael Wade	Dear Mr Wade
Knight*	Sir Thomas Eccleston	Dear Sir Thomas
Knight's wife*	Lady Eccleston	Dear Lady Eccleston

* Courtesy Titles: Should a woman bearing a courtesy title in her own right marry an 'Hon' or a baronet, she keeps her own title, eg Lady Hermione Esmond married to a baronet, would be Lady Hermione Aubyn. Married to the younger son of an earl, or the son of a viscount or baronet, she would remain Lady Hermione. A female 'Hon' married to a peer's younger son, would be 'The Hon. Mrs James' rather than 'The Hon. Mrs Hugh James'. If married to a baronet or a knight she would be 'The Hon. Lady Aubyn'.
**For Dowagers, see under Women's titles
*** non-hereditary

Introductions and Verbal Address	Place cards
Introduced as 'Lady Hermione Esmond' *Addressed as* 'Lady Hermione'	Lady Hermione Esmond
'Lord Dalsany'	Lord Dalsany
'Lady Dalsany'	Lady Dalsany
'Mr Trevor'	Mr Hugh Trevor
'Mrs Trevor'	Mrs Hugh Trevor
'Miss Trevor'	Miss Caroline Trevor
'Lord St Edmunds'	Lord St Edmunds
'Lady St Edmunds'	Lady St Edmunds
Introduced as 'Sir Arthur Aubyn' *Addressed as* 'Sir Arthur'	Sir Arthur Aubyn
'Lady Aubyn'	Lady Aubyn
'Lord Frognal'	Lord Frognal
'Lady Frognal'	Lady Frognal
'Mr Wade'	Mr Michael Wade
Introduced as 'Sir Thomas Eccleston' *Addressed as* 'Sir Thomas'	Sir Thomas Eccleston
'Lady Eccleston'	Lady Eccleston

Women's titles

	Envelopes	Opening of letter
Hereditary Peeress in her own right	The Countess of Bannockburn	Dear Lady Bannockburn

If the husband of an hereditary peeress has no title, he remains 'Mr'. Her children take the same titles as the children of a peer of her rank, and the title descends to her eldest son or, if she has no son, to her eldest daughter.

Widows of hereditary Peers	The Dowager Marchioness of Belchamber or Cecilia, Marchioness of Belchamber	Dear Lady Belchamber

Life Peeresses	Baroness Brown	Dear Lady Brown

The husband of a life peeress takes no title. Her children take the title of 'Hon.' for their lifetime.

Dames (The female equivalent of a knighthood)	Dame Augusta Marchant	Dear Dame Augusta

Widows of baronets	Lilian, Lady Aubyn or Dowager Lady Aubyn	Dear Lady Aubyn

Divorcées	Rosamund, Viscountess Dalsany	Dear Lady Dalsany

For all ladies of title, whether ex-duchesses or former wives of knights, the form is the same; the Christian name precedes the title.

NB See also footnote on women's courtesy titles, page 216

Scottish and Irish titles:

There is little difference between the peerages of England, Scotland, or Ireland with the notable exception that Irish Peers do not automatically have a seat in the House of Lords and can therefore stand as members of the House of Commons. Many Scottish peerages can descend through the female line and the heir to a peerage is called 'Master' (see below).

Eldest son of a Scottish peer (or peeress in her own right)	The Master of Glamis	Dear Master of Glamis

Wife of a Master	The wife is called 'Mrs' unless her husband (or herself) has the right to use a title such as 'Hon.'	

Introductions and Verbal Address	Place cards
'Lady Bannockburn'	Lady Bannockburn
'Lady Belchamber'	Cecilia, Lady Belchamber
'Lady Brown'	Lady Brown
Introduced as 'Dame Augusta Marchant'	Dame Augusta Marchant
Addressed as 'Dame Augusta'	
'Lady Aubyn'	Lilian, Lady Aubyn
'Lady Dalsany'	Rosamund, Lady Dalsany
Introduced as 'The Master of Glamis'	The Master of Glamis
Addressed as 'Master'	

	Envelopes	Opening of letter
Irish Hereditary Knight	The Knight of Glin	Dear Knight
Wife of Irish hereditary Knight	Madam Fitzgerald	Dear Madam Fitzgerald
Scottish Chief or Chieftain	The MacKinnon of MacKinnon	Dear MacKinnon
		(A member of a Clan or Name writes 'Dear Chief')
Female Chief	Madam MacLachlan of MacLachlan	Dear Madam MacLachlan of MacLachlan
Wife of Scottish Chief or Chieftain	Madam MacKinnon of MacKinnon NB Some wives prefer Mrs to Madam and this varies depending on the family.	Dear Madam MacKinnon
Eldest son of a Chief	John MacKinnon of MacKinnon, yr. ('yr.' means 'younger')	Dear Mr MacKinnon
Wife of Chief's eldest son	Mrs MacKinnon of MacKinnon, yr.	Dear Mrs MacKinnon
Other children of a Chief	The sons are addressed without special titles, eg Hugh MacKinnon, Esq. but the daughters bear the designation of the house, eg Miss MacKinnon of MacKinnon (the eldest) and Miss Jane MacKinnon, the younger daughter.	
Irish Chieftain	The McGillycuddy of the Reeks (O'Conor Don is the only Irish chief whose name is *not* prefixed by 'The')	Dear McGillycuddy
Irish Chieftain's wife	Madam McGillycuddy of the Reeks	Dear Madam McGillycuddy
Children of Irish Chieftain	Children of Irish Chieftains have no special titles or designations.	

Untitled People

Men	Charles Newby, Esq.	Dear Mr Newby
Married Women	Mrs Charles Newby	Dear Mrs Newby

Introductions and Verbal Address	Place cards
Introduced as 'The Knight of Glin'	The Knight of Glin
Addressed as 'Knight'	
'Madam Fitzgerald'	Madame Fitzgerald
Introduced as 'The MacKinnon of MacKinnon'	The MacKinnon
Addressed as 'MacKinnon'	
(verbal address is by clan or territorial designation, not by surname, eg Col. Donald Cameron of Lochiel is addressed as 'Lochiel')	
'Madam MacLachlan'	Madam MacLachlan
'Madam MacKinnon'	Madam MacKinnon
'Mr MacKinnon'	Mr John MacKinnon
'Mrs MacKinnon'	Mrs John MacKinnon
Introduced as 'The McGillycuddy of the Reeks'	The McGillycuddy of the Reeks
Addressed as 'MacGillycuddy	
Introduced as 'Madam McGillycuddy of the Reeks'	Madam McGillycuddy of the Reeks
Addressed as 'Madam McGillycuddy'	
'Mr Newby'	Mr Charles Newby
'Mrs Newby'	Mrs Charles Newby

	Envelopes	Opening of letter
Daughters	Miss Lily Newby (sometimes the eldest daughter is addressed as 'Miss Newby')	Dear Miss Newby
Widows	Mrs Charles Newby	Dear Mrs Newby
Divorcées	Mrs Betty Newby	Dear Mrs Newby

Government and Parliament

The designations given here apply to official or parliamentary life, and events connected with it. In ordinary social life it is correct to address members of the government by their own names and *personal* titles, eg 'Mr Mildmay', 'Sir Marmaduke' etc.

All members of the House of Commons have the initials 'M.P.' (Member of Parliament) after their names on envelopes. In the case of Cabinet Ministers (and some other ministers) this is preceded by the initials 'P.C.' (Privy Councillor). This also entitles them to the pre-fix 'The Rt. Hon.' (For information about initials signifying awards or decorations see the Appendix.)

The Prime Minister	The Rt. Hon. William Mildmay, P.C., M.P. (personal)	Dear Prime Minister
	The Prime Minister (official)	
The Lord Chancellor	see 'The Law'	
Lord Privy Seal	The Rt. Hon. The Earl of Brentford, P.C. (personal)	Dear Lord Privy Seal
	The Lord Privy Seal (official)	
Chancellor of the Exchequer	The Rt. Hon. Plantagenet Palliser, P.C., M.P. (personal)	Dear Chancellor
	The Chancellor of the Exchequer (official)	
Chancellor of the Duchy of Lancaster	Sir Marmaduke Morecombe, Bt, P.C., M.P. (personal)	Dear Chancellor
	The Chancellor of the Duchy of Lancaster (official)	

Introductions and Verbal Address	Place cards
'Miss Newby'	Miss Lily Newby
'Mrs Newby'	Mrs Charles Newby
'Mrs Newby'	Mrs Betty Newby
by appointment or by name	The Prime Minister
as above	Lord Privy Seal
Introduced by appointment or by name	Chancellor of the Exchequer
Addressed as 'Chancellor' or by name	
Introduced by appointment or by name	Chancellor of the Duchy of Lancaster
Addressed by name or as 'Chancellor'	

	Envelopes	Opening of letter
Secretaries of State	The Rt. Hon. Phineas Finn, P.C., M.P. (personal)	Dear Secretary of State or
	The Home Secretary (official)	Dear Home/Foreign/Chief Secretary
The Lord President of the Council	The Rt. Hon. The Duke of St. Bungay, P.C. (personal)	Dear Lord President
	or by official title as above	
Ministers	John Grey, Esq., M.P.	Dear Minister
	or by official title as above	
Back Benchers	Barrington Earle, Esq., M.P.	Dear Mr Earle

The Law — The designations given here refer to occasions when the person is acting, or being addressed, in an official capacity. In private social life, legal applications would not normally be used, eg Lord Clarendon, the Lord Chancellor would be addressed, introduced and written to as Lord Clarendon (see Peers). Circuit judges and retired High Court judges are often called 'Judge'. In court, High Court judges are called 'My Lord'; Circuit judges are called 'Your Honour' save when they sit at the Central Criminal Court when by usage they are called 'My Lord'

	Envelopes	Opening of letter
The Lord Chancellor*	The Rt. Hon., The Earl of Clarendon, The Lord Chancellor or The Lord Chancellor	Dear Lord Chancellor or My Lord
The Lord Chief Justice*	The Rt. Hon., The Lord Chief Justice of England, P.C.	Dear Lord Chief Justice or My Lord
Lord* Justice-General (of Scotland)**	The Rt. Hon., the Lord Justice-General, P.C.	Dear Lord Justice-General or My Lord
The Lord Chief Justice of Northern Ireland***	The Rt. Hon. Sir David Bowen, Lord Chief Justice of Northern Ireland	Dear Lord Chief Justice or My Lord

* a member of the Privy Council
** For details of Scottish judiciary, see 'Debrett's Correct Form'
***other legal forms of address are as in England.

Introductions and Verbal Address	Place cards
by appointment or by name	Mr Phineas Finn
Introduced as above	The Duke of St. Bungay
Addressed as 'Duke' (or other personal title) or as 'Lord President'	
Introduced as 'Mr Grey'	Mr John Grey
Addressed as 'Minister' or 'Mr Grey	
'Mr Earle'	Mr Barrington Earle
Introduced as 'The Lord Chancellor'	The Lord Chancellor
Addressed as 'Lord Chancellor'	
Introduced as 'The Lord Chief Justice'	The Lord Chief Justice
Addressed as 'Lord Chief Justice'	
'Lord Justice General'	The Lord Justice-General
Introduced as 'The Lord Chief Justice'	The Lord Chief Justice
Addressed as 'Lord Chief Justice'	

	Envelopes	Opening of letter
Master of the Rolls	The Master of the Rolls	Dear Master of the Rolls
The President of the Family Division (always knighted and a P.C.)	The President of the Family Divison	Dear President or Dear Sir William
Lords of Appeal	The Rt. Hon. The Lord Howe, P.C.	Dear Lord Howe
Court of Appeal Judge	The Rt. Hon Lord Justice Pimm, P.C.	Dear Lord Justice or My Lord
High Court Judge	The Hon. Mr Justice Allen	Dear Judge
Woman High Court Judge	The Hon. Mrs Justice Harris	(Dear) Madam

NB Though referred to as 'Mr Justice' and 'Mrs Justice' officially, high court judges are knights (or dames) and socially are addressed accordingly.

Circuit Court Judges	His Honour Judge Jones, Q.C. (If a knight, His Honour Sir John Bates) (If the judge was a Q.C. before his appointment, he retains his patent.)	(Dear) Sir
Queen's Counsel	Philip Euston, Esq., Q.C.	Dear Mr Euston

The Armed Services

NB The rank of an officer should always be on the envelope, so should his decorations. The usages given here are social, for more details of forms of address, see 'Debrett's Correct Form'.

ROYAL NAVY officers from Admiral of the Fleet to Lieutenant	Admiral of the Fleet, the Earl of Matcham, G.C.B., K.B.E.	Dear Lord Matcham
	Admiral Sir William James, G.C.B.	Dear Sir William (Admiral James if he has no title)
	Commodore Hugh Lessing, C.B.E., Royal Navy (or R.N.)*	Dear Commodore Lessing

NB Captain, Commander and Lieutenant, as for Commodore but with appropriate title.

Introductions and Verbal Address	Place cards
Introduced as 'The Master of the Rolls'	The Master of the Rolls
Addressed as 'Master of the Rolls'	
By title or as Sir William Dawson	As for introduction
Lord Howe'	Lord Howe
Introduced as 'Lord Justice Pimm'	Lord Justice Pimm
Addressed as 'Lord Justice'	
Introduced as 'Mr Justice Allen' or 'Sir Peter Allen'	Mr Justice Allen
Addressed as 'Sir Peter'	
Introduced as 'Mrs Justice Harris'	Mrs Justice Harris
Addressed as 'Dame Elizabeth'	
(members of the bar may address High Court judges as 'Judge')	
Judge Jones'	Judge Jones
Mr Euston'	Mr Philip Euston
Lord Matcham'	Lord Matcham
Introduced as 'Sir William James'	Sir William James or
Addressed as 'Sir William' (Admiral James if he has no title)	Admiral James
Commodore Lessing' or 'Commodore'	Commodore Lessing

	Envelopes	Opening of letter
Sub-Lieutenant and all ranks below	Sub-Lieutenant Harold Ross, Royal Navy (or R.N.)	Dear Mr Ross

* All officers below the rank of Rear-Admiral are entitled to the words 'Royal Navy' after their name, followed by decorations etc. This may be abbreviated 'R.N.'

| **ROYAL MARINES** | As for the army, below. The rank of Lieutenant-Colonel and ranks beneath it are entitled to 'R.M.' or 'Royal Marines' after their name, followed by any decorations. | |

| **THE ARMY**

Officers from Field Marshal to Captain | The form is as for the higher ranks of the Navy, but with appropriate titles: however, if a general does not have a knighthood and is not a peer, he is referred to as 'General Paine' except on envelopes where his rank as a general is designated, eg Major-General John Paine, C.B., C.B.E. | |
| | | Dear General Paine (or Dear General) |

| **Lieutenant and Ranks below** | John Harris, Esq. Grenadier Guards

(The regiment or corps may be added on the next line as shown here) | Dear Mr Harris |

| **ROYAL AIR FORCE** | As for the other services: the full rank plus any personal titles and decorations goes on the envelope. 'R.A.F.' may follow the name; Flying Officers or Pilot Officers are 'Mr'. | |

NB As a rule in the Services, titled people are addressed by their titles rather than service rank, except by special preference, eg Admiral Sir William James is 'Sir William' not 'Admiral James'. On envelopes his service rank appears before his title, eg Admiral Sir William James (followed by 'Bt' if appropriate) then decorations, etc.

The Clergy

CHURCH OF ENGLAND

| **Archbishops** | The Most Reverend and Rt. Hon. the Lord Archbishop of Canterbury (or York) | Dear Archbishop |

Introductions and Verbal Address	Place cards
'Mr Ross'	Mr Ross
'General Paine' or 'General'	General Paine
'Mr Harris'	Mr Harris
Introduced as 'The Archbishop of ...' *Addressed socially as* 'Archbishop'	His Grace, The Archbishop of Canterbury (or York)

CORRECT FORMS OF ADDRESS

	Envelopes	Opening of Letter
Bishops	The Right Reverend the Lord Bishop of Durham	Dear Bishop
	(exception: the Bishop of London, Rt. Rev. and Rt. Hon. the Lord Bishop of London)	
Deans	The Very Reverend, the Dean of Plumstead	Dear Dean, or Dear Mr Dean
Other ranks	The Very Rev. the Provost of Coventry	as above, but substituting appropriate titles
	The Venerable the Archdeacon of Exeter	
	The Rev. Canon John Smith	
Vicars and Rectors	The Reverend John Pike	Dear Mr Pike, or
	(if wife is included the correct form is The Rev. John and Mrs. Pike)	Dear Father Pike
Wives of the Clergy	Wives are addressed as other wives are. Queen Elizabeth I disapproved of the Protestant innovation of married clergymen, and refused to grant even bishops' wives the titles of their husbands.	
CHURCH OF SCOTLAND		
The clergy (for other ranks see 'Debrett's Correct Form')	The Reverend Peter Jones (The Reverend Mary Jones, if a woman)	Dear Mr /Mrs Jones Dear Minister
JEWISH		
The Chief Rabbi	The Chief Rabbi Dr Immanuel Jakobovits	Dear Chief Rabbi
Rabbis	Rabbi P. Wiseman, or Rabbi Dr P. Wiseman (if appropriate)	Dear Rabbi Wiseman Dear Dr Wiseman (if a doctor)
Ministers	The Reverend Peter Wiseman	Dear Mr Wiseman
	The Reverend Dr Peter Wiseman (if a doctor)	Dear Dr Wiseman

Introductions and Verbal Address	Place cards
as above, except 'Bishop'	The Lord Bishop of Durham
Introduced as 'The Dean of Plumstead' *Addressed as* 'Dean'	The Dean of Plumstead
as above, but substituting appropriate titles	The Provost of Coventry The Archdeacon of Exeter The Rev. Canon John Smith
Introduced as 'Mr Pike' or 'Father Pike' according to *his* preference *Addressed as* in introduction, or 'Vicar' or 'rector' if appropriate	The Rev. John Pike
'Mr Jones', 'Mrs Jones'	Mr Peter Jones Mrs Mary Jones
'Chief Rabbi'	The Chief Rabbi
Rabbi Wiseman' 'Dr Wiseman'	Rabbi Wiseman Dr Wiseman
'Mr Wiseman' 'Dr Wiseman'	Mr Peter Wiseman Dr Peter Wiseman

227

THE ROMAN CATHOLIC CHURCH	Envelopes	Opening of letter
The Pope	His Holiness the Pope	Your Holiness, or Most Holy Father
Apostolic Delegate	His Excellency Most Reverend Lorenzo Giotto or His Excellency the Apostolic Delegate	Your Excellency
Cardinals	His Eminence the Cardinal Archbishop of Westminster His Eminence Cardinal Jones (if not an archbishop)	Dear Cardinal Jones or Your Eminence
Archbishops	His Grace the Archbishop of Armagh	Dear Archbishop Boland or Your Grace
Bishops	The right Reverend James Evans, Bishop of Castletown	My Lord Bishop or Dear Bishop Evans
Monsignors	The Reverend Monsignor Patrick Penn, or The Reverend Monsignor	Dear Monsignor Penn
Priests of other ranks	The Reverend John O'Reilly	Dear Father O'Reilly

Local Government

Lord Mayor (this applies to Lady Mayors as well)	The Rt. Hon. the Lord Mayor of (London, York, Belfast and Cardiff only) The Right Worshipful the Lord Mayor of (for all except above)	Mr Lord Mayor (formal official) Dear Lord Mayor (social official)
Lady Mayoress (the Consort of a Lord Mayor*)	The Lady Mayoress of Castletown	My Lady Mayoress (formal official) Dear Lady Mayoress (social official)

*see end of section

Introductions and Verbal Address	Place cards
Introduced as 'His Holiness the Pope'	
Addressed as 'Your Holiness'	
Introduced as 'His Excellency (Lorenzo Giotto) the Apostolic Delegate'	H.E. The Apostolic Delegate
Addressed as 'Your Excellency'	
Introduced as 'His Eminence Cardinal Jones' or 'Cardinal Jones'	H.E. Cardinal Jones
Addressed as 'Your Eminence' or 'Cardinal Jones'	
Introduced as 'His Grace the Archbishop of Armagh, or 'Archbishop Boland'	as for introduction
Addressed as 'Your Grace' or 'Archbishop Boland'	
Introduced as 'Bishop Evans of Castletown' or 'His Lordship Bishop Evans of Castletown'	Bishop Evans
Addressed as 'My Lord' or 'Bishop Evans'	
'Monsignor Penn'	Monsignor Penn
'Father O'Reilly' or (in address) 'Father'	Father O'Reilly
Introduced by appointment or appointment plus name	The Lord Mayor
Addressed as 'My Lord Mayor' or 'Lord Mayor'	
as for Lord Mayor, substituting appropriate title	The Lady Mayoress

	Envelopes	Opening of Letter
Mayors	The Right Worshipful the Mayor of Liverpool (and other cities; also correct for Hastings, Hythe, New Romney and Rye)	Mr Mayor (formal official) Dear Mr Mayor (social official)
	The Worshipful Mayor of . . . (for all town Mayors)	
Lady Mayoress and Mayor's Consort	as for Lady Mayoress above	
Alderman (Corporation of London only)	Mr Alderman Jones, Alderman Sir Peter Jones Bt., Alderman the Rt. Hon. Lord Jones, Lieutenant-Colonel & Alderman Jones, or Mrs Alderman Jones, as appropriate (official) or by name (social)	Dear Alderman (formal official) By name (social official)
City, Borough or District Councillor	Councillor followed by name, (preceded where applicable by rank, Mrs or Miss) (official) or by name (social)	Dear Councillor

* A female Lord Mayor's husband is called the Lord Mayor's (or Mayor's) Consort but is addressed by name.

Professional and Civil

MEDICAL PRACTITIONERS	John Jekyll, Esq., M.D., F.R.C.P. or Dr John Jekyll, M.D., F.R.C.P. (if knighted, Sir John Jekyll etc)	Dear Dr Jekyll Dear Sir John
Surgeons	Harold Hyde, Esq., M.S., F.R.C.S.	Dear Mr Hyde
	Sir Harold Williams, M.S., F.R.C.S. (if knighted)	Dear Sir Harold

Introductions and Verbal Address	Place cards
Introduced as by appointment or name plus appointment	The Mayor of Liverpool
Addressed as 'Mr Mayor' (Exception: several mayors would be addressed collectively 'Your Worships')	
Alderman followed by name or title (in the case of a woman, Alderman Mrs Jones)	Alderman Jones
	Alderman Mrs Jones
Introduced as on envelope	Councillor Allen
Addressed as 'Councillor' or with name added as above	Councillor Mrs Allen
'Dr Jekyll'	Dr John Jekyll
'Sir John (Jekyll)'	Sir John Jekyll
'Mr. Hyde'	Mr Harold Hyde
'Sir Harold (Williams)'	Sir Harold Williams

	Envelopes	Opening of letter
DENTISTS	A Dental Surgeon is addressed as a Surgeon above, but with the appropriate intitials following. He may be referred to as 'Doctor' provided he has a medical degree in addition to dental qualification.	
POLICE **Police Commissioner** **(Metropolitan and City** **of London)**	Sir Peter Evans (plus decorations) or Commissioner of Police of the Metropolis (or, for the City of London)	(Dear) Sir, Commissioner, or by name
Police: Deputy or Assistant **Commissioner**	as above, but with appropriate titles	
Police: Deputy **Assistant** **Commissioner,** **Commander, Chief** **Superintendent and** **Superintendent**	Rank plus name, followed by 'Metropolitan Police' or 'City of London Police', plus decorations or Name followed by appointment etc.	as above, but with appropriate designations
Police: Chief Inspector, **Inspector, Police** **Sergeant and Police** **Constable**	Rank precedes name. Rank is often abbreviated to P.S., P.C., D.S., D.C. 'Metropolitan Police' or 'City of London Police' follows	Dear Chief Inspector (or other rank) Allen The prefix 'Detective' is added if a member of C.I.D.; Detective Chief Inspector Allen
Police, other forces: **Chief Constable** **(this style applies also** **to Deputy or Assistant** **Chief Constable)**	Sir John Harris or John Harris, Esq. (as appropriate, followed by decorations) or Chief Constable, Barsetshire Constabulary	Dear Chief Constable or by name
Police, other forces	all other ranks are as for Metropolitan police	
Police: women	It is the custom to precede the designation with 'W', eg W/Chief Inspector Curran, or W.D.C. James (Detective Constable)	
CIVIL SERVICE	Members of the civil service are addressed by names, not by appointments (except by other members of their departments)	

Introductions and Verbal Address	Place cards
Introduced by name or office	by name
Addressed by name or as 'Commissioner'	
by appointment or by name	by name
by appointment or by name	by name
by appointment or by name	by name

9 VISITORS AND HOUSEGUESTS

□Ideally, a visit, of whatever duration, should be a relaxed and congenial occasion, and between good friends this is nearly always assured. But if people do not know each other very well, tensions are likely—and rarely because someone is behaving badly. Rather, people may be trying too hard to please and to fall in with each others' wishes, without quite knowing what these are. Of course, all guests and hosts must 'find their footing' but it is up to the hosts to take the lead, to try and put guests at ease and (if the occasion demands) outline what is on the agenda.

PAYING A VISIT

□The old tradition of paying calls is long since gone and its nearest equivalent, 'dropping in', is a practice that has inherent drawbacks in modern households (see 'Unexpected visits' below). The majority of visits therefore are the result of invitations and these tend to be founded on an activity of some kind—usually drinking or eating. 'Come and see us', when translated into a fixed date and time, becomes 'come for a drink' or 'dine with us' or 'come for the weekend'. Most of these occasions have been described elsewhere, under Table Manners, Parties, etc. ('Houseguests' are described below). In fact, almost the only occasion one is invited to that is not a party (or dinner) is for a drink, and in such cases about 45 minutes to an hour is the proper length of time to stay. After that, even the most conscientious host may understandably fail to notice empty glasses.

Unexpected visits

□Not surprisingly perhaps, these inspire mixed feelings and it is up to the visitor to play things by ear: to perceive if he has chosen the wrong moment and, if so, to make a rapid departure. Whenever possible, it is kind to telephone first, as this gives friends all sorts of options—to say that they are just about to go out, to have a hasty conference about asking you to stay to dinner, to turn off the television they swear they never watch, or do any one of a thousand other things to preserve

234

either privacy or dignity.

☐If, by the way, an unannounced visit does prove inopportune and the red carpet is not unrolled, it is hardly fair to act as though it had been pulled out from under one's feet.

Receiving uninvited guests

☐If someone calls at a genuinely inconvenient time, it is perfectly in order to say as politely as possible that you cannot invite him/her in — you are just going out, putting the children to bed, etc.— and perhaps fix another time. But more often than not uninvited guests are asked in and then of course they must be offered something to drink. What and how much is up to you.

☐Sometimes, friends or a neighbour who drop by are very welcome but only for a limited time, and if they overstay their welcome it may be necessary to allow the conversation to flag and not refill cups or glasses. If they do not take the hint, one has to say brightly something like, 'Well it has been so nice to see you but I'm afraid I have to finish ...'. It may even be advisable to stand and deliver this parting shot but a sensitive guest will jump up and begin leave-taking before you get beyond 'Well, it's been so nice ...'. The inevitable awkwardness of such confrontations can often be forestalled by letting guests know when you invite them in that you have to be at the dentist at four o'clock or whatever.

VISITS TO THE ELDERLY OR INFIRM

☐Two types of visit that demand a special approach are visits to someone in hospital, and visits to someone who is at home but is very elderly or infirm.

Visiting hospital

☐Many hospitals still have fixed visiting hours and it is essential to abide by these (but not of course necessary to stay the full span of time). While a too-brief visit can make a patient feel like a 'duty' has been got out of the way with all possible speed, a too-long visit can overtire the patient and, as most people try to rise to an occasion, the effects may

not be felt until the visitor has left. As with so much
else, the situation must be played by ear. It is
wisest not to arrive with any preconceived ideas,
but to see how things go.

☐If the hospital allows visits at any time and you
arrive at a mealtime or when the patient is having
treatment, you will simply be asked to wait outside
the ward. The most convenient times are still those
chosen by hospitals with restricted visiting—that is,
mid-afternoon or mid-evening. Anyone who is
visiting more than once can obviously arrange the
second and subsequent visits with the patient, who
will by then know the routine of the ward.

What to take   ☐Flowers and fruit are reliable stand-bys. If the
stay in hospital is to be a long one, a small and
robust pot plant is a good idea (but check with the
florist that it will thrive in a hot hospital ward—a
plant that drops its leaves or dies is not a tactful
addition to a bedside). Reading matter should be
lightweight and short—newspapers, magazines,
short stories, or a compendium of humorous articles.)

Conversation   ☐This is the one occasion when it is quite in order
to talk about one's operation. The truly squeamish
visitor may certainly ask to be spared the details
but anyone who can bear to hear the tale should
listen attentively. It is, after all, the big event of the
moment.

☐The outside world seems extraordinarily remote
to a patient, even one who is only in hospital for a
very few days, and often the most entertaining and
reassuring thing the visitor can do is to relate tiny
anecdotes from the world they both share outside
the hospital. The aches, pains, anxieties and
tribulations of the visitor are taboo of course, unless
told strictly as a funny story.

Visiting the elderly   ☐Probably the most important, yet oddly the most
or infirm   difficult, thing to remember when visiting people
who are elderly, infirm, or both, is that they are not
fundamentally different from anyone else and do

not need or enjoy being patronised. It may be necessary to speak more loudly or more clearly than usual, but that does not mean that the content of the conversation should be any more banal than it would be with anyone else—that is, unless the person is actually senile. If help is needed, or requested, it is pleasant to give it, but if the person in question genuinely wants to offer hospitality then it must be accepted gracefully.

HOUSEGUESTS

☐Going to stay with relations or good friends rarely presents problems of either behaviour or dress, but the first visit to people who are not particularly close friends, or who perhaps entertain rather formally, can be daunting. Equally, entertaining people who are used to a formal life-style can be daunting for their hostess. (With the exception of all-male households, the burden of entertaining still falls on the hostess.)

The invitation

☐Whether issued by letter or telephone, the invitation should convey as much information as possible. Most important is the expected time of arrival: the hostess should either suggest a suitable train and offer to meet it, or the time of a meal. For instance, an invitation from Friday to Sunday might mention what time dinner is served on Friday so that the guest can arrange to arrive about an hour beforehand, allowing time for greetings, unpacking and possibly changing before dinner.
☐The invitation should also make it clear when the guest is expected to leave, either by mentioning a useful train or by words to the effect of 'We do hope you will be able to stay for tea on Sunday'. This means what it says but it also means 'please leave soon afterwards'.
☐Finally, the guest should be given an idea of what to bring. If the household 'dresses for dinner' this should be indicated, as should any special entertainments that are in the offing which call for special clothes or equipment, such as walking, riding, tennis, shooting or a cocktail party.

If the invitation is unclear

☐If your arrival and departure times have not been made clear by the hostess, it is perfectly correct to ask what time would be convenient to arrive. But do not say, 'Shall we come on Friday or Saturday?' because this makes it difficult to say 'Saturday'.
☐The usual time to leave after a weekend visit is between four and five o'clock on Sunday afternoon, that is, after lunch and either before or after tea.

What to pack

☐This needs some thought because bringing a large amount of luggage on a weekend visit can look rather silly; it may also involve others in a lot of carrying. At the other extreme, borrowing gumboots or another sweater from hosts is even more irritating. When in doubt, it is better to ask the hostess in advance.
☐If you are going to stay at a rather grand house that is fully-staffed it is worth bearing in mind when packing that your suitcase may be *unpacked* by someone else.

The good hostess

☐The good hostess makes sure that guests' rooms are in order before their arrival: fresh towels and coathangers are of course essential, but a bedside book or two, thoughtfully selected, and a small vase of flowers from the garden are the sort of touches that give special pleasure.
☐The hostess should make clear what the pattern or timetable of the day is likely to be so that guests can fall in with it. Most guests who disrupt households only do so because they have been expected to fit in with norms that they know nothing about and to conform with unwritten laws that they only discover after they have infringed them. The hostess must, for example, make it clear at what time breakfast is served and not say politely 'Come down when you like', and then greet the 11 o'clock riser with a frosty look and a cleared table.
☐If there is a shortage of bathrooms (and there usually is), the hostess should let guests know at what times the bathroom is free in the morning, at

the end of the afternoon (if people are going to change for dinner), and last thing at night.
□If guests are to amuse themselves, they must know what options are open to them, and a thoughtful hostess will draw their attention to books, the garden, the sunchairs, or whatever facilities and amusements the house affords; also to what is available in the vicinity—the shops, places of interest, local scenery and so on. Guidebooks and maps of the area are tremendously useful to have on hand. The hostess must also inform guests when this self-amusement should cease for meals or other pre-arranged events.

The good guest □The good guest falls in with the hostess's arrangements with a good humour and, preferably, with obvious enjoyment. It is vitally important to be able to judge the true meaning of the words 'Make yourself at home' when uttered by a specific hostess as they rarely mean exactly that. Usually they mean, 'Please fit in with the household and look after yourself up to a point.' The overly polite guest, who catches cold because he does not ask for an extra blanket, or refuses the cheese at dinner because someone has inadvertently removed his plate, is not making life easier for anyone.

Households without staff □In households without domestic help, houseguests inevitably cause extra work, and here again it is necessary to judge accurately the wishes of the hostess about offers to help with the cooking or washing up. The offer must certainly be made, but sometimes the best thing to do is to slip in to the kitchen unnoticed and perform some small task, such as washing up the tea things or preparing the potatoes for dinner. It must be said that the onus to help is on female guests, unfair though this may be, and the male guest who offers help or unobtrusively performs a helpful task, such as washing up or clearing the table, is in line for special praise from his hostess.
□All guests in houses without staff must of course

239

make their own beds in the morning and tidy their own rooms.

Households with staff

☐Because they are increasingly rare, domestic staff are all the more daunting if unexpected.

☐The butler, if there is one, is the most senior; he will open the door, arrange for luggage to be taken to the rooms, cars parked and so on. He also announces meals and serves drinks.

☐In a fully staffed house, suitcases are normally unpacked by a maid or valet and re-packed by them at the end of the visit. A maid will sometimes come to a female guest who is changing for dinner and ask if there is anything she needs. The maid will fasten a dress with a back zip or a necklace with an awkward clasp (and if asked to do these things, she may return at the end of the evening to release the wearer). She may be asked any practical information—the whereabouts of the bathroom for instance—but she should not be asked to run errands, and never in any circumstances should she be asked for personal information about members of the household.

Tipping

☐All members of the staff who have been of help must be tipped: the butler (if there is one); the chauffeur if he meets or takes you to the station; the bedroom servants; and the cook.

☐Tips for bedroom servants may be left in the bedroom, but it is courteous to tip as many people in person as possible, thanking them at the same time for their assistance. To do this, you may have to find your way to the kitchen or garage, but it is worth the effort as a marked courtesy.

☐If you are uncertain about how much to leave, ask your hostess's advice rather than take the chance of leaving either far too little or much too much.

Thanking

☐A houseguest must always write a letter of thanks. (For details of writing 'thank you' letters see Chapter Eight.) Guests should also sign the visitors' book before departing, if there is one.

BEARING GIFTS ☐See also 'Visiting hospital' on page 235.

Houseguests ☐When going to stay at a very grand house, it is not correct to take a gift. Almost everywhere else it is nice to do so but not absolutely necessary and the nature of the gift depends very much on the circumstances. For instance, if joining close friends at their country cottage for the weekend, food or drink will probably be appreciated and a brief chat about it on the telephone may establish exactly what would be useful. But if staying with people one does not know very well, bringing something that is peculiar to you or to your area might be considered—a book you have mentioned before, a cutting from an unusual plant you have grown, or a local delicacy that is unlikely to be widely available. Sometimes these presents are better sent after the visit, when you have had a chance to establish your hosts' interests.

Visitors ☐Sometimes people who are coming to dinner or for drinks bring gifts. While this is a thoughtful gesture, the givers ought to keep in mind that the hostess is liable to be very busy and will not have time to arrange flowers, or look at a 'coffee table' book. Equally, the wine to be served at dinner will already be uncorked, so it is too late to try the amazingly good Californian burgundy you have discovered. Most people of course are happy to store this away for future use, but a few are apt to think of it as a slur on the adequacy or generosity of their cellar, and for this reason it is particularly unwise to take drink to the houses of people you do not know well.

SPECIAL PROBLEMS ☐Visiting people one does not know very well is in many ways like visiting a foreign country. It means accepting others' customs and ways of doing things, and adapting to them in as agreeable a fashion as possible. Often, as with foreign visits, a certain amount of diplomacy is needed. Three examples are given here.

Children and Animals
☐These have at least two things in common: the first is that they rarely behave well in company, or in someone else's home; and the second is that other people are unlikely to love them as much as their parents or owners and so are more likely to find their 'funny little ways' annoying rather than appealing.

Their children
☐Guests who genuinely like children, or at least genuinely like the children in question, have no problems, but those who do not must make an effort to take an interest, enquire into their progress and development, examine their new toys and so on.
☐As for courtesy towards children, there are rules:
☐Do not remind a child of something silly he did when much younger, especially in front of siblings.
☐Do not offend the dignity of a child over six by talking to him only about childish things—he is just as likely to be interested in your trip to Marrakesh as are his parents.
☐Do not cross-question a shy child in order to get a response—include him in general conversation and assume that he will talk when he wants to (and when he does, reply normally and don't say, 'So you have got a tongue, then').
☐Never discipline a child in his own home unless he is actually interfering with your belongings or your person.
☐In your own house you may ask him not to touch certain things, not to jump on the furniture and so on. Ask politely first (he may be allowed to do such things at home). If he persists, then you may be stern, but bear in mind that a child who likes you is far less likely to damage your possessions or torment the budgie than one who does not.
☐Do not expect a child to sit quietly, keeping out of the way of conversation in a strange house,. unless you have provided him with something to do or look at.
☐One very important point to be remembered about children, especially by those who are not

used to them, is that a silent child is listening hard. Anyone who says anything indiscreet in front of him must be prepared to take the consequences of hearing it repeated at a most inopportune moment.

Your children

☐ See also 'Introducing children' Chapter Eight.
☐ Children should be taught how to greet a guest properly, to join in conversations when they are old enough but to spend all or most of a visit amusing themselves elsewhere (which they are likely to prefer in any case).
☐ The guest room should be wholly out of bounds at all times unless the guest invites the child in. Just as guests should not make personal remarks about children, so children should be taught never to make personal remarks about guests.
☐ The hostess should try to be aware if a guest is actually enjoying playing with the children or is hoping for rescue. In someone else's home the strain is greater, especially if the children are small and the host and hostess do not have children of their own. It is always better to ask if you may move the china shepherdess to a higher shelf than to hear it smash later on.
☐ Ideally, the child should not touch anything or interfere with anything unless told he may. He should bring some toys and books (not paints) to amuse himself with.
☐ No parent should ever make disparaging remarks about a child in front of strangers. This is not only disloyal, but it makes it almost impossible for the child to behave well.

Their animals

☐ A guest who is genuinely allergic to, or phobic about, a particular animal should make this clear to the hostess before arriving, or immediately on arrival if the animal comes as a surprise. It is then up to the hostess to keep the two apart. The guest who just does not like animals must simply put up with them.

Your animals

☐ All pets should be discouraged from making

advances to guests who clearly are not enamoured of them. No dog should be allowed to jump up, and no cat should be allowed to sit on a guest's lap unless expressly encouraged to do so. Animals that do party tricks are a little like boxes of holiday slides—some guests are fascinated to see them, most are not.

☐No one should take an animal visiting without asking first, and the question should be phrased in such a way that it is easy for the hostess to say she prefers it to be left at home.

Bedrooms ☐The days of clearcut policy when married couples were put together and unmarried couples kept apart have vanished. A hostess who knows that an unmarried couple are living together must choose whether to put them in the same room or not. It is a courtesy to put them together, but if she has strong feelings against doing so she does have the right to make the rules in her own house. If she chooses not to, she is of course expressing personal disapproval, unless there is some other reason and this is made clear. For instance, a weekend party might include an elderly relation who would be shocked or upset by the arrangement and it is only fair to separate the couple in this case, explaining privately the reason.

10 ROYAL, DIPLOMATIC AND FORMAL OCCASIONS

ROYAL AND STATE OCCASIONS

☐Royal and State occasions probably give rise to the most formal standards of behaviour currently in use, but even in these areas there has, in recent years, been a general relaxing of protocol which means that nothing is quite as cut and dried as it once was. This makes life both easier and more difficult; easier because there are fewer rigidly defined patterns of behaviour to remember, and more difficult because there are now 'grey areas' governed only by normal courtesy and common sense. For example, at one time the rule in conversation with royalty was 'never speak until you are spoken to, do not introduce topics of conversation and do not ask questions'. Now, although it is still true that royalty initiate the conversation in the first place, it is perfectly in order (especially on an occasion such as an informal lunch at Buckingham Palace) for a guest to introduce a subject or ask a question—which of course means that it is now equally up to the guest to avoid controversial topics and impertinent questions. However, there are still some guidelines that can be laid down and some practical information that can be given.

☐Probably the most useful piece of general information is the fact that any Royal or State function is minutely organized from Buckingham Palace and anyone invited to such a function is guided every step of the way, first by the information on the invitation and then by members of the Household and staff, so that there is really no opportunity to get lost or do the wrong thing. (After all, the essence of successful entertaining is that the guests have a happy time and feel relaxed and at ease—and royalty do know how to entertain!) If still beset by specific worries, further advice and information can always be obtained from the Queen's Lady-in-Waiting or Private Secretary, from Prince Philip's Equerry or Private Secretary, or from the press office (all at Buckingham Palace); or from the staffs of other members of the Royal Family, who each have their own office.

245

Meeting royalty   ☐It is usual for men to bow and women to curtsey
on being introduced to and taking leave of royalty.
If the Royal hand is extended, take it lightly and
briefly, at the same time executing a brief bob with
the weight on the *front* foot, or a bow from the neck
(not from the waist). If she wishes, a woman may
bow instead of curtsey: it is the acknowledgment
that counts, not the exact form it takes.

Direct address   ☐The Queen and the Queen Mother should be
addressed as 'Your Majesty' for the first time and
as 'Ma'am' (pronounced like 'am' not 'arm') on
subsequent occasions. Prince Philip, as a prince in
his own right, is first addressed as 'Your Royal
Highness' and subsequently as 'Sir'. Other
members of the Royal Family should also be
addressed for the first time as 'Your Royal
Highness' and subsequently as 'Sir' or 'Ma'am'.
☐The wife of a royal prince takes on her husband's
status and should be addressed as 'Your Royal
Highness' and then as 'Ma'am'. However, the
husband of a royal princess does not take on his
wife's status and should not be bowed or curtseyed
to, nor addressed as 'Sir' unless his seniority is such
that he would be addressed as 'Sir' in any case.
☐See also 'Correct forms of address', Chapter Eight.

Description in   ☐When referring to a member of the Royal Family
conversation   in his or her presence or in the presence of other
royalty, the following descriptions are correct: Her
Majesty or The Queen; Her Majesty or Queen
Elizabeth, The Queen Mother; His/Her Royal
Highness followed, if necessary, by the appropriate
title (The Duke of Edinburgh or The Prince of
Wales). The prefix 'The' before 'Prince' or
'Princess' is only used for the children of a
sovereign, as in 'Her Royal Highness, The Princess
Royal' but 'His Royal Highness, Prince Michael of
Kent'.

You and your   ☐It is correct to substitute 'Your Majesty/Royal
Highness' for 'you' and 'Your Majesty's/Royal

246

Highness's' for 'your'. For example, 'I hope Your Majesty had a pleasant journey' or 'May I confirm the arrangement with Your Royal Highness's Private Secretary'. However, although the rule should be adhered to when making a formal speech, it isn't necessary to overload an informal conversation with formal references.

Introductions

☐Use only the name of the person being introduced, never the Royal name. For example: 'Your Royal Highness, may I present Mr John Smith?'

Foreign royalty

☐The above applies, except that an emperor or empress is addressed for the first time as 'Your Imperial Majesty' (referred to as 'His/Her Imperial Majesty') and a reigning prince or princess is addressed as 'Your Serene Highness' (referred to as 'His/Her Serene Highness'). Often invitations to occasions where royalty are to be present indicate their presence and also indicate the correct form of address:

A dinner in honour of

His Serene Highness

Prince Rainier III of Monaco

Entertaining royalty

☐The normal rules of good manners and etiquette apply, but perhaps a little more so than usual. The following are the areas where protocol demands a slightly different approach.

The invitation

☐Unless you are a very close friend of the royal guest (in which case you will not need this section) the invitation should be made through a member of the Household, such as the Lady in Waiting or Private Secretary (who can be telephoned or written to by office rather than by name). This intermediary will indicate whether or not the royal guest is willing or able to accept the invitation, and will answer any questions including, if necessary, questions about the suitability of the guest list, the menu and the form of dress. (Conceivably a royal dinner guest might prefer dress to be informal if having to come straight from another engagement). If the invitation is accepted at this stage, it should be confirmed in writing to whichever member of the Household is handling the matter. It is not correct to send a printed invitation to royalty unless it is enclosed with a letter of confirmation, purely for interest (for example, a wedding invitation).

Procedure ☐The Queen, and each member of the immediate Royal Family is always accompanied by a police officer, who makes his own decision about whether to wait inside or outside the house. Royal ladies are only accompanied by a lady in waiting at formal occasions (in which case the lady in waiting is a guest). The Royal guest is always accorded the position of guest of honour: the days when the reigning monarch was regarded as the owner of the establishment throughout the visit are over.

Departure ☐No one should leave an occasion where royalty are present before the royal guest or guests (although exceptions are made at garden parties and state banquets, see below).

Charity or official functions ☐A similar procedure should be followed when inviting a member of the Royal Family to attend a charity ball or dinner, to open a new building, unveil a plaque, lay a foundation stone or attend a film premiere. It is worth remembering that royal diaries fill up rapidly and are usually running some months ahead, so it is wise to make the initial approach as early as possible.

The invitation ☐The invitation should ideally be extended through the Lord-Lieutenant of the county if outside London, or through the Private Secretary (who can be addressed by office rather than by name). The approach should come from the most senior person concerned with the arrangements. It is usual first to

make an informal enquiry about the likelihood of the particular member of the Royal Family considering the invitation favourably and then, if this seems to be the case, to follow up with a formal letter of invitation, addressed to the Lord-Lieutenant or Private Secretary, setting out the nature of the function, the place, date and time.
□If the invitation is declined, it is perfectly in order to invite another member of the Royal Family instead (although obviously it would not be correct to invite the Queen or the Queen Mother if a more junior member of the family had declined). It is not correct to invite more than one member of the Royal Family (apart from a consort) to the same function, except in very unusual circumstances.

Procedure   □If the invitation is accepted, every last detail of the programme from the arrival to the departure of the royal guest, will be worked out by the Private Secretary, or other members of the royal staff, in consultation with the organizer of the event. The programme will be written down and strictly adhered to, right down to details such as who is to be presented, how and when. A member of the royal staff will very likely make a reconnaissance trip to the venue, so that nothing is left to chance. The organizer will find that advice and information are readily available (even advice on the most suitable size for the presentation bouquet, if necessary.)

Invitations from royalty   □Invitations from the Queen or the Queen Mother are royal commands and should be answered as such, first presenting compliments to the member of the Household who forwarded the invitation, and then using the wording 'have the honour to obey Her Majesty's command to...' in place of the usual 'have pleasure in accepting the kind invitation to...'. If it is necessary to decline such an invitation the reason must be given, and it should be a substantial one—such as illness, a long-standing business engagement the cancellation of

which would have an adverse effect on future work,
or an engagement such as a lecture tour which
could not be put off without letting down other
people.

Replying to a royal
invitation

Mr and Mrs Anthony Lawrence
present their compliments to the
Master of the Household and have
the honour to obey Her Majesty's
command to luncheon on July
8th at 12.30 o'clock.

☐Invitations from other members of the Royal
Family are not commands and should be replied to
in the usual way, except that the reply should be
addressed to whichever member of the Household
forwarded the invitation.
☐For details of replies, see Chapter Eight.
☐The occasions for which invitations from the
Queen are most frequently issued are royal garden
parties, investitures, the biennial party for winners
of the Queen's Award for Industry, and informal
lunches at Buckingham Palace.

Garden parties   ☐An invitation to a garden party at Buckingham
Palace comes from the Lord Chamberlain. As well
as the usual information about date, time and place
it carries a map and specific parking instructions.
An admission card is enclosed with the invitation
and anyone unable to attend must return this card
with their letter of explanation. An acceptance
letter is *not* necessary, but it is important to
remember to take the admission card which has to
be shown when parking, and again on entering the
palace grounds.

What to wear	☐The majority of women wear afternoon dresses and hats, or national dress. Men wear morning coats, lounge suits, national dress, service uniform or official dress (for example, parsons wear cassocks). Medals are worn on uniforms but, on the whole, mayors and mayoresses are discouraged from wearing their chains of office. No one is permitted to take in a camera.
Procedure	☐The gates open at 3.15pm. At 4pm the Queen, Prince Philip and the Queen Mother, together with any other members of the Royal Family attending on that day, walk from the palace and among the guests, who form avenues to let them pass. Some presentations are made at this stage. Later, all members of the Royal Family mingle with the guests, who form avenues to let them pass Household—a lady-in-waiting, private secretary or equerry. About 5pm the Royal Family retire to the royal tea tent. Guests are served in other tents.
Presentations	☐Should a member of the Royal Family wish to meet you, a member of the Household will make the first approach, asking for your name (which should be given complete with rank and title) and possibly some information about you. This information should be quite brief (perhaps your job or the fact that you have just published a book or climbed a mountain). If you have met the particular member of the Royal Family before, you should make this clear to the member of the Household who approaches you, with brief details of where and when. He or she will then lead you to the member of the Royal Family and formally present you (see 'Meeting royalty'.)
Leaving	☐At 6pm the National Anthem is played and the party is officially over. The Royal Family leave, without ceremony, and there is a general drift towards the gates. It is perfectly in order to leave a garden party before the Royal Family, but the party is short and people rarely do so.

Thanking □It is not necessary to write a letter of thanks after a garden party (although many people like to write, and all such letters are shown to the Queen). The practice of signing the Palace visitor's book in lieu of a letter of thanks is beginning to die out. Nowadays it is perfectly correct either to sign or not to sign.

Investitures □Most of those whose names have appeared on one of the two annual Honours Lists will in due course be invited to an investiture at Buckingham Palace to which he or she is entitled to bring two guests (usually immediate family or close friends).

The invitation □This will come from the office called Central Chancery of the Order of Knighthood and will give all relevant details—date, time, place, where to park (usually in the inner quadrangle of Buckingham Palace) and what to wear. The invitation is a royal command. Recipients respond by completing and returning the form provided.

What to wear □Women generally wear a smart day dress, suit or coat. It is not essential to wear a hat, but in fact most women do. Large hats should be avoided because there is always the possibility of blocking someone else's view of things. Men wear a morning coat, a lounge suit or service uniform. Cameras may not be taken into the palace, but may be used outside later—see 'Leaving'.

Procedure □The invitation usually suggests an arrival time of 10am to 10.30am. There are members of the Household and staff at the front entrance to the palace, and at every point between there and the ballroom, so it is not possible to get lost. Guests are taken straight to the ballroom and allocated their seats. Some of these are on rows of chairs facing the dais and others on raised banquettes on either side of the ballroom. The recipients are taken into other rooms where they are briefed on every stage of the short ceremony.

☐At 11am the Queen arrives in the ballroom and the guests stand. When the Queen has reached her place the National Anthem is played and Her Majesty asks the guests to be seated once more. The recipients are guided one by one to the door of the ballroom where each name is called out by the Lord Chamberlain. They then follow their recently received and quite explicit instructions on how to approach the Queen, receive their honour, and move on to take their places with the rest of the guests and recipients.

☐The entire ceremony usually lasts for about an hour and ten minutes. When it is over the guests stand, the National Anthem is played, and the Queen leaves.

Leaving

☐Once the Queen has left the ballroom, everyone else is free to go. Many people choose to have their photographs taken in the inner quadrangle of the palace, or outside the gates, before leaving.

Party for the winners of the Queen's Award for Industry

☐This takes place in February, every other year, when three people from each of the firms who have received awards are invited to attend a drinks party at Buckingham Palace from about 6pm to 8pm. The trio is made up of one representative from management, one from middle management, and one from the shop floor, or equivalent.

The invitation

☐The invitation, which is issued on the command of the Queen by the Master of the Royal Household, carries full details about exactly where to park and when to arrive. A presentation card is also enclosed; this must be taken to the party and handed to the member of the Household presenting the guests.

Procedure

☐Upon arrival, each guest is given a name tag to wear. As at every other party at the palace, the guests are looked after by members of the Household and staff from the moment they arrive until the moment they leave. They are taken to the rooms where the party is held, and given drinks. The Queen, Prince Philip and any royal guests circulate and talk to as many guests as they can.

Leaving □The party ends when the Queen withdraws.

Letter of thanks □A letter of thanks may be written by the head of each firm, on behalf of the firm and its three representatives, to the Master of the Household (he may be addressed by title only), presenting compliments to him and asking him to 'convey thanks to Her Majesty for . . .' etc.

Lunch at Buckingham Palace □For many years now, the Queen and Prince Philip have been entertaining certain members of the public from different professions, trades and callings, at informal lunches at Buckingham Palace. These are made up of eight guests and two members of a royal Household. People are asked as individuals, and the invitation does not extend to husbands and wives.

The invitation □The prospective guest is first telephoned by the Master of the Household to discover if the date is suitable. (The invitation, when it comes, is a royal command, so the palace avoids embarrassing people by commanding their presence on a day when complying would present serious difficulties). The initial telephone call is followed up by a formal invitation card, giving full details of time of arrival, where to park, how to enter the Palace and so on. The invitation should be accepted in writing (see 'Invitations from royalty', page 249) and taken along to be shown to the policeman on the gate at the Palace and to the member of the Household who meets the guests at the main door to the Palace.

Procedure □When coats have been taken (at which time there is an opportunity for a wash and brush up) a member of the Household takes the guests to one of the drawing rooms on the ground floor. Guests are introduced to one another and offered a drink

(usually gin, sherry or a soft drink). Just before one o'clock the guests are asked to line up. The Queen and Prince Philip come into the room and each guest is presented in turn. (See 'Meeting royalty'.) After the presentations, everyone stands around chatting for about ten minutes, and then the Queen and Prince Philip lead the way into lunch.
□Members of the Household show the guests to their seats. When the Queen is seated, all sit down. A three course lunch, followed by cheese and fruit, is served by footmen. The food is always simple and not too rich or heavy. Wine is offered, and soft drinks and water are also available. As this is an informal lunch, there are no toasts.
□After lunch, the Queen and Prince Philip lead the way back to the drawing room where everyone stands, drinking coffee and liqueurs, and the Queen and Prince Philip circulate once more. At this stage, members of the Household make sure that those, if any, who have not yet spoken to their hosts get their chance.

Leaving □At about 2.30pm the Queen and Prince Philip say goodbye and go. The party is over, and members of the Household see the guests out.

Thanking □It is usual to write the letter of thanks to the Master of the Household, asking him to be kind enough to convey thanks to the Queen. However, anyone particularly wanting to thank the Queen direct should begin their letter 'Madam, with my humble duty' and end it 'I have the honour to be Your Majesty's humble and obedient subject and servant.'

State functions □Now that formal presentations at court, in the form of levées, no longer happen, the two State functions most likely to be attended by the public are State banquets and the State Opening of Parliament.

State banquets □State banquets are formal occasions and very large, with 170 guests present. They almost invariably take place at Buckingham Palace, though occasionally at Windsor Castle, and are given in honour of a visiting head of state.

Invitation ☐This is issued, on the command of the Queen, by the Lord Steward of the Household. It is a royal command and should be replied to as such (see 'Invitations from royalty'). In common with all royal invitations, this one carries full details of time, what to wear and where and how to arrive. A presentation card is also enclosed. A seating plan for dinner is given on arrival. Both cards should be taken along—the invitation card to be shown when arriving and the presentation card before being announced. The seating plan is for guidance later.

What to wear ☐Dress is very formal. Men wear white tie or national dress. Decorations are worn. Women wear long dresses (with long white gloves if the dress is sleeveless) or national dress. This is an occasion for those who have them to unpack their tiaras and take the family diamonds out of the bank.

Procedure ☐There are footmen to guide guests from the front door to, usually, the green drawing room, where they are greeted by the Lord Chamberlain and the Mistress of the Robes. They are then ushered through to congregate in the picture gallery, where drinks are served. Members of the Household are on hand to look after and guide all the guests. (Ladies-in-waiting are distinguished by discreet badges and male members of the Household by the Household coats which they wear, with velvet collars and gold buttons.)
☐Guests are then shepherded gradually towards the white drawing room where the Queen and Prince Philip are waiting. The Lord Steward of the Household is ready to receive each presentation card and present the holder.
☐Having been presented, the guests continue through to the ballroom where, with the help of their seating plans and/or members of the House-

hold, they find their places and stand behind their chairs. When everyone is in place, the Queen and the royal party process in to dinner. When they are seated, the guests may sit.

☐A four course dinner (usually soup, fish, meat and pudding) followed by fruit, is served by footmen, on gold plate, to the accompaniment of a small string orchestra which plays in the minstrel's gallery. Because of the mixture of nationalities and religions so often present, each with particular eating habits, the food is quite plain, so that no one has difficulties. Wine, although liberally available, is not obligatory, even for toasts, and soft drinks and water are at hand.

☐At the end of the dinner, silence is called for and the Queen rises and makes a speech of welcome to the visiting head of state. She then proposes a toast to this guest of honour. Everyone rises, drinks the toast, and sits again. The visiting head of state rises, makes a speech in response, and then proposes the loyal toast, 'The Queen'. Everyone rises, drinks, and sits again. Up to twelve pipers then process twice around the tables, playing pipe music. When they have gone, everyone rises and stands while the Queen and the royal party leave the ballroom. When they have gone, everyone else follows. Coffee and liqueurs are then served in the various drawing rooms.

Leaving ☐At the end of the evening, the National Anthem is played and the Queen and her party leave. This is the signal for everyone else to go. Strictly speaking, it is not correct to leave a state banquet before the Queen, but in exceptional circumstances (ill health, a last train to catch) it is quite in order to approach a member of the Household and explain the circumstances. Permission to leave is always given.

Thanking ☐The letter of thanks may be written to the Lord Steward of the Household, asking him to be kind enough to 'convey thanks to Her Majesty, the Queen.'

257

State Opening of Parliament

☐At the State Opening of Parliament the chamber itself and the galleries (usually the public galleries) are reserved for members of the Royal Family and their guests, for the cabinet and for various dignitaries (representatives of the church, the diplomatic corps and so on). However, the royal gallery, which leads to the chamber, is for the invited guests of peers and MPs, and a place on the pavement outside can be booked by anyone.

The royal gallery

☐Guests who are allocated positions here can see the procession pass through into the House of Lords and return again after the ceremony. The invitation carries quite explicit instructions about dress, asking that women wear a day dress and a small hat (a large one could block someone else's view) and that men wear a morning suit, service dress or a lounge suit.

Pavement

☐A few pavement tickets are obtainable each year from the Lord Great Chamberlain's office at the House of Lords. The ticket holders, who will see the arrival and departure of the Queen and various distinguished guests, should be prepared to stand for a long time. They, obviously, can wear what they like—but it would be unfair on others to choose a large hat.

Royal Ascot

☐This is an unusual royal occasion in that it is possible to apply for tickets to the Royal Enclosure, yet it is a very formal occasion at which no exceptions are made regarding dress. Anyone who arrives 'improperly dressed' is simply not admitted. See also 'Horse racing', Chapter 11.

The ticket

☐Each December, the court pages of *The Times* and *Daily Telegraph* carry instructions about applying for tickets to the Ascot Office at St James's Palace. Applications should be made in the third person, stating clearly which members of the family the applicant hopes to bring. He or she will then receive a sponsorship form and must arrange to have this signed by someone who has received vouchers to attend Royal Ascot on at least four occasions, or else by someone known personally to the Queen. Because of the demand, tickets can only be allocated to some of those who apply.

☐Visitors from overseas who hope to attend should contact their own embassy in London. The ambassador's secretary usually deals with such requests and the ambassador is empowered to sign the sponsorship form.

What to wear ☐Women wear very formal day dresses, with hats obligatory. Most men wear morning coats. Service dress for men, although acceptable, is in fact rarely worn. No cameras are permitted in the Royal Enclosure.

Trooping the Colour ☐Each year, on the official birthday of the Queen, the colour, or flag, of one of the five regiments of foot guards (the Grenadiers, the Coldstream, the Scots, the Irish and the Welsh) is ceremoniously trooped, or displayed, before the Queen to the music of massed bands. This is a military rather than a Royal occasion, but is included here because of the presence of the Queen and, frequently, other members of the Royal Family.

The ticket ☐Between 1st January and 1st March requests for tickets should be sent, together with a stamped addressed envelope, to The Brigade Major, The Household Division, Horseguards, Whitehall, London S.W.1. It is important to state whether, if you are unlucky, you would like tickets for the first or second rehearsals instead. A ballot is held to award tickets—only two per application.

Rehearsals ☐Although lacking the presence of the Queen, the rehearsals do not lack the pageantry of the real thing. At the first rehearsal the salute is taken by the Major General commanding the Household division, at the second by the Colonel of the regiment of the Colour.

What to wear ☐Instructions appear on the ticket. For men, morning coat, service uniform or a lounge suit and for women a day dress, or coat and skirt. Most women wear hats, but large view-blocking ones should be avoided.

Procedure ☐Instructions on behaviour are included in the programme. It is correct to stand when the Colour passes by, when the Queen rides on to the parade ground, and when the National Anthem is played at the end. Applause is usual at the very end of the ceremony.

DIPLOMATIC OCCASIONS ☐Diplomatic etiquette is also less formal than once it was, but there are still certain rules and conventions which are set out below. Perhaps the main difference between a diplomatic social occasion and a more ordinary social occasion is that, because of the mixture of nationalities present at any diplomatic function, and because of their different customs, it is on the whole unwise to initiate a conversation on a political or religious subject.

Precedence ☐The order of precedence should be strictly adhered to because ambassadors and high commissioners are representatives of their head of state and an innocent mistake could be taken as an insult to the country concerned. The order of precedence of the ambassadors of (not 'for') foreign countries and the high commissioners for (not 'of') Commonwealth countries, accredited to the Court of St James's, London, is determined by the date on which they took up their duties in London—so that the longest serving is the most senior and the most recent arrival the most junior, regardless of the size or prestige of their country. *The London Diplomatic List*, arranged first alphabetically and then in order of precedence, is published every two months by H.M.S.O.

Form of address ☐On a formal occasion, an ambassador or high commissioner should first be addressed as 'Your Excellency' and subsequently as 'Sir/Madam' or by name. On a social occasion, the correct address is 'Ambassador' or 'High Commissioner' or by name.

In conversation □A foreign ambassador is correctly referred to as 'His/Her Excellency the Ambassador of (France)', or 'His/Her Excellency the (French) Ambassador'. A Commonwealth high commissioner is also referred to as: 'His/Her Excellency' followed, if necessary, by the name of the country, either in the form 'His/Her Excellency the High Commissioner for (Canada)' or 'His/Her Excellency the (Canadian) High Commissioner'.

Wives □The wife of an ambassador or a high commissioner has no specific title (unless she has one in her own right). The term 'ambassadress' can be used, but only for the wife of an ambassador, never for a female ambassador.

Writing to □In writing, 'His Excellency' always precedes any other title (royal, military, and so on) which in turn precedes the name. Formal letters should begin 'Your Excellency' and social letters 'Dear Ambassador/High Commissioner'. A formal letter to an ambassador should end 'I have the honour to be, with the highest consideration, Your Excellency's obedient servant'. A formal letter to a high commissioner should end 'I have the honour to be Your Excellency's obedient servant'. A social letter to an ambassador should end 'Believe me, my dear Ambassador, Yours (very) sincerely'. A social letter to a high commissioner should end 'Believe me, Yours (very) sincerely'. 'Your Excellency' should appear once in the opening and once in the closing paragraph.

Further information □If in need of further information on specific points (such as what to wear for a particular occasion, or what food to serve to a particular foreign ambassador) then approach the embassy in question. The larger ones have a protocol section, which always includes someone with a good command of English. All ambassadors have private secretaries, who can be asked for by office rather than by name, and who are happy to help. If still at a loss, approach the protocol department of the Foreign and Commonwealth Office.

Entertaining □A printed invitation may be sent direct to an ambassador or high commissioner in the usual way (See 'Form of address', above). Although it is not essential, it is sometimes wise to telephone the private secretary first to sort out a suitable date and then to follow this up with the invitation card.

Procedure □For precedence and forms of address, see above. When entertaining any overseas visitor it is courteous, if in doubt, to make enquiries about suitable food and drink. (The three trickiest areas are alcohol, beef and pork, but there are others.)

Cards □The practice of leaving a visiting card with an ambassador of a foreign country after meeting him/her socially is dying out. It is still correct, but no longer essential.

Invitations from □An invitation from a foreign embassy might be for
an embassy a lunch or a dinner but is statistically more likely to be for a reception. Receptions are large multinational gatherings, sometimes held in the embassy itself and sometimes in a large hotel, at which drinks and canapés are served and a certain amount of diplomatic business may be conducted along with the social pleasantries. The purpose of the reception is stated on the invitation—it might be in honour of a new or departing ambassador, in honour of visiting royalty or dignitaries, or to mark the national day of the country in question. The guest lists for national day celebrations are sometimes limited to nationals only. Those which include guests from the host and other countries are held at lunch time and each guest is invited in

his/her official capacity. Husbands and wives are not included, nor is the wife of the ambassador, because these are official occasions rather than parties. Evening receptions, on the other hand, are parties, and husbands and wives are invited.

The invitation ☐The invitation will give details of time, place, what to wear (probably) and the purpose of the occasion. Replies should be written in the third person and sent to the person issuing the invitation. If a telephone number is given, it is correct to use it rather than to write a formal letter.

What to wear ☐The invitation usually indicates this, and the conventions are much the same as for any party, except that it is wise for European women to 'dress modestly' (avoiding sleeveless dresses and low necklines) in order not to offend Muslim hosts or guests.
☐'Dress informal' on an invitation to an embassy probably means a lounge suit or equivalent for a man and a day dress or equivalent for a woman. 'Dress formal' could mean either white or black tie. 'Decorations will be worn' usually means white tie, but sometimes black tie. If in any doubt, enquire.

Food and drink ☐Food served at an embassy lunch or dinner in London is usually English. It is only rarely that the food of the country is served, but if it is, it is perfectly all right to ask questions about what it is and how it has been prepared (so long as the questions sound interested rather than fearful). Both alcoholic and soft drinks are generally available at embassy gatherings. Even Muslim countries tend to serve alcohol to those who want it.

General behaviour ☐As different countries have different codes of behaviour it is just possible that, for instance, a remark that would be regarded as a compliment by a European would sound unfortunate to a visitor from an Arab country. If unaware of the mores of the country in question, it is wise to try and talk to a more experienced guest at the party to ask if there are any pitfalls to be avoided. (People love airing their knowledge, and for the nervous or tongue-tied it is a useful line of conversation.) Anyone who discovers too late that an innocent remark was rather unsuitable would do better to hope that it was taken in the spirit in which it was intended rather than to try and put things right.

Thanking   □The letter of thanks should be written to whoever issued the invitation. The practice of signing the embassy's visitor's book in lieu of a thank-you letter is also correct.

OTHER FORMAL OCCASIONS   □Other formal dinners and banquets which differ from ordinary large dinner parties include civic dinners (such as the Lord Mayor's banquet) and the dinners given by City livery companies, at Inns of Court, at universities and by the armed services on guest nights. They all tend to have individual peculiarities and to include traditional patterns of behaviour. As they all differ, not only from each other but also within groups, there is not space to set down the precise procedure followed by each one. There follows some general guidance about high tables, rose bowls, port, toasts, the loving cup ceremony, snuff and smoking.

High tables   □At state and civic banquets, and also at university and legal banquets and dinners, there is often a high table whose occupants process in to dinner after the rest of the guests have reached their seats. Sometimes the high table guests are clapped in to their seats and clapped out again at the end of dinner, sometimes they are not. This can even vary between, for instance, different livery companies, so it is wise not to be the first to clap unless you are absolutely certain that you are correct.

The rose bowl   □At livery company and civic dinners, and some others as well, one or more rose bowls are passed

around the table. They are large communal finger
bowls—made of glass or silver, or even gold plate—
filled with rose water and sometimes floating rose
petals as well. You may rinse your fingers and dry
them on your napkin, and it is also correct to dip
the corner of the napkin in the rose water and dab
it on the temples.

Port   ☐Port is served at the end of dinner. The decanter
is often placed on the table for guests to help
themselves and pass it on. Traditionally, port is
always passed to the left, and is never drunk before
the loyal toast (if there is one) which is usually
drunk in port in any case. There is no obligation to
take port (toasts may be drunk in water without
insult) but if you let the port pass by, thinking you
do not want any, and then change your mind, you
may pass your glass to the left, in pursuit of the
decanter, and the guest currently in possession of it
should fill the glass for you.

Toasts   ☐Toasts are drunk at the end of formal dinners
and banquets. They vary enormously—and
sometimes there is a short preamble before a toast,
sometimes a whole speech, sometimes nothing at
all. Never be the first to stand when a toast is
made, because some are drunk sitting down. The
toast most frequently met with is the loyal toast,
and the usual wording is simply 'The Queen'. The
navy always drinks the loyal toast seated (the
commonest explanation for this is that anyone
standing to attention on the mess deck of a ship
would concuss himself on the beams). Some
regiments of the British army also have a special
dispensation to drink the loyal toast sitting down.
Some do not drink it at all (for instance, the Royal
Fusiliers, to whom George IV said, 'Gentlemen, pray
be seated, there is no need to drink the health. The
loyalty of the officers of the Royal Fusiliers could
never be in doubt!'. At the other extreme, the Royal
Regiment of Artillery cause the main lights to be
switched on and hold their glasses at arm's length

before drinking so that each one can be seen to respond to the toast.) The rule seems to be, if you do not know how it is done, do not make the first move.

Loving cup ceremony   ☐This is most likely to be met with at a livery company dinner or at the Lord Mayor's banquet. The ceremony of passing a large cup or bowl full of wine round a gathering, for each guest to raise in both hands and drink to his neighbours, is very old indeed, but the present loving cup ceremony is said to date from the time when the Saxon King Edward was perfidiously stabbed to death while standing and drinking from such a cup, his face buried in the cup and both hands occupied. After that, no man was prepared to make himself vulnerable in this way and so always asked a companion to 'stand too', sword drawn, to protect him.

☐Nowadays, when the cup is passed round the table from the host (usually circulating to the left, although sometimes two cups are set in motion, one travelling in each direction) the ceremony goes like this: When a guest receives the loving cup he or she turns to the neighbour who will drink next. The neighbour stands and they bow to each other. The neighbour then removes the cover of the cup with his/her right (dagger) hand, and holds it high. The bearer of the cup drinks and then wipes the rim with the napkin tied at the foot of the cup. The neighbour replaces the cover and they bow to each other again. The one who has just drunk passes the cup on to the neighbour and turns to stand back to back with him/her. The neighbour, now the cup bearer, turns to his/her neighbour, who rises and the procedure is repeated. When the cup is in the hands of the next person (the neighbour's neighbour) the first guest sits again. In other words, there are always three people standing—he who has just drunk, he who is drinking, and he who is about to drink.

Snuff   ☐At a few formal dinners snuff is still passed round the table. It, like port, travels to the left, after the port and the toasts. There is no obligation to take snuff, and it might be unwise to experiment for the first time at a formal dinner. For those who want it, and wish to observe traditional practice, it is correct to hold the box with the left hand, tap it twice with the knuckles of the right hand (to settle the contents), open the lid, take a small pinch between the right forefinger and thumb, place it on the back of the left hand (in the hollow between the base of the first finger and the base of the thumb), close the lid, tap it, pass it to the left, raise the left hand and sniff. The result is unpredictable and a novice is advised to experiment at home first.

| Smoking | □Traditionally, you may never smoke until after the loyal toast. Sometimes the toastmaster announces that you may smoke (but this is regarded as unnecessary, and once gave rise to one of the worst toastmaster's gaffes of all time—'Gentlemen, you may smoke. The Queen is drunk.') However, if there are no toasts, then an announcement is often made. Smoking goes with coffee and liqueurs, and at State and other banquets where these are served to everyone in another room, it is preferable not to smoke at table, but to wait. At dinners where the ladies retire to powder their noses and leave the gentlemen in possession of the port, smoking begins at the parting of the sexes. |

EMERGENCIES □This section is not for the confident or assured but for people who are anxious to do the right thing, nervous about attending large formal dinners (or even an informal lunch if it happens to be with the Queen) and haunted by recurring worries which fall into five main groups—food ('What if I'm allergic to it?'), drink ('What if I don't?'), choking at table ('What if I do?'), leaving the table in the middle of dinner ('What if I have to?') and leaving the occasion early ('What if the last train goes before the Queen does?').

Food	☐It is never necessary to eat anything that is going to produce a violent allergic reaction, nor is it necessary or desirable to explain, or to describe expected symptoms. Usually at formal banquets, and certainly at lunch at Buckingham Palace, food is brought round by waiters or footmen, so it is easy to accept all but the dangerous vegetable, or whatever it might be. If the problem food is the only thing currently on offer—perhaps the first course is allergy-producing salmon mousse and to refuse it would mean to sit with an empty plate—it is best to take a small portion and toy with it while the others eat. No one will notice, or comment, that it has not been finished.
Drink	☐It is always acceptable to refuse alcoholic drink, or to accept one glass and refuse subsequent offers. Water or soft drinks are always available and it is not an insult to the recipient of a toast to drink it in water.
Choking	☐If it happens, it happens, and the only hope is to bury your face in the napkin and do it as discreetly as possible. If a neighbour chokes, put a glass of water within reach (discreetly summoning a footman or waiter if necessary) and then keep the conversation going and do not watch. Avoid dramatic back-thumping except in the (extremely rare) case of someone who actually cannot breathe. ☐Peter Barkworth's recent book *About Acting*, gives a useful hint which is really meant for actors who have to eat and drink on stage—breathe in before putting food and drink in the mouth. This means you breathe out while you eat and are less likely to inhale a crumb or breathe in a mouthful of wine.
Leaving the table during dinner	☐Best avoided, if at all possible, but if you have to you have to. The main thing is to get out and back again with as little fuss as possible.
Leaving early	☐If you know in advance that this will be

necessary, talk to whoever issued the invitation, or to his or her representative, explaining the reason. If you only realise the problem when, for example, drinking coffee and liqueurs after a state banquet, find one of the surrogate hosts or hostesses and explain the problem. Someone will always usher you out discreetly.

11 PUBLIC OCCASIONS AND EVENTS

EVERYDAY OCCASIONS

☐Many of the traditional courtesies and conventions which used to be observed by those who were 'out and about' have been dropped or modified. There is of course less time for mere formalities, but sometimes it means, in effect, less time for the consideration of others. This is unfortunate since in even the most prosaic situations—queuing for a bus, perhaps—elementary courtesies go a long way towards ironing out and preventing tensions.

Queueing

☐The British queue for almost everything—buses, taxis, full restaurants, theatres, cinemas, and to be served in shops. The latest arrival must join the end of the queue and wait his or her turn. Few ordinary occurrences generate more bad feeling than a group of foreign tourists, who do not understand the procedure, pushing their way on to a bus and leaving a long-standing queue on the pavement in the rain.

Escalators and travelators

☐If you want to stand still on an escalator (moving stairway) and be carried, stand on the right. If you prefer to walk, walk on the left. On a travelator, or moving pavement, (most often encountered at airports) you are really supposed to keep walking, but if age or infirmity make standing still more suitable, stand on the right.

Pavements

☐By tradition, the man walks on the street side if he is accompanying a woman (to protect her from splashes and marauders) and although this custom is dying out (splashes and marauders being rare), if a man is courteous enough to observe it, a woman certainly ought to be polite enough to allow it.
☐It is inconsiderate for a group of friends to walk abreast along a crowded pavement thereby blocking the passage of others.

Pedestrian crossings

☐By law, a car must stop to let pedestrians cross, but it is thoughtless and dangerous for a pedestrian suddenly to launch himself on to a crossing, forcing a car to brake suddenly.

Driving □The Highway Code contains the rules of the road but some basic courtesies are often overlooked. A driver who chooses to go slowly must make it easy for others to pass. A driver loses virtually no time by slowing down to allow someone from a side road, or garage, to join the stream of traffic. No one should ever nip forwards into a parking space if he can see that another car is already being lined up to reverse into the same space. No one should hoot in a traffic jam—people would move if they could and hooting achieves nothing more than frayed nerves.

Taxis □See queues, above. It is still the custom for a man to open the taxi door, see the woman in first, speak to the driver through the side window, then get in himself. The man should get out first and turn to help the woman out.

Cars □Strictly speaking, a man should open the door for a woman, see her in, close her door and then walk around to the driver's side. On arriving, he should get out, walk round the car, open the passenger door and help her out. But this is not always practical—the woman may be driving, or she may be independent and used to opening her own doors, or they may both be in a hurry. If this courtesy is abandoned, it should be revived on occasions when the woman genuinely needs a little help—because she is wearing a long dress, or carrying a baby, or a lot of parcels.

Buses □See queues, above. When boarding a bus or going upstairs in a doubledecker bus, the woman goes first, when getting off or coming downstairs, the man goes first (in both cases, to catch her if she falls). □It is discourteous and pointless to berate the conductor if the bus is late. It is not his fault, there is nothing he can do, and yours will be the hundredth complaint he has had to hear that day.

Doors and seats □Courtesy has long demanded that a man should open a door for a woman and that a younger person should open a door for an older one. It is no longer practical to uphold this rule when getting on and off crowded commuter trains, or in extremely crowded shopping centres when anyone holding a door for one person is likely to be trapped in that position for some time while dozens of others file through. However, on less crowded occasions it is still correct practice to open doors for those who take precedence. In any circumstances, it is unforgivable to walk straight through a swing door and let it go in the faces of those following behind—it should always be held until the next person can take hold of it. A woman may assume that a man she is with will hold a door for her and, if he is opening a series of doors, need not acknowledge this each time it happens; but any stranger, including and perhaps especially a child, who holds a door should always be thanked.

□Similarly, courtesy used to demand that on any form of public transport a man should give his seat to a woman and a younger person should give a seat to an older. The influx of women into working life has changed this rule, at least in the big cities, and there is now no real reason why a working man should give up his seat to a working woman. However, it is still correct for a man or woman to relinquish a seat for an elderly or infirm person, for a pregnant woman and for anyone, man or woman, carrying a baby or small child. A seat that is offered should be accepted with thanks. A refusal can make anyone, especially a child, feel silly.

Deportment

□One of the features of a civilised country is every person's right to privacy, even in public, and for this reason distracting behaviour of any kind— speaking loudly, shouting in the street, excessive gesticulation, whistling, singing, playing radios, or arguing—breaches good manners.

Altercations

□It sometimes happens in public that differences of opinion, or a sense of frustration or indignation, leads to excited or rude behaviour. A person who cannot get service in a shop loudly demands to see the manager, or a motorist who is in a hurry repeatedly blows his horn at the inept driver who is blocking the way. The victim of such an harangue should let the matter drop if at all possible. If the occasion demands a reply, speak clearly and firmly in a calm, dispassionate voice. One diminutive gentleman claims that on such occasions he tries very hard to pretend he is John Wayne being challenged to draw by a 'dude' whom he knows he can kill.

Unexpected meetings

☐It can happen that when walking down the street with one friend or acquaintance, you bump into another. If you simply greet the second friend and walk on there is no need to perform introductions, but if you stop for a chat, and if the friend you are with remains by your side, you must introduce him. If a person you are with meets a friend, and stops for a chat, it is sometimes tactful to wander a little way on, perhaps looking in a nearby shop window. This gives the person you are with the choice of not bothering with introductions or of making a point of calling you back to introduce you. (See also 'Introductions', Chapter Eight).

In a restaurant

☐If, on arriving at a restaurant, you see friends at a table, it is acceptable to go over to them to greet them. If you want to go over by yourself, first make sure that your companion is settled at your table, and make the visit very brief. If you are a woman, it is polite to ask any men at the other table not to stand up. If the friends ask you to join them, you must gauge whether or not they really want you and consider, too, the wishes of your own companion(s), before accepting. You are perfectly at liberty not to join them if you do not want to. If friends come to your table, the men should rise if there are women present—unless asked not to—but there is absolutely no obligation to ask people to join you.

Stage, film and TV stars

☐Celebrities should be allowed to dine or attend a

273

theatre in peace, without having autograph books thrust at them. If they are performing in a theatre, then the stage door is the natural place to find them and here they will be 'on duty'. Otherwise the autograph hound should write to them, care of the theatre, film studio or their agents. But it must also be said that celebrities *do* like to be noticed and tend to be unhappy if they think no one knows who they are. Therefore it is acceptable to look at them and even to smile if you catch their eye, but you should not cause interruption.

RESTAURANTS   □The conventions of ordering food and of general behaviour are more or less the same no matter how elegant or simple the restaurant. There is some difference in the style of dress expected, however, and sometimes in the degree of informality shown by and to the waiters.

What to wear   □This decision has been made more difficult by the general relaxing of conventions, but it is still wise for a man to wear a tie and a dark suit to a restaurant where he does not know the form. Trousers for women are now acceptable almost anywhere but, because there are still exceptions, the best rule is, if in doubt, don't, or telephone the restaurant and enquire. Restaurants in the lower price ranges, bistros and many neighbourhood restaurants have few rules, diners dress up or not as they like. At lunch-time more casual dress is acceptable everywhere but, even in summer, shorts and beach wear are rarely welcomed.

The female host   □All the suggestions below apply equally to a male or a female host, unless stated otherwise. For further comments see Business Manners.

Arriving   □It is not correct for a host to arrive after the guests but this is sometimes unavoidable. If the host is late then the guest may ask to be shown to the table, if it is booked, or may wait in the cocktail bar or reception area if there is one.

☐If everyone arrives together, the host should take care to move to the head of the party so that he is the one to say to the advancing *Maître d'Hôtel* or head waiter, 'I have booked a table in the name of...' If the head waiter proceeds to lead the way to the table, the rule is 'ladies first'. If, on the other hand, the table is not booked and no member of the restaurant staff comes forward to give guidance, then the host should move ahead and take the responsibility of finding a table.

Arriving separately ☐The host should make it clear, when he is shown to his table, that he is expecting a guest or guests. The guests, on arriving, should tell whoever meets them at the door the name of the person they are meeting. A nervous host entertaining several people will find there are at least two advantages to arriving early; one is that it is possible to examine the menu and wine list and make a few tentative decisions so that when the guests arrive they may have his undivided attention; the other is that it allows some time to discuss the manner of paying the bill. For instance, a host who thinks an overbearing guest may try to pay, or a hostess who thinks a male guest may be embarrassed to see her pay, can ask the advice of the head waiter, or proprietor, who may suggest a way of paying in advance, or signing the bill and having it sent to home or office later.
☐The host should rise at the approach of the guest(s) and, if there is more than one, indicate where they should sit. If the host is female it is only necessary to rise when greeting a much older woman or a very senior man (royalty, for instance).

The menu ☐This is likely to be large and written in French. Only in a few restaurants do the English descriptions of the particular dishes appear underneath. It is often divided into two halves—one offering *table d'hôte* which is the set meal, and the other *à la carte* which means that you choose each course from among things listed. *À la carte* generally works out

275

more expensive unless you decide to have only two courses, which is quite normal.

□ Underneath the main headings are likely to be the following sub-headings: *Hors d'oeuvre* which is the first course; *Potages,* soups; *Coquillages,* shellfish, such as oysters, mussels and scallops. (Any one of these may be ordered as a first course.) The *Entrée* is always eaten as a main course, and there may be a choice between *Entrée, Rôtis* (roast), and *Grillades* (grills). *Légumes* are vegetables: *Poissons* refers to fish. Puddings, if listed, are headed *Desserts* or *Entremets,* but often they are simply displayed on a trolley which is brought to the table: you may point and ask questions. *Fromages* (cheeses) are usually an alternative to pudding.

Choosing the food

□ It is not recommended that anyone choose the most expensive dish on the menu, unless expressly urged to do so by the host. It is always acceptable to ask how a dish is cooked, or to ask for advice in choosing the accompanying vegetables (a good waiter will usually offer advice to a guest who hesitates too long over the vegetable selection). In the extreme situation of a guest who is so confused by the menu as to be rendered incapable of any kind of choice, it is quite acceptable to ask the host what he recommends—on the assumption that he chose the restaurant because he knows and likes the food.

Choosing the wine

□ This is entirely the responsibility of the host, and is normally ordered from a wine waiter. Beyond establishing that the guest drinks wine, and possibly checking whether red or white is preferred (though this should really be dictated by the food), a host should not involve the guest, who cannot know whether to aim for the house carafe or the chateau bottled. The exception to this is if the host knows himself to be in the company of a guest with a special knowledge of wines—it is then a compliment to seek the advice of this guest. Nevertheless, it is

still up to the host to make the price range clear—
perhaps in the form, 'I had thought of ordering the
Beaune, but I'd much rather take your advice'. If in
doubt it is always all right to ask for the house wine,
specifying white or red. For more information about
what kind of wine to choose to accompany various
foods, see Table Manners.

Ordering   ☐It is usual to order the first and main course
together and then to order pudding or cheese when
the main course has been cleared away. Coffee and
liqueurs (if any) are normally ordered after the
cheese or pudding is finished. As has been said,
there is no need to order three courses and some
people prefer a first and main course only, while
others like a main course and a pudding.
☐Strictly speaking, all orders should be given to
the host who then relays them to the waiter. This is
because the host is giving the meal, the waiter is
only bringing it to the table. In practice, what often
happens is that the dish is ordered through the host
and the finer details negotiated with the waiter.
(For example, the guest will say to the host
'I'd like the steak, please'; whereupon the host will
say to the waiter, 'One steak and I'll have the trout',
after which the waiter is likely to say directly to the
guest, 'How would Madam like her steak?' In this
case, it is unnecessarily pedantic to say to the host,
in effect, 'Tell him I'd like it underdone', and far
more natural to make the request directly to the
waiter. If, on the other hand, the waiter directs all
his enquiries to the host, then that is where the
guest should direct his or her answers.)
☐In large parties, the men often attend to the
orders of the women beside them; alternatively
everyone looks after themselves.
☐It is important to be aware of the degree of
formality operating in the restaurant. If it is very
relaxed, then it is usual to involve the waiter more
directly in the proceedings whether you are male or
female—although it is by no means obligatory to do
so. But whatever the atmosphere, the waiter should

be addressed politely and not treated as though he was a useful robot.

Tasting and drinking wine

☐The wine waiter will put a small amount of wine into the host's glass for him to taste it and see that it is all right. If it is, and it usually is, the host indicates his approval and the waiter then fills the guest's glass, topping up the host's glass last. If it is not all right, the host must have the courage of his convictions and send it back. (Wine buffs do not taste the wine but merely sniff at it delicately. They also tend to refuse the offer of tasting the house wine, saying 'I'm sure it's all right' and indicating that the waiter should carry on pouring.) At smart restaurants, the waiter will keep an eye on the glasses and top them up as necessary, but it is also perfectly in order for the host to top them up if the waiter is slow off the mark. Anyone who does not want any more wine for the moment may either say so, or cover the glass with a hand.

Calling the waiter

☐A good waiter will keep an eye on his tables and it will not take much to attract his attention—usually leaning back in the chair and looking expectantly around is enough, coupled with catching his eye the moment he looks over. It is unfair, and also pointless, to attempt to gain his attention when he is in the middle of cooking *crêpes suzette* at another table. Shouting, table banging or finger snapping are not appreciated by waiters, other customers or embarrassed guests, but saying 'Waiter' when he is within range, or raising a hand to catch his attention, is correct and may be necessary.

Problems

☐If the wrong food is brought, or if it is badly cooked, or underdone when the request was for well-done (which can happen because chefs who believe that meat should be rare cannot bear to overcook it) it is up to the host to call the waiter and explain the problem. The best plan is to explain it politely, simply and clearly and then to continue to talk to the guest(s). This leaves no chance for the waiter to enter into discussions and explanations. In practice, most waiters will simply remove the dish and return with an improved version. It is polite for the host to ask his guest if the food is all right and, if it is not, it is up to the guest to say so, particularly if there is any question about, for example, the freshness of seafood. The guest who nobly eats a suspect oyster in order not to make a fuss may not survive to write a thank-you letter.

Smoking

☐This is often an anti-social practice, particularly in a small restaurant. You may have reached the coffee and liqueur stage, but your close neighbours may only be beginning their meal. If you must smoke, make sure that the smoke does not blow over any other tables. It is correct to ask if your companion(s) mind if you smoke. However, it is difficult to refuse permission. If you are sharing the table and others are in the middle of their meal, it is inconsiderate even to ask if you may smoke.

Paying the bill

☐It is usual to ask for the bill to be brought to the table, to check it and pay it there and then, by cash, or cheque or credit card. There is nothing wrong with asking if a service charge has been included, or with querying an apparent overcharge, so long as the latter is done discreetly and courteously (so avoiding upsetting the guest and also saving your own face if the bill turns out to have been correct after all).

☐If there is any reason to think a guest may be embarrassed by the paying of the bill, or may feel that he should offer to pay, then it is best either to have made an arrangement to pay beforehand (see 'Arriving separately') or to excuse yourself after the coffee and pay discreetly in the head waiter's corner.

Tipping

☐Ten per cent to 15 per cent of the bill is usual—add a little more if you have had exceptionally good service. If there is a service charge on the bill it is only necessary to leave a tip if you have had special service. If you pay cash and put the exact amount of the bill, plus the tip, on the saucer, you can, as the waiter collects it, say 'That's all right', indicating that you do not expect any change. If you do want change, perhaps because you only have large notes, allow the dishful of change to return to you, pick off what you should have, leave the tip in the saucer and then ignore it. If you pay by cheque, add the tip to the total.

Taxis ☐If you wish it, almost any restaurant will call you a taxi. Make the request when you pay the bill and then continue to sit at your table until someone comes to you with the information that the car has arrived.

COCKTAIL BARS AND PUBS ☐In a cocktail bar, the customer chooses a table and sits down; a waiter approaches, takes the order and brings the drink to the table. The waiter expects a tip of between ten per cent and 15 per cent of the cost of the drink—although if having several drinks, it is not necessary to pay each time; the total bill is settled up at the end. Conversations rarely spring up between tables, unless the customers already know each other. Pubs are different.

Pubs ☐(Literally, public houses, although they are not public because the landlord reserves the right to refuse admission.) Many pubs are still divided into three separate rooms; public bar, lounge or saloon bar and private bar, designed so that the bar itself cuts through the divisions and one barman can serve all. Traditionally, the public bar was for beer, darts and men only; the lounge or saloon bar for more genteel, often mixed drinking; and the private bar for assignations. It is still true that in pubs which keep these divisions the public bar tends to be uncarpeted and to house the games, the lounge bar to be more comfortable with carpets and more

seating, and the private bar to be small with tables, sometimes booths, for two. Drinks are often slightly more expensive in the lounge or private bar.
☐In a pub the customer goes up to the bar to buy a drink and either drinks it there or conveys it himself to a table. The person serving behind the bar is never given a direct tip—but if she or he is helpful and friendly, you might ask him or her to have a drink with you. There are two possible responses to this, both equally correct—one is to charge you for a drink, pour it and be seen to enjoy it; the other is to charge for a drink 'to have later' and keep the money.

Sociability

☐Pubs are sociable places and conversations often begin between strangers. In general, those standing at the bar are more open to chat than those sitting at tables, who may want privacy. A customer who accepts a drink from a stranger is expected to chat with him at least until the drink is finished. Although it is perfectly in order, in a crowded bar, to sit at a table where others are already sitting, it is polite to ask if they mind before sitting down.
☐Anyone who spills a stranger's drink, however accidentally, is expected to buy him another, even if most of it is still left in the glass.

Buying rounds

☐If a group of people in a pub are taking it in turns to buy a round, it is a cardinal sin for one of them to opt out. If the round-buying stops before his turn, he must make sure of buying one at the next session. Anyone who has to leave before the end of a session should make sure of buying a round early on. If someone else is buying, it is perfectly all right to ask to be left out 'this time round'.

The non-drinker

☐A non-drinker is an unusual person to find in a pub, but may turn up as a guest of a drinker. It is extremely bad manners to force a non-drinker to drink, or to force anyone to have one more than he wants. For the non-drinker himself, it is important that he sounds firm in his refusal and not as though

281

he hopes to be persuaded. Anyone who is given a drink he does not want, in the face of firm and unambiguous refusals, is entirely within his rights to ignore it.

Women in pubs ☐For many years, the pub was an entirely masculine world and in some areas this has not been forgotten. While a woman going in to a West End London pub on her own, to meet a male or female friend, will probably not feel out of place, a woman doing the same thing in the North-East would be likely to inspire catcalls from the young men, glowers from the old men, and exceptionally slow and sulky service from the barman. It is the pubs that have grown accustomed to women that welcome them. The area, the décor and the layout of the pub are the best guides. Although there are exceptions, the pub most likely to accept female customers is the one in the centre of a large city or, alternatively, in a country village; one where all the bars have been knocked together, one with a garden, or one which serves 'hot bar snacks'. On the whole, the South still tends to be more tolerant of women in pubs than the North.

☐It is difficult everywhere for a woman to buy a round of drinks in a pub. For a married woman who does not work, the problem does not arise, since her husband buys drinks on behalf of them both. For a single woman, or a married woman earning her own money, there is a problem. In general, young men feel that everyone in the group should take his or her turn, but there are still older men who would be genuinely upset to be bought a drink by a woman. The young men are right, but until the practice becomes more accepted, the woman should remember that good manners are about not making people unhappy, and should back down in the face of real distress.

**PUBLIC
ENTERTAIN-
MENT**
☐Good manners in all public places of entertainment are principally concerned with not disturbing

the other members of the audience, or, indeed, the performers. In practice, this means arriving in time to be seated and settled before the curtain rises, not wearing noisy jewellery, and not talking or unwrapping sweets and chocolate during the performance. It also means bearing in mind that a surprisingly large amount of the auditorium can be clearly seen from the stage, and that obvious yawns and glances at one's watch can be very off-putting to any performer who happens to notice them.

The theatre □Tickets can be bought from the theatre in person or reserved on the telephone either by giving a credit card number or paying by post (enclosing s.a.e.). Some theatres will put on you on a mailing list so you are informed of forthcoming productions. In London, tickets can also be bought from a ticket agency, but because agencies take block bookings you may have more choice of seats if you approach the theatre direct. On the other hand, if a show is heavily booked you may stand more chance with an agency.

Where to sit □Most theatres are divided into stalls (downstairs, expensive at the front and cheaper further back); dress circle (one floor up and, like stalls, expensive at the front and cheaper further back); boxes (on the same level as the dress circle, expensive but with seats for four to six people. They are cosy and slightly exclusive but often give a lop-sided view of the performance). Above dress circle level theatres differ slightly, according to size. Almost all have an upper circle, where the seats are cheapest, and which is often entered by a side door and not through the main foyer. The larger ones have a still higher level, called a gallery or balcony. These are the cheapest and least comfortable seats, are not always bookable (you may have to get your ticket on the night) and are always reached through a side door and up a great many stairs.

What to wear □Going to a West End theatre is not the

smart occasion it once was. Generally, the more expensive the seats, the more smartly dressed the audience. An increasing number of theatregoers turn up in whatever they happen to be wearing.

Taking your seat
☐On taking your seat, enter the row as discreetly as possible, by whatever method causes least inconvenience to those already seated.

Intervals
☐Because intervals often last only ten or fifteen minutes and theatres are very crowded, it is wise to order and pay for interval drinks in the theatre bar before the performance begins. In all theatre bars you will be told where (on which table or shelf) you will find your drinks; some write your name on a slip and put it on top of the glasses, some give you a ticket with a letter on it and your drinks are to be found in the relevant patch of a long, lettered shelf.

Opera and ballet
☐Good manners for opera-goers and balletomanes are very similar to those for theatre-goers. Two points which differ slightly are arrival and applause.

Arriving
☐Late arrivals will be asked to wait until a suitable moment before taking their seats. In an opera, this can mean waiting until the first interval, often watching the performance on closed circuit television in the meantime.

Applause
☐As well as applauding at the end of each scene, and at the end of the performance, it is customary to applaud at the end of a well-sung aria, ballet solo or special dance. In an opera, do not begin to applaud until the last note of the music has completely died away. If the aria or performance is exceptionally good, cries of 'Bravo' are sometimes mingled with the applause. Standing ovations at the end of an opera are rare in Britain, although quite common on the Continent and in America. This kind of appreciation is usually welcomed by the artists but if moved to rise, be warned that you may rise alone.
☐Because the facilities and degree of formality

vary, the three principal houses—The Royal Opera House, The Coliseum and Glyndebourne—have to be treated separately.

The Royal Opera House Covent Garden ☐This huge, colonnaded 19th century building is the London home of grand opera and ballet.

Tickets ☐Both opera and ballet are booked up well in advance. It is wise to send for monthly programme details which will indicate when booking opens for each series of performances.

What to wear ☐Black tie and an elaborate, long dress are rare, except on gala nights. (White tie is requested at the rare state galas.) As with the theatre, people in the expensive seats tend to dress up more than the rest, while those in the cheapest seats rarely dress up at all. There are those who feel it is still nice to make a special occasion of a visit to the opera, but no one is turned away for being casually dressed.

Intervals ☐As at the theatre, drinks can be ordered and paid for in the nearest bar to one's seat before the performance begins. It is possible to buy or order sandwiches before the performance, and in the interval, and tables can be reserved in the Crush bar for a lucky few. All the boxes have waiter service, and here it is the waiter's responsibility to see that glasses are removed before the performance recommences.

The Coliseum ☐Ballet and opera are performed here, but the opera is in English from the English National Opera. The occasion is less formal than Covent Garden, as regards dress, but comments about arriving and applause still apply.

Glyndebourne Festival Opera ☐This is a summer opera festival, from May to August, held in the opera house attached to an elegant Tudor manor set in beautiful grounds near Lewes in Sussex. It begins at about five o'clock in the afternoon and there is one long (seventy

285

minute) interval in the middle when people either dine in the restaurant or, more traditionally, eat a picnic on the grass and wander by the lake.

Tickets   ☐These are expensive and much sought after. For members of the Glyndebourne Festival Society, postal booking opens in February. For non-members it opens in the first week of April. (Anyone may apply for membership, with its preferential booking opportunities, but the waiting list is some years long.)

What to wear   ☐The programme requests that men wear 'black tie' and women wear long evening dress. Virtually everyone accedes to this request, although no one is turned away for wearing a lounge suit or a short dress. If planning to eat or stroll in the grounds, it is wise for women to take wraps of some kind.

Arriving   ☐For drivers, Glyndebourne is marked on most maps and well signposted once you draw near. Trains run from London Victoria to Glynde where coaches connect the station and the opera house. The grand arrive in Rolls Royces or even by helicopter (although these may only land by prior arrangement with Glyndebourne Transport Office).

The interval   ☐Those intending to eat in the dining room should book in advance, but it is part of the experience of Glyndebourne to take a picnic. (There is a marquee for bad weather, but it will not hold everyone). Picnics tend to be elegant affairs with smoked salmon; pâtés and terrines; mousses; cheese; strawberries and cream; champagne or good wines. Most people take glasses, crockery and cutlery; some set up table and chairs. The knowledgeable arrive early, set out the picnic furniture in the chosen spot, and put the champagne to cool in the lake before it is time to take their seats for the performance.

Concerts   ☐At a concert, and more especially at a song recital, extraneous noises are seriously disturbing. In the latter case they may even distract the singer. The commonest breach of courtesy is to rustle the programme pages when following the English translation of a song. A page should never be turned until the end of the song.

What to wear

☐For men, a lounge suit, and for women a short dress, although more casual clothes are not necessarily out of place.

Applause

☐At a symphony concert it is incorrect and distracting to applaud between movements. It is essential to wait until the end of the symphony. At a song recital, it is incorrect to clap each song. Applause should not come until the end of the song sequence (always clearly marked on the programme). On no account should any applause begin until the last note of music has completely died away.

The St Matthew Passion and the Hallelujah Chorus

☐Convention dictates that the St Matthew Passion, which is usually played in a church, is not applauded, and that the audience rises and stands throughout the Hallelujah Chorus.

SPECTATOR SPORTS

☐Several popular British sports such as sailing, cricket, tennis and racing have special occasions at which it is customary, by long-established traditions, to behave or dress in a given manner. Deviation is considered ill-bred and in some instances may mean you are barred from the event.

Horse racing

☐Flat racing is the oldest form. The flat racing season runs from 25th March to the second week in November and the classic flat races are The Derby, The Oaks, the St Leger, the One Thousand Guineas and the Two Thousand Guineas. National Hunt Racing, or 'steeplechasing', means racing over fences or hurdles. The season runs from the 1st of August to the end of May the following year, and because of the overlap of seasons, mixed meetings

287

are sometimes held. Two of the great 'steeplechases'
are the Grand National and Cheltenham Gold Cup.
□See also Royal Ascot, Chapter 11.

Stands and enclosures □There are three types—the Club or Members'
Enclosure, which is the most expensive and
comfortable but no longer limited to members;
Tattersalls, which is the middle range and is
where the bookmakers are; and the Silver Ring
which is the cheapest and has its own bookmakers.
Spectators in the Silver Ring do not have access to
the paddock and so cannot look over the horses
before a race. The Tote, see 'Betting' below, is
available in all three Enclosures.

What to wear □Grand summer race meetings, such as Royal
Ascot, mean a suit for a man and a dress and a hat
for a woman (although the Royal Enclosure at Ascot
is more formal, see page 258). Goodwood has a
tradition of panama hats for men. Winter steeplechases usually see men in tweed suits and women in
boots, smart coats and probably headscarves.

Betting □For those who do not understand its intricacies,
the best plan is to ignore the bookmakers and bet
on the Tote. Here, the sum you may bet appears
over each window and you can bet on a horse for a
'win' or a 'place'. The latter means that you expect it
it to be one of the first three.
□Give the number, rather than the name, of the
horse and keep the betting slip because you will
have to hand it over at the cash-out if you win.

Food and drink □This is liberally available, at a price.

Point-to-point □This is a less formal version of the above. The
course may be edged only with ropes and the cars
of spectators (many of whom watch from inside
them). Most people take simple picnics.

Lord's □Lord's cricket ground is the home of the MCC
(Marylebone Cricket Club) the premier cricket club
in Britain. It is where the Eton and Harrow Match,

the Oxford and Cambridge Match, the Test
Matches and the One-Day Finals are played.

Tickets □Write in or call for tickets in advance of a match,
or risk buying them at the gate on the day. Test
Match tickets should be acquired well in advance.
They become available to MCC members in
January and to the general public in March.

What to wear □On the public terraces there are no rules. A few
men still wear morning dress to the Eton and
Harrow Match, and dark suits to the Oxford and
Cambridge, but they are now very much in the
minority. Those with seats in the pavilion (and
these are only available to MCC members and their
guests, or to members of the Club playing and their
guests) must wear a collar, tie and jacket at all
times. This rule is so strict that when it was relaxed
in 1976 as the temperature reached 96°F the fact
was announced on the national news. No women are
permitted in the pavilion during the hours of play.

Applause □Traditionally, the correct form of applause is a
slow gentle clap, with the occasional approving
'(Well) played, Sir', from the gentlemen. But today
even Test Cricket often evokes the kind of
responses once reserved for 'village cricket'—
shouts, whistles, hand clapping and foot stamping.
On the public terraces there is nothing to stop you
from indulging in the latter. In or near the pavilion
you will cause serious offence unless you stick to
the former.

Photography □This is not allowed, unless with the written
permission of the Secretary. It is never, in any
circumstances, allowed in or from the pavilion or
the long room (which is the inner sanctum of the
pavilion).

Henley Royal □The regatta, which takes place annually during
Regatta the first weeks of July, was founded in 1839 and
became royal when, in 1851, Prince Albert gave it

his patronage. It is held along Henley Reach which is slightly more than a mile and a quarter of straight river, and oarsmen from Britain and overseas compete for some of the oldest established trophies in rowing history. There are three ways of enjoying the regatta—from the Steward's Enclosure, from the Regatta Enclosure, or from the public stretch of river beyond both, where there is no entry fee and no facilities and you wear what you like.

The Regatta Enclosure □You pay at the gate to go in and, once inside, you find the comfort of deckchairs, public lavatories, refreshment tents and an amplified commentary. There are no restrictions on dress.

The Steward's Enclosure □The regatta is managed by forty elected stewards—and to be elected a steward at Henley Royal Regatta is one of the most coveted honours in the rowing world. The Steward's Enclosure is the inner sanctum and admission is by invitation only. No children under 11 are ever admitted.

What to wear □Men must wear jackets and either ties or cravats—women must wear dresses, not slacks or trouser suits, however smart, and certainly not shorts. Although a hat is not obligatory for a woman, and there are always several women in simple summer dresses, the majority dress as for a garden party, either in very pretty or very smart dresses, with large hats, and sometimes, parasols. Those men who are entitled to, wear club or university rowing blazers, socks, caps or boaters peculiar to their fraternities—the rest wear sports jackets and trousers, or suits.

Food and drink □Those who take picnics must go outside the Steward's Enclosure to eat them (anyone with a pass may go in or out as he or she pleases). Buffet lunch is served in a large marquee, at a price, and you may buy champagne to drink while you queue to get in. The bar, in a smaller marquee, serves a wide selection of drinks but custom dictates that the majority choose Pimms or champagne.

The stands   □Those who choose to attend to the rowing rather than the socialising can get a good view from deckchairs at the water's edge or from raked stands where they can hear an amplified commentary.

Applause   □Applause is evident but restrained.

Wimbledon Fortnight   □The World Championships which are held at the All England Club in Wimbledon for two weeks each summer are the most important events in the year for tennis players from all over the world.

Tickets   □Send a stamped addressed envelope to the All England Club in December for booking details.

What to wear   □In the royal box, where admission is only by the invitation of the chairman and committee, men wear a jacket and tie and women tend to be fairly smartly dressed, though hats are not necessary. The same applies to the Member's Enclosure, which is reserved for Club members and their guests. Everywhere else, people dress for comfort, depending on the weather, but large view-blocking sun-hats should be avoided.

Behaviour   □Spectators are asked only to move from their stands when the players are changing ends. Applause should be reserved until the end of a game, a set or a match. Many people do applaud in the middle of a rally, but it is incorrect, and distracting for the players.

Food and drink   □A small picnic area is provided for those who take their own food. For those who do not, various buffets serve lunches, snacks and soft drinks. There are always strawberries and cream. It is impolite to distract players and other spectators by eating or drinking in the stands.

Cowes Week   □The regatta held at Cowes, on the Isle of Wight, for a week every August, is one of the most important events in the sailing world. Yachts arrive from far and wide to take part in the events, and spectators gather to watch and to socialise. Cowes itself is a maritime arena with a long parade and esplanade where onlookers can stroll or lean on the railings for a good view. There are five principal yacht clubs with headquarters in Cowes; the Royal Yacht Squadron, the Royal Corinthian Yacht Club, the Royal London Yacht Club, the Island Sailing Club and Cowes Corinthian Yacht Club. The Royal Ocean Racing Club, the Royal Thames and Royal Sutton and Household Brigade Yacht Clubs hold regattas at Cowes using the facilities of these five clubs.

□Guests enter the clubs, or attend parties on yachts, by invitation only. Members of other yacht clubs may obtain temporary membership through the secretary—except in the case of the Royal Yacht Squadron, when the introduction must be through a member.

What to wear   □The Royal Yacht Squadron is the most formal of the clubs and members' guests should dress accordingly when in the castle grounds; women wear dresses and, quite often, hats, and the majority of men wear a collar and black tie, a yachting suit or reefer jacket with either grey or white flannels. The Royal Corinthian and Royal London Yacht Clubs are somewhat less formal. Men may still dress as above, but fewer women wear hats, and smart trousers for women are acceptable. If men choose to cover their heads when afloat, yachting caps are considered more elegant than 'bobble hats', but the latter are perhaps more practical when actually sailing. Yachtsmen coming ashore from races usually change before mingling with the guests. The Island Sailing Club and Cowes Corinthian Yacht Club are still less formal; there are no restrictions on dress and yachtsmen may not change between races.

□To evening parties on large yachts on the 'roads',

men wear collar and tie without going so far as black tie, and women bear in mind the hazards of climbing aboard and of steep companionways and wear short, not long, dresses—full, not tight, skirts—or trousers. In the marina, anything goes.

Shoes □A vital consideration. Those expecting to be invited aboard any yacht should have with them a pair of rubber-soled shoes with a good grip—the soles in white or red composition, not black which can mark the deck. Many yachts, and, indeed, yacht clubs, still bear the scars from the stiletto heels of the inconsiderate.

12 BUSINESS MANNERS

BUSINESS VS SOCIAL MANNERS

☐Business manners have the same roots as social manners, but there are many occasions when the two diverge. Then too, circumstances arise in a business context which would never arise in a social one.

☐Strictly speaking, business and social manners ought not to diverge as much as they do. It is not true that it is unnecessary to be polite to a subordinate; it is not true that a curt and hectoring manner is good enough—even useful—for business contacts. People should be treated with courtesy regardless of the environment in which they are operating. That said, a certain amount of divergence is only practical. In a busy office where one person has regularly to give instructions to another, 'please' and 'thank-you' may be time-wasting and superfluous. (Just as a surgeon is not expected to say, 'Please would you pass me a scalpel, Sister? Thank you so much.')

Women

☐Oddly enough, it is the influx of women into business and professional life which has caused the most recent rift between the two codes of behaviour. A man who, in a social context, would always rise when a woman enters the room, and always open the door for her to leave, is not expected to leap up and down each time his secretary walks in and out of his office. Professional and managerial women prefer to be treated with no less, but equally no more, courtesy than their male colleagues. After a meeting of eight men and one woman (a not uncommon ratio) it would be silly for all the men to stand back for the woman to pass through the door first—although in a social context they should do just that.

Hierarchy

☐The business circumstances which differ from social circumstances are principally connected with hierarchy, relationships and meetings. In business, as in the services, hierarchy is arranged by rank within the company, and not by social status. (Prince Andrew would call his commanding officer

294

'Sir', rather than the other way about.) No social relationship equates with that between secretary and boss, solicitor and client, superior and subordinate, and no social occasion parallels a board meeting or a meeting between an executive and a representative of a client firm.

Degrees of
formality

□One of the marked similarities between business and social situations, on the other hand, is the way in which degrees of formality vary. When entering an unfamiliar world, it is necessary to notice the dress and general behaviour patterns of those already in it because, within reason, new employees are expected to adapt to the 'manners of the country'. For example, the worlds of the arts and the media are traditionally informal, both about dress and address, while the worlds of banking and the civil service tend to be conservative in dress and strictly hierarchical in behaviour. But even within these broad outlines, firms differ and the advice given below should be modified and adapted as appropriate.

DEPORTMENT

□This overall heading refers to the ways in which people should conduct themselves in business or professional situations with regard to dress, pecking orders, women in business, foreign business contacts and professional relationships. The basic, and frequently offered, social advice holds good in this area also— that one should behave in a relaxed and natural manner as far as possible, and play difficult situations by ear. However, this is not very helpful if the natural bent of the individual is to be morose and argumentative, and if the ear is not true. It might therefore be useful to say that the attributes a well-mannered business person should nurture in him or herself are awareness of the needs and moods of others, a willingness to carry out instructions from above, and a sympathy for complaints or dissent from below. If a particular service is part of the job it should be rendered willingly (service with a smile was always a useful

slogan). If the service is irksome (perhaps a
secretary resents being asked to stop her own work
to make tea for her boss's visitors) then a suitable
moment should be found to explain this and to
initiate a discussion about altering the situation. If
the situation cannot be changed then the service
must still be given with at least an appearance of
willingness.

□No superior should ever ask for a service that is
not part of the job. For example, a subordinate
known to be good with cars should not be expected
to spend any part of his free time with his head
under the bonnet of the managing director's
Rolls.

Dress □How to dress for the office presents more of a
problem to those about to start a new job than to
anyone else, because it is harder for them to put
into practice the best advice of all—dress as the
others dress. Customs vary so much from office to
office that it is not possible to generalise, and there
are few unvarying rules. The man in the pin-striped
suit, and the man in the jeans and tee shirt may
both be correctly dressed for their respective
offices. The best solution is to be alert during the
interview, notice what others of the same sex, age
and status are wearing, and use that as a guideline.
This, of course, still leaves the problem of what to
wear for the interview. Here, it is better to err on
the side of being too formal than of not being
formal enough. It is actually possible that an
applicant who is dressed too casually to suit the
taste of a particular firm might lose the job to an
applicant who is dressed more correctly, if all
qualifications are equal; an applicant dressed too
smartly is less likely to be turned down for that
reason. If in doubt, a man should wear a dark suit
and a plain tie, unless his old school tie seems
relevant, and a woman should wear something
smart but very simple and plain with a minimum of
jewellery. A hat is unnecessary and gloves need only
be worn in winter.

General rules of dress   ☐There are still a few of these. A man who removes his jacket in the office should remove his waistcoat, if any, also. A man who wears braces should either keep his jacket on or remove the braces completely (that is, not leave them hanging around the hips). A man who rolls his shirt sleeves up should not roll them above the elbow. It is hard on the eyesight of colleagues to wear a strongly-patterned tie with a strongly-patterned shirt.

☐A woman who wants to be taken seriously in a business context should not wear low necklines, see-through blouses, very short or split skirts or noisy jewellery. Some offices still bar women from wearing trousers and, if in doubt, it is wise to ask about this.

☐There are of course exceptions. A woman in the fashion industry might be expected to dress exactly as described above. It is also possible to find several examples of extremely successful businessmen who take off their jackets to reveal patterned shirts and ties, dangling braces and shirtsleeves rolled up to the armpits, but in this case they may have succeeded in spite of, rather than because of, these attributes.

☐For more information about correct dress, see Chapter 16.

Pecking orders   ☐The pecking order in an office is usually as clearly established as that in a hen-house, which is just as well, because in an office with a rigid hierarchy it is possible to cause great offence by claiming privileges reserved for those of a higher status. Within the pecking order, treatment of superiors, subordinates and equals should not differ as much as it often does.

Equals   ☐Good behaviour between equals should in theory be the easiest to maintain, but a certain amount of tension can easily be generated if one party has the stronger personality and instinctively takes the dominant role. This shows itself most of all when it becomes necessary for two equals to have a meeting

in one or the other's office. In this case, the correct
procedure is for the person initiating the meeting to
go to the other's office—it is not correct to
'summon' an equal to your own office unless you
are entertaining a visitor you would like him or her
to meet. In this case, if the situation is a formal one,
you should rise when your colleague enters the
room, perform the introductions and indicate a
chair before sitting again, so making it clear to the
visitor that you and your colleague are at least of
equal status. It is not correct to barge into someone
else's office, sit down and expect full attention. If
there is an intercom system it is courteous to ring
through first and ask if it is convenient. If not,
pause to ask if he/she can spare the time while you
are still in the doorway.

Superiors ☐It is in the nature of things that superiors must
be deferred to, but that does not mean they cannot
be disagreed with, so long as it is done politely.
Never volunteer a contrary opinion in the presence
of visitors or clients. Take genuine grievances to the
superior and ask if something can be done;
grumbling and scowling in private is rarely
productive. Often, a busy executive doesn't even
realise he is overloading a subordinate with work
unless it is pointed out to him.

Subordinates ☐Apart from the obvious difference in who gives
and who obeys instructions, subordinates should
not be treated very differently from superiors or
equals. Everyone has a right to expect courtesy and
consideration. The superior must remember that
the subordinate has a life outside the office and
should not initiate an impromptu meeting at lunch
time or the end of the day without first checking
that it is convenient.

Clients ☐The visiting client's temporary place in the office
hierarchy depends on whether he or she is offering
or receiving a service. Even so, the degree of
courtesy should not change, only the degree of

formality—and that will largely depend on the age and status of the client.

Criticizing others ☐Modern management practice suggests that this should never be done at all because it is counter-productive and produces anger and resentment rather than better results. However, if it is essential, then it must be done in private, never in front of other members of staff, of whatever status, and never in front of a client, even if the client has lodged a complaint. Contrary to popular belief, the client has no right to dictate office practice and demand to witness a dressing-down. The executive concerned should be polite, apologetic, firm in assuring that the matter will be dealt with, and then deal with it as seems fit after the client has gone.

Christian names ☐In a formal business-client relationship it may never be appropriate to use first names. The slight distance caused by the use of formal address can actually be conducive to efficiency—less of the 'I'm sorry, George old boy, but I haven't got around to it, you know how it is'. But if Christian names do seem appropriate it is up to the senior of the two people concerned to make the move—either by saying, 'Please call me Mary. May I call you John?'—or else by beginning a letter with the use of the Christian name and commenting on it in the first line, 'I hope you don't mind, but . . .'. Anyone who takes the second course must remember to sign the letter with his/her Christian name, even although the full name is typed after the signature.
☐When making a first approach to someone, by letter or telephone, it is rarely correct to presume first-name terms. The person who is making the approach, however, gives both first and last name: 'Mr. Lamb? This is Sarah Bell' and, if writing, signs the letter Sarah Bell, putting Mrs, Miss or Ms in parentheses, as part of the typed name beneath her signature.
☐The use of Christian names should work both ways except where there is a substantial age gap. It

is arrogant of a superior to choose to be addressed formally, yet to call subordinates by first names (or by last names only). For example, a man who wishes his secretary to call him 'Mr Dunn' should address her as 'Miss Smith' unless she specifically asks him to call her 'Mary'.

Shared secretary ☐The shared secretary can be a source of great irritation if sharers seek status by competing with each other as to who can hand out the most work and who can persuade the secretary to do his/her work first. The chief sufferer is the secretary.
☐It is essential that the sharers get together and come to some reasonable arrangement about division of time. It is then up to the other sharer to tell the secretary she may put his/her work aside for the time being. It is totally incorrect for both parties to insist to the secretary that their work is the more important. Similarly, anyone wanting to borrow anyone's secretary should ask her direct boss first. This is not only courteous to the boss but also to the secretary, relieving her of the responsibility of what may be a very difficult decision.

Interviews ☐An advertisement always makes it clear whether to telephone or write in. If it requires you to write, note if it asks for specific information and be sure to supply it. The letter should be straightforward and simple, clearly set out and, if possible, typed.
☐If the job in question requires typing skills, it is essential that the letter of application be typed. A brief first paragraph should state that you are writing in response to the advertisement for the position of —in—paper of—date. The main paragraph should mention any relevant jobs or qualifications (this is the paragraph in which you are, in effect, telling the prospective employer why he or she should consider you for the job). A final brief paragraph should mention any enclosures, C.V. perhaps, and conclude on the lines of 'I look forward to hearing from you if you feel my qualifications are suitable'.

The C.V.	□A prospective employer may ask for a C.V., or *curriculum vitae*. A full C.V. will list education (from secondary school level to higher education), resulting qualifications, and every job held from leaving school or university to the present day. In the case of an older applicant it may be sufficient to list no more than the last two or three jobs in some detail—responsibilities, position in company and so on.
What to wear	□See Dress, above.
The interview	□Expect to be asked questions about previous jobs, responsibilities and qualifications; reason for wishing to leave your present job; reason for wanting advertised job; general health; willingness to take on new responsibilities and, possibly, how you would organize the work if you were successful. □The prospective employer should give a clear idea of what the job entails; of where (in which office) you will work; of the hours; of holiday allowances, salary and whether or not it is negotiable; the likelihood of rises or promotion; details of perks such as luncheon vouchers, pension scheme, interest-free loan for season ticket etc. If the job would entail moving house, he should make it clear whether or not the firm will help with expenses, and to what extent. He or she should then offer to answer questions, and these may be on any subjects mentioned above. (If you are seriously interested in the job, questions about the work and the company itself should outweigh questions about perks, or your sincerity may be doubted.)
References	□If previous employers have furnished you with letters of reference, these may be handed over on request. If not, and if the prospective employer asks for the names and addresses of previous employers, you may give these, and hope for the best. If, however, as sometimes happens, the prospective employer asks for the name of someone prepared to give a character reference, and if you decide to offer

the family doctor or vicar, or a friend of the family who is in one of the professions, it is correct first to ask this person if you may use them as a referee.

The follow-up

☐It is not usual to contact a prospective employer after the interview to ask if you have got the job. Therefore, once the employer has made a selection and informed the successful applicant, he or she must inform every other applicant, however many there may be, that the job has been filled, and must do this as soon as possible. The practice of forcing unsuccessful applicants to come to their own conclusions after weeks of waiting is rude and inconsiderate.

Letter of agreement or contract

☐The successful applicant should be sent a letter of agreement, or contract of employment, setting out the terms of employment, salary, notice required on either side, holiday arrangements and so on. This should be read very carefully because, once signed, it is legally binding on both of the parties.

Women in business

☐Even today, a woman in any role other than that of secretary is only truly accepted in certain business areas, specifically the female-oriented ones such as fashion and cosmetics, and also the arts. This means that a woman may have to try harder than a man in an equivalent job because male colleagues and clients are likely to be less tolerant of mistakes, and also likely to be on the look-out for 'feminine' behaviour, by which is meant tears and hysterical outbursts.

Modifications of social behaviour

☐The requirements of social good manners include standing up when a woman enters a room, opening a door for her and allowing her to go through it first, and seeing that she has a chair if there is a shortage. But all these have to be modified in a business context. This is partly in order that the normal workings of office life are not seriously disrupted, and partly because it is in itself a courtesy to treat a business woman in accordance

with her place in the hierarchy of the firm rather than in accordance with her sex. People in business are people, not men and women.
□But changes in conventions may make it harder for a man to know how he should behave and the most useful guideline is to observe the usual courtesies in the case of a senior woman—just as he would for a senior man—and if the woman is his equal or junior, behave as seems natural in the particular situation—for example, if he happens to reach the door first, the courtesy of opening it for her will be appreciated, but if she reaches the door first she is quite likely to open it for him and there is no need for him to make elaborate efforts to get ahead of her.

The woman boss □The rules for a female boss are no different than those for a male boss. It is just as important to treat a subordinate with courtesy as it is to treat a superior with courtesy. However, a woman with a male subordinate should be aware that a man may feel at a disadvantage and should be prepared, for this reason, to take particular care to follow the rules. See also, 'Business entertaining'.

Foreign business contacts □When dealing with business people from abroad, and especially when entertaining them or being entertained by them, it is important—apart from the obvious courtesy of not criticizing the politics or religion of the country in question—to be aware of relevant differences in attitudes and manners. In many cases, the differences are not great. Africans have often been educated in Britain, or brought up in former British or French colonies; Europeans may be a little more formal than the British, and North Americans a little less so, but no one behaving with normal courtesy is likely to cause offence or confusion. The most serious pitfalls probably occur when dealing with someone of the Muslim faith—this includes many Africans as well as Arabs—or with Japanese.

303

Muslims ☐Because Islam is a way of life, its customs extend into business areas. Friday is the day of rest and government departments of Muslim countries are closed, though it is not against the law to work on a Friday and it is possible to arrange a business meeting for a Friday.
☐The month of Ramadan is a time of fasting during which a Muslim will not eat, drink or smoke from dawn to dusk. The Islamic calendar is different from ours, and Ramadan begins eleven days earlier each year, so it is wise to check exact dates. Business is as usual, but it is discourteous and thoughtless to invite a Muslim to lunch at this time, although inviting him to a dinner party beginning at sunset is perfectly all right.
☐It is also courteous to avoid party-giving during the first month of the Islamic year because Mohammet's grandson was murdered in that month.
☐The Muslim faith forbids pork or alcohol at any time.

Arabs ☐The majority are Muslim, so the above applies. Also, in an Arab household, food is eaten with the right hand only—the left hand is never used to pass or receive food and is never placed on the table (if a British business person overlooked this rule it would probably not be taken as an insult).
☐Anyone finding himself in a situation where it is necessary to sit cross-legged on the floor should remember that the sole of the foot must never point towards anyone.
☐A business woman would find dealing with an Arab extremely difficult, perhaps impossible, since a woman's place is considered to be in the home.
☐A business man is unlikely to meet his business contact's wife and should not enquire about her in person but rather to ask after 'your house'. The surest way to avoid causing offence is to pretend that women don't exist at all.

Japanese ☐Japanese and European cultures have differed for thousands of years and any European conducting business with a Japanese company will be immediately aware of differences of approach and attitude which are often extreme.

Approach □In Japan, the approach to a business transaction is slower and less direct than it would be in the West. The first move should be to discover which individual should be dealt with and to exchange cards with him. After this, a meeting can be arranged. It would not be expected that business would be discussed during the first meeting— hobbies and interests are better topics.

Cards □These are vital. A British business man should have cards for Japanese contacts printed in English on one side and Japanese on the other. A Japanese will bow on receiving your card and touch it briefly to his forehead.

Status □It is extremely important to deal with someone of your own status. This is assessed by age, position in the company and the status of the company itself. That is, an older man usually has higher status than a younger unless the older occupies a position too low for his age and in a company without high standing. Also, a buyer has higher status than a seller.

Greeting □The Japanese do not shake hands, they bow, and the depth of the bow is related directly to the amount of respect due to the person being greeted.

Names □A Japanese is never called by his first name, except by his family. He should be greeted by surname followed by 'San', which means 'Sir', although a European will not give offence by using the surname preceded by 'Mr'. If the time comes for greater familiarity, the surname is abbreviated.

Presents □These are important, and so are 'treats' (a trip to a nice golf course, perhaps). They are always reciprocated.

Yes and No
☐When a Japanese says 'Yes' he means 'I have heard and understood what you said'—he does not necessarily mean 'I agree with you'. He will not say 'No'. He will say 'That might be difficult' or 'I must think about that' and slide gently out of the situation.

Ending a business or professional relationship
☐It is courteous to write a letter to indicate that you intend to sever such a relationship and in some cases, for example if you are changing solicitors, it is essential because it is not ethical for a new solicitor to take on a case until it has been formally relinquished by the previous one. If you are leaving a solicitor, doctor or other professional person because you are dissatisfied, you are at liberty to make this clear in the letter, but it is not wise to discuss the inadequacies of the person you have left with whoever takes you in his or her stead.
☐If you do not wish to express dissatisfaction, the letter may be couched in vague terms, 'I feel a change may be beneficial'. If you have always been satisfied and are leaving solely because of a change of address or perhaps because, in a family wrangle, you feel that separate solicitors would make life easier all round, make this clear in the letter.
☐Your medical card tells you how to go about changing a National Health doctor.

CORRESPOND-ENCE
☐Business stationery is important. Often it is the first 'image' of a firm or a business person that another firm or business person sees, and cheap stationery does not inspire confidence. Although personal writing paper, and also business and professional cards are often engraved, a business letterhead is normally printed; the printing should be of good quality, on good quality bond paper, and the design and layout should be chosen to reflect the character of the business—formal or informal, 'olde-worlde' or modern, and so on.
☐Business stationery should have on it the name, address and telephone number of the firm, the registered office address (if different), the VAT

number, company registration number, and the names of the directors.

When to write ☐Write rather than telephone when it is necessary to have a record of what was said; when presenting new ideas that need to be thought about; when accepting formal invitations (unless a telephone number is given on the card); when thanking for hospitality; when offering apologies, condolences or congratulations.

Dictating letters ☐Nowadays, it is acceptable for all but the most personal letters to be dictated and typewritten. Many people dictate on to cassettes, a useful system which means that letters can be dictated at the convenience of the dictator, and typed back at the convenience of the secretary. It is important, however, to speak clearly into the microphone and not look away from it around the room or out of the car window so that the volume of the voice constantly rises and falls. It is rude and inconsiderate, but not uncommon, to cough or sneeze into the microphone.
☐Those who dictate letters directly to a secretary should do just that, and not pace the room expecting him or her to catch words directed out of the window or into a bookcase. It is also a matter of courtesy to choose a time of mutual convenience for dictation and not emit a string of letters late in the afternoon and expect someone to stay late until they are all typed up.

Opening and closing a letter ☐Strictly, a letter which begins 'Dear Mr/Miss Smith' should end 'Yours sincerely', and one which begins 'Dear Sir' should end 'Yours faithfully'. 'Yours truly' is rarely used now except when writing to shops or the bank. Naturally a letter written to a friend may end any way you choose—'Yours ever', 'With best wishes' and 'Kind regards' are examples—and many people evolve their own ways of ending letters to people they address by name and write to frequently. These are only incorrect if a misjudgement is made about the degree of familiarity which is acceptable. It is a pleasant, though dying, courtesy to handwrite the opening and closing of all letters in which the recipient is addressed by name. For the correct opening and closing of letters to those with ranks and titles, see the charts in Chapter Eight.

Letters to someone whose name is unknown

☐It is sometimes impossible to find out a name and title, and if the information is not available, 'Dear Sir' is still the best alternative. If the person's sex is unknown, some people write 'Dear Sir/Madam', others continue to write 'Dear Sir'.

Letters to women

☐The opening of a letter to a woman who does not have a professional title (Doctor etc.), and whose marital status is unknown, presents problems. The contraction 'Ms' (pronounced miz) was created to overcome the difficulty, and although not yet fully established, it is certainly the best solution.
☐Some married women retain their maiden names for business purposes, especially if they became established in business before marrying, and in this case, a woman would be addressed, for example, as Miss Mary Bennett at the office but as Mrs John Harris if an invitation were sent to her home.
☐A good secretary should endeavour to find out the preferred mode of address before typing the letter. Equally, it is helpful for women who are writing letters to make their preferred mode of address clear by typing it beneath their signature.

Personal letters

☐A personal letter sent to an office address may be marked 'Personal', but a letter sent to someone's home must not be. Very personal letters—of condolence, of thanks for hospitality in someone's home, or responses to invitations sent to home and not to office—should be written by hand on personal writing paper.
☐However, if a letter of condolence is to a representative of a firm in which a member of staff

has died, and if the member of staff was no more than a business acquaintance of both, the letter may be typed on office stationery. Similarly, if a letter of thanks is sent to a business person in response to business hospitality, it may be typed on office stationery. (See also 'Letters of sympathy', Chapter Eight).

By hand ☐The envelopes of letters sent by hand should be clearly marked 'by hand'. If the letter is sent by a paid messenger or employee, it may be sealed. If a friend or colleague is to deliver it, it is considered impolite to seal it and it is customary for the colleague to seal it when it is handed over.

Office memos ☐These are useful for passing on information which a colleague would otherwise have to write down him/herself, and also for making statements which need to go on file. It is usually a sign of insecurity to dictate dozens of memos when a moment on the internal telephone would make them unnecessary. Most firms have their own customs with regard to styles of memos.

TELEPHONE MANNERS ☐Because the telephone is potentially a source of irritation, good telephone manners are particularly important. Brevity and clarity are the two most essential qualities. (For personal calls, see Chapter Eight.)

When to telephone ☐Telephoning is done in preference to writing when no record of the conversation is needed, when you want to make or change an appointment or warn that you may be late; ask for information which can be given immediately and does not involve a lot of thought or searching; ask for leaflets or 'details' to be sent; have an informal discussion.

Making a telephone call ☐It is important to get any necessary papers together and in order before making a call. It is neither polite nor efficient to keep someone waiting while you shuffle through your notes. It is also practical to make a brief list of points to be covered, in the relevant order, and to work steadily through it, rather than rely on memory and risk backtracking to related topics.

☐If the call is likely to be a long one, it is courteous to mention this at the beginning and to check if another time would be more convenient—in effect, to make an appointment for a long call.

Answering the telephone

☐A telephonist should answer with the name of the company, preferably adding 'good morning/afternoon' and sounding reasonably cheerful. When outside calls come straight through to an office, whoever answers should state his or her name; 'John Smith (here)'. A colleague's telephone should be answered, 'John Smith's telephone'. When a secretary or telephonist has found out who is on the telephone, and has passed on the information, then it is best to begin by greeting the caller by name.

Asking the caller to wait

☐If the person asked for is speaking on another line, the telephonist or secretary should ask the caller if he would like to wait. If the caller chooses to wait, and if the wait proves to be a long one, the telephonist or secretary should cut in regularly, saying, 'I'm sorry, I'm afraid he/she's still engaged', giving the caller the opportunity perhaps to leave a message.

☐If the person asked for proves difficult to locate and the telephonist is forced to try several extensions, she should cut in regularly to explain to the caller what is happening. On no account should a caller be left holding a silent telephone, not knowing whether the connection has been cut off, forgotten, or is still intact.

Putting people off

☐The phrase 'I'm sorry, he/she's in a meeting' has become a euphemism used to put people off. 'I'm afraid he/she's busy' is not an acceptable alternative because it carries the implication 'with more important people than you'. 'I'm afraid he has someone with him', or 'I'm afraid she's out of the office at the moment' are both currently acceptable, but whatever phrase is used it should be followed with 'May I ask him to ring you back?'. If this offer is accepted, it is very discourteous of the person in question not to ring back—even though this is a favourite way of dodging unwanted callers.

Disconnections □If, for whatever reason, a call is disconnected before it is finished, the person who originated the call should be the one to ring back.

APPOINTMENTS AND MEETINGS □Making and keeping appointments are an essential part of efficient business life. It is not discourteous to call on someone without an appointment, just impractical, since the person in question may have an appointment with someone else, or be out of the office. It is not discourteous to refuse to see someone who arrives without an appointment if it is genuinely impossible to fit in a meeting. But if it is possible, it is foolish to refuse in order to make the point that you are busy. Before turning away an unexpected caller, whoever is in charge of the appointment book should offer to arrange for a meeting at some other time.

Making a visit □A visitor should arrive on time or a few moments early. If visiting a large firm it is wise to arrive at the main door five or ten minutes early, to allow time to find the relevant department. It is usually impossible for a visitor to guess how much time has been allocated to the appointment, so it is prudent to be brief and direct rather than embark on a long preamble and find that is all you have time for.

Receiving visitors □A visitor who arrives early may be asked to wait until the pre-arranged time, but one who arrives on time should not be kept waiting. If, however, a delay is unavoidable—because a sudden emergency has arisen— the person with whom the appointment has been made should personally take the time to ask the visitor to wait, to apologise, and to indicate that the situation is unusual and acute. The executive who deliberately keeps visitors waiting in order to demonstrate extreme busyness only succeeds in demonstrating inefficiency.

☐Before receiving a visitor or visitors it is obviously necessary to arrange that there are sufficient chairs in the room and to set out any relevant files. Both a man and a woman should rise to greet visitors, indicate where they may sit, and give them undivided attention during the meeting. It is for the senior of the two, or the woman, to be the first to extend a hand.

☐A visitor whose appointment is at tea or coffee time, or one who has made a long or difficult journey to keep the appointment, should be offered tea or coffee at the beginning of the meeting. The exception to this is if both parties intend the meeting to be very short and refreshments would prolong it unnecessarily.

Incoming calls

☐If at all possible, an instruction should be given that no calls are to be put through during a meeting. This is not practical in every business, but if an urgent call does come through it should be dealt with as promptly as possible, after an apology to the visitor. On no account should a long telephone call be conducted in front of a visitor unless it relates directly to the business in hand.

Ending the visit

☐It is usual for the senior of the two people to indicate that the visit is over. If the visitor is the supplicant—seeking a job, business, or free advice— it is up to the owner of the office to make some kind of concluding statement and rise. If the visitor has been invited to the firm in the hope that he will offer it business, or capital, or if he is paying for the visit (with a solicitor, perhaps) the visitor is usually the first to make a move. In practice, the majority of visits are ended by mutual agreement.

☐Both a man and a woman should rise when visitors leave and see them at least as far as the office door. If the way out is difficult to find they should be seen to the head of the stairs, or the lift, by the host or a secretary.

Cards ☐These should be engraved, not printed, on good quality card and are supposed to be used for business purposes only. (For personal visiting cards, see Chapter Eight.)

Professional cards ☐For professional cards the correct size is 3″ x 1¾″ The name should be in the middle and followed by the professional degrees, except in the case of a lawyer who will leave out the degrees but add the word 'solicitor' or 'barrister-at-law' below the name. The address goes in the bottom left-hand corner and the telephone number in the bottom right-hand corner.

Humphrey Baker
Solicitor

4 Bedford Row
London, W.C.1.   01 - 437 6591

Business cards ☐Because business cards often carry more information than professional cards, they may be slightly larger. An executive's card usually has the name in the middle, followed by any qualifications or decorations; the company name is underneath or bottom left with the address, and the telephone number bottom right. A sales representative's card usually has the name of the company in the middle, the telephone number in the top left-hand corner, the address in the bottom left-hand

corner and the representative's name in the bottom
right-hand corner. But any lay-out is acceptable as
long as it is clear and neat.

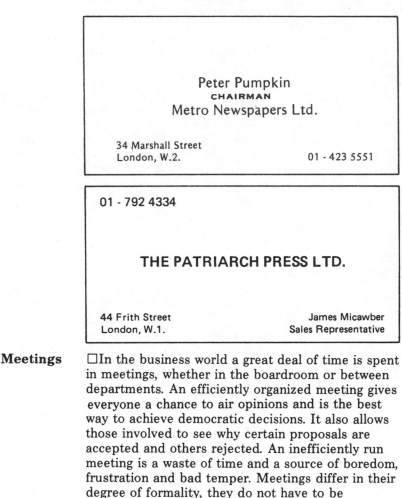

Peter Pumpkin
CHAIRMAN
Metro Newspapers Ltd.

34 Marshall Street
London, W.2.   01 - 423 5551

01 - 792 4334

THE PATRIARCH PRESS LTD.

44 Frith Street   James Micawber
London, W.1.   Sales Representative

Meetings   ☐In the business world a great deal of time is spent
in meetings, whether in the boardroom or between
departments. An efficiently organized meeting gives
everyone a chance to air opinions and is the best
way to achieve democratic decisions. It also allows
those involved to see why certain proposals are
accepted and others rejected. An inefficiently run
meeting is a waste of time and a source of boredom,
frustration and bad temper. Meetings differ in their
degree of formality, they do not have to be
extremely formal in order to be efficient.

Bye-laws   ☐In the case of board meetings and committee
meetings, there are often company bye-laws in force
which state exactly how a meeting should be

convened, how many people constitute a quorum, and how the meeting should be conducted. If these exist, it is essential that the chairman is aware of them and bound by them.

Chairman (male or female) □At a large formal meeting, a candidate for the chair is usually proposed, seconded and voted for. At a board meeting or inter-departmental meeting, it is not uncommon for the senior executive present to assume the chair as a matter of course. Even at a small and relatively informal meeting it is helpful if one person is chosen to take charge and to sum up the results.
□The chairman's job is to open the meeting; declare its purpose; ask that the minutes, if any, be read; ask that any relevant correspondence be read; work through the agenda and close the meeting. The chairman must exercise impartiality, give equal time to both sides of any argument and be scrupulously fair in declaring the result of a vote.

Secretary (male or female) ⊔At a formal meeting the secretary (and any other officer) is also proposed, seconded and voted for. At a board or inter-departmental meeting, the personal secretary of the chairman usually fulfils this role. It is up to the secretary to send out notices of the meeting, prepare and circulate the agenda, arrange seating, supply the chairman with any necessary documents during the course of the meeting, read the minutes and the correspondence and take notes of the proceedings in order to write up the new minutes afterwards.

Agenda □Unless the meeting has been called to discuss, informally, a single topic, an agenda is extremely helpful. A formal agenda will itemize the reading of the minutes from the last meeting, matters arising from these, correspondence, reports, election of new officers (if necessary) and any other business. An informal agenda will simply list the topics to be discussed in the most practical order. It is usually helpful if the secretary circulates copies of the agenda in advance so that people can gather their thoughts and their notes together before the meeting opens. An agenda enables a meeting to move more quickly and efficiently by ensuring that items are not left out, and by giving the chairman a chance to gauge roughly how much time to allow for each.

Minutes   ☐If these are considered necessary, they are usually set out as follows: date, time and place; name of chairman and other officials present; the names of others present, or their number, depending on the size of the meeting; a note of the opening formalities (including the reading of the minutes from the previous meeting); notes of points covered and decisions made, including specific tasks undertaken by specific people; the date of the next meeting; the time when the meeting finished. ☐Sometimes the reading of the minutes is waived, by common consent.

Speaking in turn   ☐At an orderly meeting a member will catch the chairman's eye in order to be invited to speak, and the chairman must be alert enough to notice this and react to it. If, however, people start shouting each other down, it is up to the chairman to restore order. The accepted method is to insist that the original speaker be heard out, and then to make a point of inviting the shouter, or shouters, to take their turn. Everyone's views must be heard before a fair vote can be held. A wise chairman who notices someone shifting and frowning, but not actually speaking, will choose a pause to say, 'Would you care to comment on that, Mr/Miss . . . ', but will not force the issue if the person declines. (Anyone who declines the chance to air views at the meeting should not expect to be listened to by selected colleagues after the meeting.) When all views have been heard, the chairman should put the matter to the vote. The time-honoured way of doing this is to ask first that those in favour say 'Aye' and then that those against say 'No', but, unless the vote goes

overwhelmingly one way or the other, it is
sometimes difficult to be certain of the outcome.
A show of hands, and a careful count of same,
is safer.

Concluding   ☐When winding up the meeting it is essential that
the chairman ensures that everyone knows exactly
what, if anything, he or she has agreed to do before
the next meeting. This should also be noted down
in the minutes, if any, so that, at the next meeting,
people may be specifically asked for the results of
their labours or enquiries.

BUSINESS   ☐Lunches and dinners are the two commonest
ENTERTAINING   forms of business entertaining and the normal social
conventions apply with two main differences. The
first is that it is, for once, perfectly in order to 'talk
shop'; the second is that seating arrangements are
unusual because the order of precedence is
different and because there are often few if any
women present.
☐The third mode of business entertainment is
notorious—the office party.

Lunches and   ☐Assuming that there is no hostess, the principal
dinners   guest should sit on the host's right, the second most
important guest on his left. Unless one of them is
the guest of honour, any women are placed at more
or less equal intervals among the company.
Business precedence overrides social precedence—
that is, a senior executive takes precedence over a
junior even if the junior is an earl. Sometimes
precedence is ignored altogether and people are
placed next to those to whom they can most
usefully talk—or else members of staff are
interspersed with guests. Any of these arrangements
is correct.
☐At a large dinner, place cards and a prominently
displayed seating plan are essential. If foreign
business contacts are being entertained, special
attention may have to be given to the choice of
food, drink and even the date. See also 'Foreign
business contacts' above.

The female host   □There are still men who are seriously embarrassed to be entertained at a restaurant by a woman, even for a business lunch. The woman should be sensitive enough to be aware of this and should do all she can to minimize this embarrassment.
□One possible way round the problem is to arrange for a buffet and wine in the office (this presupposes that it is reasonably large and comfortable and equipped with crockery, cutlery and glass). This is an efficient way of entertaining two or more business men (especially if they actually need to discuss business, since a peaceful office is more suitable than a noisy restaurant). But any woman entertaining one man on his own in this way is likely to have her motives misconstrued, especially if he is a man who already finds it hard to accept women in business.

Restaurants   □If entertaining a man in a restaurant, she should make it clear both when issuing the invitation and at the beginning of the meal that he is the guest of the firm rather than of herself. She might even arrange in advance to have the bill sent to her office, or, arriving first, (preferably choosing a restaurant where she is known) she may make it clear to the head waiter that she is the host. She should not rise when the man arrives, but apart from that should behave as suggested in the section on restaurants in Chapter 11.
□As host, she chooses the wine but, remembering that her guest is used to doing this, it might be courteous to ask his approval. If he instinctively takes over and orders the meal she should let this happen without comment. If at the end he begins to insist on paying the bill, she must be in a position to say with assurance that it is all taken care of, and then change the subject.
□For his part, the man should conduct himself exactly as if his host were male, except that after the meal he may help her on with her coat and open the restaurant door for her.

Business and press previews

☐Because there are so many of these, invitations are sometimes ignored and as a result the organizers rarely have a clear idea of how many people they will have to accomodate. Any business invitation which asks you to respond should be replied to just as any social invitation should, and it is discourteous not to attend once you have accepted. If, however, it is impossible for you to attend at the last minute, it is often acceptable to send along another representative of the company. ☐The invitation should state clearly what is offered, not only with regard to food and drink but also whether there is to be a film, a speaker or a lengthy tour around a large construction. All this helps people to decide if they have the time or the inclination to attend. If a great many members of staff are to be present they should all wear name tags. It is helpful if the most relevant members of staff—that is, the ones best equipped to answer questions—wear name tags of a different colour to everyone else's. Press releases may have been sent out with the invitations, but they should still be handed out at the door.

Office parties

☐These divide into two main types—the staff-only party and the party to which each member of staff is invited to bring one guest. If the party is of the second type it is discourteous to limit the invitation to husbands and wives only, thereby penalizing the single.
☐Office parties have a bad reputation and this is largely because people tend to drink too much, let their hair down too far, and in a sudden surge of drunken courage insult the superior they have always disliked, or make a bee-line for the one they have always fancied. If the office is small, friendly and non-hierarchical there are few dangers, but if it is large it is wise for anyone tempted to get carried away to remember that he or she has to face everyone else not just on the morning after, but five mornings a week after.
☐As on other social occasions, it is up to the older

319

to look after the younger, the senior to look after the junior. A wise chairman will simply drift away from a heavy-drinking junior executive who is treading on dangerous ground and not give him the opportunity to commit an indiscretion. It is in the worst possible taste for older members of the staff to persuade the very young to drink more than they can cope with. It is extremely difficult for a very young secretary to refuse a fourth drink from a forceful senior executive, and it is inexcusable of him to make use of this fact. As far as possible, people should protect each other from making fools of themselves.

Guests   ☐A guest at an office party should remember that he or she is in a unique position to embarrass the person who took him/her along. It is unkind to wear wildly eccentric clothes without finding out first if your companion minds. It is foolish to treat the party as anything other than a social occasion. Wives should not inform the boss that their husbands are overworked and underpaid; husbands should not explain that their wives find coping with a job and a home a bit much; no guest should correct a story told by the person who brought them, even if they know it to be a bare-faced lie; every guest should, for the course of the evening, forget all the snippets of information that have been told about various members of staff and *never* repeat them to other members of staff.

Dancing   ☐If there is dancing, each man on the staff should dance with as many company women as possible (while remembering that the first and last dance should be with his own partner). It is discourteous for senior male executives to dance only with their own and each others' wives and ignore the younger female members of staff, who are often in a majority and forced to dance with each other or stay off the floor. It is cruel to dance only with the younger female members of staff and leave the office dragon to sit alone.

Thanking □After a dinner or other major social function, a letter of thanks should be written to whoever issued the invitation. If invited as a couple, the wife should write the thank-you letter, even if the husband was the sought-after business contact. There is no need to thank for an office party but if you bump into the managing director during the day or two following, an enthusiastic comment would almost certainly be appreciated.

13 COURTSHIP

☐Establishing a relationship with someone of the
opposite sex leads into one of the most delicate of
all the areas of human communication. It is at the
same time the one that has been thrown into most
confusion by the general relaxation of the old rules.
There was a time when the correct mode of
behaviour was so firmly laid down that it could be
used as a blueprint for establishing, or trying to
establish, any new relationship. Although there was
less freedom it is probable that there were fewer
misunderstandings. Even those who chose to break
the rules had the advantage of knowing exactly
which rules they were breaking. It certainly did
not mean that no one ever got hurt, but what it did
mean was that two people embarked on a
relationship with much the same expectations and
under much the same constraints.
☐Today, expectations have broadened radically
and most constraints have been removed. It
used to be assumed that all so-called 'respectable'
attentions paid to an unmarried woman
had marriage as the object, if all went well;
now such attentions, on the part of either sex, may
legitimately have as their object sex, a close
personal relationship with no permanently binding
ties, marriage, or, sometimes, simply friendship.
The great hazard is of course that each partner may
misunderstand the other's intent or may want
something different; one may wish to live together
amicably with no long-term plans whereas the other
may be set on marriage and children. The
difficulties become very great indeed and few rules
can be reasonably set down beyond saying that it is
important not to hurt the other person, who,
assuming that he or she is emotionally involved, is
extremely vulnerable. It is also important to be
honest with oneself about one's own needs and
feelings. There is little that can be stated that
cannot be shown to be inappropriate in certain
circumstances. However, as good manners are a way
of showing consideration for others, they are very
relevant in this area.

'FIRST DATES' ☐The convention that demands that the man should issue the first invitation dies hard. The idea that the girl might do so is gradually becoming acceptable among the young in North America but it has not taken hold in Britain. It is no longer incorrect, but at this stage of social development it is certainly ill-advised. Therefore, it is to be assumed that on the first date he will be the host and she will be his guest.

The invitation ☐It is up to the host to decide what form the first 'date' will take. He does not have to offer an elaborate and expensive dinner and certainly should not choose something he cannot comfortably afford. A drink or even a walk in the park are perfectly acceptable suggestions.
☐There are two forms of invitation to a first date that are incorrect and unfair (although perfectly acceptable when people know each other better). It is wrong to ask if the other person is free at a specified time without giving further details about the evening. The girl might like the opportunity to say she will be busy on that particular day, and if she chooses to accept she will need a rough idea of what to wear, and whether or not to eat first.
☐It is also unacceptable to arrange to meet or collect her and then to greet her by saying 'What would you like to do?' What is she to say? Apart from the fact that the responsibility should be taken by whoever issued the invitation, it is very unlikely that she will know what he is prepared to spend or how far he is prepared to travel.

Refusing an invitation ☐Acceptance is easy, but refusal can be trickier, depending on what is meant by it. Someone who wants to discourage further invitations should refuse *politely* but *firmly*, give no explanation and wind up the conversation as quickly as possible. On the other hand, someone who is genuinely unable to accept, and genuinely regretful, should make this clear—perhaps by mentioning the nature of the earlier engagement and certainly by saying that she would have liked to have been able to accept.

The host ☐The host should arrive on time and should know at what time the concert begins, whether there is time for a drink or a meal before or afterwards, the best way to get to the concert hall (especially if public transport is involved) and so on. It is also up to him to have booked anything that needs booking, so avoiding sudden changes of plan and possibly fruitless searches for food or entertainment elsewhere.

The guest ☐The guest should be ready when called for or should arrive only a little late at a public meeting place (to give her host a reasonable chance of getting there first). She should have been sufficiently forewarned to be dressed suitably, and if in any doubt should follow the general rule of underdressing rather than overdressing. A bad start can colour a whole evening, and it is unnerving to a young man who is planning a meal in a simple restaurant to be faced with a girl in all her finery, obviously expecting something better.
☐If a meal is on the agenda she should remember that it is thoughtless to choose the most expensive dish on the menu, but also that it is irritating and faintly insulting to choose the cheapest.
☐The nicest guest for anyone to take out is the one who gives every appearance of having a happy time, without going too far and overwhelming the host with gratitude.

Getting home ☐At one time it was obligatory for a young man to see a girl to her door after an evening out. It is still true that if he has a car he should drive her home, but if he does not, and if they live at opposite ends of town, it may be wholly impractical to take her home and risk missing his own last bus or train. However, he should show a genuine concern, see her to her bus or train, and safely on it, or else call a taxi for her. If the girl, when asked how she is going to get home, says quite firmly that she wants a taxi, he may assume that she is prepared to pay for it

and it is entirely up to him whether or not he offers
to pay. If, on the other hand, he insists that she
take a taxi when she would have been happy with
the bus, then he must be prepared to pay. It is then
up to her whether or not she accepts this. (The old
rule that said that a girl should always carry her taxi
fare is still very sensible and practical.)
☐If he does take her home she is under no
obligation to invite him in, but she should be quite
clear about her decision and ideally should make it
known to him before he embarks on a long journey.
If he takes her home by taxi she might recommend,
before getting out, that he keeps it for himself. He
should then walk with her to her door and she
should say her thank-yous and goodnights before
opening it. If he takes her home in his car, she
should say goodbye inside it and then get out.
Again, he should see her to her door. If he takes her
home by public transport and walks the last stretch,
she should again say goodnight before opening the
door. This avoids embarrassing indecision with the
door ajar.
☐If she does choose to invite him in for coffee or a
drink, he ought not to assume she inviting him into
her bed.

Thanking ☐When courtship was more formal it was the
custom for the man to thank the girl for a pleasant
evening, even though he had planned it, organized it
and paid for it. Of course it is equally in order for
the girl to thank him, but a subsequent telephone
call or a thank-you letter is an indication of interest
and should not be indulged in by anyone unless he
or she hopes to see the other person again.

WHO PAYS ☐Here is something else that has changed. It is
very much within living memory that the man
always paid, but there are two good reasons why
this is no longer always the case, both connected
with the independence of women. In the first place,
there is no reason why a young man should pay for
everything when his girlfriend may be earning as

much as he is. It is unreasonable to expect him to bear the full cost, and also rather limiting, since the likelihood is that they can go out more often if their money is pooled. In the second place, the girl has a greater sense of freedom if she pays her way. She is under no obligations and so has greater choice in the ways in which the relationship can develop, and in the way the evening is spent.

'Going Dutch' ☐Before people know each other well enough to discuss the matter openly, this is something that has to be handled with tact. Some men are perfectly happy with such an arrangement, others need gentle persuasion. It is something that can only be played by ear, but two things are worth bearing in mind. One is that it is no longer acceptable for a girl to go out with someone three or four times without sincerely offering to pay her way, or at least returning hospitality. The other is that until she has discovered the man's views on the matter she should not wave her money around at the box office or in the restaurant but should settle up with him discreetly in private.

Returning hospitality ☐Going Dutch may not always be practical. If the man earns a great deal more than the woman and, for example, desires a meal in an expensive restaurant, he will feel unable to suggest it if he knows she will insist on halving the bill. It is not necessary to limit outings to the means of the poorest in this way. Also, if the man really does not want half the cost of an outing handed to him in cash, it is not necessary to labour the point. Returning hospitality can be a far friendlier act than splitting bills, and the ideal is probably to achieve a happy blend of the two.
☐There are various possibilities, of which two are particularly practical. One is to buy tickets for a concert or play (or a cinema that is bookable), the other is to invite him to dinner and, depending on the relationship, it may be prudent to invite at least two others in case conversation flags.

FRIENDSHIP WITHOUT SEX

☐This is perfectly possible but is likely to be tricky if one partner wants a fuller relationship. It is certainly bad manners for anyone to imply that a sexual relationship is a possibility for the future if he or she has already decided that it is not. The only reasonable approach is to be completely honest about it. It may be accepted and work very well. If, however, it becomes obvious that the other person is only continuing the friendship in the hope of something more it is only fair to end the liaison, at least for the time being. The hopeful lingering swain belongs in the literature of the Age of Chivalry, not in the real world.

SEXUAL RELATIONSHIPS

☐Because sex can be an expression of such varied emotions—affection, love, lust, even aggression—its introduction into a relationship does not necessarily signify a deeper commitment between two people, although it may. It is considerate of each party to make sure that the other knows how much commitment is intended. For instance, a mistaken assumption that a relationship is an exclusive one may lead to revelations that can be quite devastating to someone who believes himself or herself to be embarking on something serious.

Courtesies due family and friends

☐Relationships between two people nearly always have wider implications, yet there is a tendency to forget about them and to overlook not only the essential courtesies due to others but sometimes others' very existence—another manifestation of love's notorious blindness.

Parents

☐Good relationships between parents and children can be difficult if there are family tensions, but they are as important as any other kind. Once someone is legally an adult there is no necessity for a parent to know everything that happens in an offspring's life, any more than he or she should expect to be told everything about the parent's life. Privacy should be respected on both sides. However, anyone still

living in their parents' home owes them the same
courtesies due to any host and hostess. This means,
among other things, respecting their views with
regard to such matters as night visitors and noisy
arrivals home in the early hours.

Friends ☐One of the commonest discourtesies meted out to
friends is to ignore them in favour of a new
relationship. Not only is this rude but it is also
extremely short-sighted. Most relationships flourish
better in a climate of friendship than in isolation,
and if the relationship should founder or end it is
better to be surrounded by reassuring, supportive
friends than by offended ones.

Rivals ☐Some people believe that a relationship should be
exclusive from its earliest stage, others that it is
perfectly reasonable to keep two or more going at
the same time until such time as one becomes so
important that it is worth foregoing all others in its
favour. Good manners express themselves in
making it clear which approach is being pursued,
thus never putting the other person in the position
of hearing from others that he or she has rivals.

Living together ☐The decision to live together must be a mutual
one and it must be possible to discuss the proposed
life style and disposal of belongings. If this kind of
discussion is not possible then it is doubtful if living
together is a good move.
☐What is almost never acceptable (although of
course there are stories which prove that it can
work well) is gradually to seep into another person's
life and home—first of all staying for weekends,
then for greater parts of the week, until at last you
forget to go home at all. As with much of this
chapter, this is a problem that usually only afflicts
the young. Older people tend to have accumulated
so many possessions that a decision to move is
necessarily a planned one.

Practical
considerations ☐When two people have made the decision to live

together, it is wise to resolve certain practical problems before they have a chance to become bones of contention. Some—especially the financial ones—are the same whether the couple are married or living together. Others are quite specifically different. There is, for example, the question of the two different surnames. If the couple are living in accommodation where it is customary to put a name over the doorbell, or against a list of apartment numbers in the lobby, then both names should appear, not just the name of the person who moved in first.

Degrees of independence

☐There is also the question of whether or not the two people wish to be regarded as an inseparable couple when it comes to invitations. In this, as in much else, it is best to be straightforward. Close friends are usually aware of the situation and the preferences of those in it. Acquaintances may need to be told and a straightforward cheerful tone—'By the way, did you know I'm now living with so-and-so'—is best. It is worth noting that the implication of this sort of announcement is that you do want to be regarded as a couple. If you do not, you will probably need to add something like 'but we don't necessarily go everywhere together'.

Money

☐Financial disagreements can cause horrible rifts between two people sharing a house or flat, whatever their relationship. These can be avoided by deciding right at the beginning how costs are to be divided. Are you going to halve the rent, is it to be divided according to each one's means, or does the original occupant prefer to continue to pay it while the newer arrival buys the food and pays for dining out? And what about the telephone bill and the electricity bill? There are probably as many different arrangements as there are people, and the important thing is not which one is chosen but that some sensible agreement is reached before someone begins to suspect, rightly or wrongly, that he or she is paying out more than is reasonable.

329

Getting married □Engagements and weddings still tend to be traditional occasions, even if they are informal. For the accepted manner of dealing with each, see chapters 2 and 3.

ENDING A RELATIONSHIP □This is always a delicate matter. The proper approach depends to a great extent on the length of time the relationship has endured and how important it is tó either party. If it is a matter of no more than a couple of dates, there is no real need to do anything formal. Simply fail to make contact with the other person and politely decline any invitations. Needless to say, it is never acceptable to fail to turn up for an engagement that has already been arranged.
□If you have been seeing someone regularly, even if for a short time, it is only polite to make a definite break, either over the telephone or over a drink. A letter is the alternative but involves the risk of being read in the wrong tone of voice and misunderstood. It is most important to present a reason for ending the relationship which avoids hurting the other person's feelings as much as possible and white lies may be necessary. It is of course far easier not to make the next telephone call, or to ignore incoming telephone calls, but it is thoughtless to leave someone wondering if they have offended you, worrying if you are all right or hoping that you will soon telephone.
□A long-standing and close relationship obviously warrants a discussion and/or explanation.
□As is the case with most points of etiquette, awareness of, and consideration for, the other person's feelings will reveal the right approach.

14 HOUSEHOLD STAFF

☐Good manners with household staff are the same as good manners anywhere else. Kindness, courtesy and consideration are no less important within the privacy of the house, or because one is with personal employees. Moreover because the relationship is so personal these qualities are even more important than usual.

☐For most people, the smooth running of the house is the key to calm and efficiency elsewhere and the most successful employer is the one who makes herself felt rather than seen or heard. If she is well organized and considerate she will be respected, and if she exhibits a real desire to promote their comfort, while at the same time demanding a steady performance of duty, good staff will be anxious to please.

Employing staff

☐It is essential to state at the first interview precisely what the duties of staff will be and to stick to this thereafter. So many traditional posts now overlap, eg cook/housekeeper, that making expectations clear at the beginning is more important than ever.

References

☐References are essential, but it is not always wise to depend solely on the written letter of reference. A word with the former employer will establish quickly whether the applicant does in fact have the qualities needed.

☐When giving a reference, it is not fair to recommend an employee whom you would not employ yourself. On the other hand, it is essential to remember the importance of good references to someone seeking a household post, so even if you are smarting with annoyance you must be scrupulously fair and explain the good points of the applicant as well as the bad.

General considerations

☐Every employer should remember that warmth and thoughtfulness work wonders in establishing a good relationship. Making time for a chat or a cup of tea indicates interest and concern for the employee's wellbeing. Everyone resents being treated as a nonentity, and as domestic staff has not quite lost its old stigma, household staff particularly welcome an attitude of respect and concern by their employer. If an employer treats her staff as she would wish to be treated in their place, all will be well.

Discipline ☐If there is disagreement, it should always be handled in private and no more should be made of the incident than is necessary. A quiet word as soon as a child or guest is out of earshot should suffice. No employee should ever be reprimanded like a naughty child, or corrected for misdemeanours in front of others.

Conflicts ☐It is important to accept that there is always potential for conflict when there are two or more staff in a house. The housekeeper may resent preparing meals for the nanny or the 'daily' may be offended when the housekeeper treads on what she considers to be her ground. Firmness and tact are needed in handling any problems but many can be avoided completely if the employer is both fair in her treatment and careful to define each job and its tasks.

Residential staff ☐See also 'Permanent staff', below.
☐There are always special considerations when staff are living in. The employer must do everything in her power to make sure there is enough privacy for both staff and family.

Accommodation ☐Each member of staff has a room and bath (although a nanny or au pair may share this bath with the children). Usually, unless the bedroom is large enough to qualify as a bed-sitting room, there is some provision made for another room in which the staff member may relax and see friends. This may be the day nursery or playroom in the case of the nanny, a breakfast room or other little-used room for other staff.

Overtime ☐When staff are living in, there is a natural

temptation to think of them as always available and this must be resisted; hours should be made clear at the time of employment and observed by both parties.

□There may of course be special occasions when the employer will want the staff to work at times that would normally be free. Provided tact and consideration are shown, there should be no difficulty. The possibility ought to be made clear at the time of employment and the employee's agreement established in principle. When the situation arises, the employer should ask staff as early in advance as possible and compensate for the time either by giving a corresponding period of time off, or by additional pay. The employer should try to keep demands of this sort to a minimum and avoid encroaching on the employee's leisure time. Asking for a few hours' work on a day off might spoil the whole day and this should be taken into consideration in giving compensation.

PERMANENT STAFF

□Several of the household positions described here—butlers, valets and ladies' maids, for instance—are rare today. These jobs are also less well-defined than they once were, owing to the tendency to combine posts. Two positions mentioned are relatively new—mother's helps and au pairs—and because these are not grounded in tradition they are particularly prone to misunderstandings and misconceptions. But whatever the position to be filled, definite expectations on the part of both employer and employee are involved and while it is hoped that the guidelines given here will provide a useful framework for arranging the details of a contract, each case must of course be treated individually according to particular circumstances.

Taxes

□The employer is responsible for deducting a percentage of national insurance contributions from wages and paying this deduction plus the employer's own contribution to Inland Revenue. Where income tax is payable, the employer is also responsible for making the necessary deductions under P.A.Y.E.

Tipping ☐Presents, bonuses and 'rises' are the province of the employer; tips are for guests to proffer. (For details, see Chapter 12.)

Butler ☐Traditionally, the butler headed the male house servants and was in charge of the cellar and the most valuable articles in daily use, such as the silver. He carved and served at meals, assisted by the footman and made sure that everything was done properly. The butler is still in demand today at large country houses, in businesses where he may run the company dining room, and in smaller houses where he may function as a general factotum, doing everything from driving his employer to the station in the morning to pressing his suits.
☐In the past, the butler worked his way up from junior footman, but today it is common to find that the butler was formerly in the armed services.

Duties ☐These are extremely varied, depending on the circumstances of the house. In a smaller household, the butler will be expected to announce visitors, care for the cellar, carve and serve at meals, act as valet (press suits, clean shoes and see that both are repaired), drive the car and generally oversee the household. He is not expected to be in charge of the children or of the kitchen, nor to perform general domestic duties, but in nearly every case there is some flexibility.

Hours ☐The butler may be required to work long hours. He may rise before 8am to warm the car for the drive to the station and finish only when the last wine glass has been polished after dinner. As with a housekeeper (see below) he will expect a two hour rest period in the middle of the day, a day and a half off each week and preferably one weekend off per month. In addition, by law he is entitled to one paid day's leave per month, or twelve working days of holiday each year, but most households give three full weeks (fifteen paid working days) a year.

Dress □In formal houses the butler may wear tails and a black tie or a dinner jacket, but in most instances he wears a dark (black or navy) lounge suit with white shirt and dark tie.

Form of address □The butler addresses his employers as 'Sir' or 'Madam' in more traditional houses, and as 'Mr' and 'Mrs' followed by the employers' surname in less formal houses. If the employers have a title they should be addressed as 'My lord/lady' or 'Your lordship/ladyship'.
□The butler is usually called 'Mr' with his surname; in old-fashioned establishments he may be addressed by his surname only, eg 'Dawson', but this is a dying practice.

Housekeeper □A housekeeper is responsible for all of the details involved in running a house including the shopping, cooking, cleaning and laundry. How much of this work is performed by her personally depends on the size of the house and the number of other staff. The larger the house and the number of staff, the greater the likelihood that she will be occupied only with the actual running of the house. There may be a cook in charge of meals, a cleaner to keep everything polished, someone to help with the washing and ironing, a nanny for the children, and a butler to direct the household generally.

Housekeeper/cook □In most houses employing a housekeeper, she functions as housekeeper/cook, with a cleaner to help, and her duties are thus extremely flexible depending on the number in the house, whether they are at home or at work, how frequently they travel, what hours they keep, how many meals are required, whether there are any pets and what other staff are kept.
□In most cases the housekeeper does expect help

from a daily cleaner for the heavier housework and she does not expect to do anything for the children except to prepare occasional meals if there is a nanny to look after them. Because of the flexibility of the role it is essential to outline clearly at the interview what the job entails.

Hours   □A resident housekeeper's day may begin at 7am or earlier when she begins to prepare breakfast, and end when the kitchen is cleaned after dinner. A rest period of about two hours in the middle of the day is required, and most housekeepers will find time for this when the house is most quiet. In addition, she receives one and a half days off each week— and some households permit one weekend each month. As with resident nannies (see below) the more free time, the more desirable the job, and an employer who wishes to attract the best applicants will be wise to allow this extra half-day per month. □The daily housekeeper arrives at 8 or 9am and departs at 5 or 6pm, or whatever hours her employer has arranged. □By law, domestic staff are entitled to one day's paid holiday for each month worked, which amounts to twelve working days per year. It is general practice, however, to give a full three weeks' paid holiday per year, or fifteen working days.

Dress   □In more formal houses the housekeeper wears a uniform; in others she wears ordinary clothes.

Forms of address   □The housekeeper is referred to as 'Miss' or 'Mrs' followed by her surname; the older custom of calling her by her surname only is superceded. □Sometimes the housekeeper is on Christian name basis with her employers, but more often she addresses them as 'Mr' and 'Mrs' followed by their surname, or occasionally 'Sir' or 'Madam'. (For titled employers, see 'Butler' above.)

Nanny   □A nanny may be trained or untrained. A trained nanny has completed two or more years of study in infant and child care leading to a Nursery Nurse Education Board diploma (NNEB) and may have followed this with a Royal Society of Health course (RSH). Her training might have been at one of the famous residential schools (Norland or Princess Christian) or within the state system, and although the diploma is the same, the training is often quite different. Some schools do not provide experience with children under three and, more importantly, not all provide intensive training in the care of newborns, ie several weeks in a maternity unit. Therefore, when seeking a nanny for a new baby or a small child, it is wise to make sure that the applicants have had the necessary experience and/or training.

Untrained nannies □An untrained nanny is someone who has had a number of years' experience in caring for young children but has not completed the NNEB or any other course. An untrained nanny may be just as capable of providing loving and responsible care for young children; this may be determined during the interview and by checking her references.

References □Any good nanny is happy to supply references as to her character and abilities and it is essential to check these to be sure that you are hiring the best person for the job. A too-brief letter of reference gives a sure clue to investigate further, and if a previous employer is less than enthusiastic about a former nanny a telephone chat will make the situation quite clear.

Duties □A nanny takes complete responsibility for everything concerning the children. She will shop for, prepare, cook and serve all meals for them and for herself; get the children up in the morning and wash and dress them; bath them and put them to bed at night; take them to school, to dance and music lessons and any other activities; arrange for them to play with other children of a similar age; buy their clothes and toys and any other play or

educational equipment; wash, iron and mend their
clothes; keep their bedrooms and play room/day
nursery clean and tidy; babysit and generally
keep them happy, healthy and occupied. (In fully
staffed houses, the cook often prepares the nursery
meals.)

☐ Obviously, the mother may wish to shop for
clothes or bath the children and, as with any
employee, it must be made clear at the beginning
what the nanny is and is not expected to do.

☐ A nanny does not expect to be asked to do
general cleaning, ironing, washing or shopping
although she may be willing to help out of courtesy
if the house is particularly busy or short-staffed and
if a good relationship exists between the nanny and
her employer.

Hours   ☐ Traditionally, a resident nanny has one twenty-
four hour period free every week plus one full
weekend off per month, plus three weeks' holiday
per year, plus additional evenings by arrangement
when the parents are at home. This still holds true
in many homes but, increasingly, young nannies
prefer jobs that allow them more free time. The
most desirable jobs are the ones that leave most
evenings and weekends free, and the employer
should make clear what free time is allowed at the
time of the first interview.

☐ A maternity nurse in residence will expect free
time to rest during the day if she has been up with
the baby at night.

☐ A resident nanny should be able to have friends
visit her in her room or in the day nursery/playroom
during her time off. Some families still do not
permit this—an unreasonable attitude, providing
the visitors do not disturb the household.

Non-resident   ☐ The daily nanny generally works an eight to ten
nannies   hour day, arriving at 9am, or earlier, and leaving
at 5 or 6pm or whatever hours her employer has
arranged. She expects three weeks' holiday a
year. Babysitting would be by arrangement.

Dress	☐A nanny may wear a uniform (with her NNEB or other badges) if desired, but in many households she wears ordinary clothes such as jeans which are suitable for romping through the park or finger-painting with toddlers. Many nannies prefer to wear a washable white coverall while caring for tiny babies as it is easier to keep clean.
Forms of Address	☐Traditionally the nanny was called by her surname preceded by the title 'Nanny'. Thus, for example, she would be 'Nanny Edwards' or 'Nanny Smith'. (In even older tradition, the nanny would be called by the name of her employer; thus she might be Nanny Windsor at one house and when she moved to a new post, Nanny Forbes-Hamilton.) Most young nannies today, however, prefer to be called by their Christian names; again, an older nanny might prefer 'Miss' or 'Mrs'. It is very much a matter of personal choice and the nanny should be asked what she prefers to be called.
	☐In traditional or more formal homes, her employers may be addressed as 'Mr' and 'Mrs' (or other title) but increasingly both employers and nannies are on a Christian name basis. In households that prefer the more traditional form of address, there is the feeling that there is greater respect if the nanny addresses her employers formally. In more relaxed homes, employers consider that respect for authority is achieved through the relationship and a warmer atmosphere is created for the children by the more intimate form of address. The employer must decide which would make everyone most comfortable and establish this preference from the beginning.
Addressing visitors	☐When there are guests in the house, strangers or less frequent visitors should certainly be addressed formally by the nanny (as should older people). Close friends, however, may be on a Christian name basis if that is the practice in the family.
Travel	☐Generally, a nanny considers trips with the family

339

a bonus and enjoys the opportunity to see new places. However, her hours are usually longer or more flexible, and if there is no opportunity to have time off during the trip she should be paid extra money or given compensatory time off in lieu on returning home. As always, careful advance planning will help the nanny organize the children successfully and make travelling far happier for them and thus for everyone.

General considerations

☐The day has long gone when a mother would knock on the nursery door before going in to see her children, but the contemporary nanny still expects to receive both respect and support from her employer and to do her job with a minimum of interference. Many problems will be avoided if the principles of child care—the daily routine, diet, bedtimes and mealtimes, discipline, spanking or no spanking—are established at the time of employment and adhered to as closely as is practical. No nanny will be happy if a peacefully sleeping child is lifted out of bed and shown to guests. Hers will be the task of calming a weeping baby and getting it off to sleep again. Similarly the two-year-old stuffed with sweets just before lunch will have no appetite for the carefully cooked meal and will be wailing again before tea. Such disruptions of the schedule are both discourteous to the nanny and upsetting for the child. If a guest or grandmother is the culprit, it is the employer's task to restrain them tactfully, perhaps by asking their help in adhering to the child's schedule.

☐More than with any other employee (except, perhaps, a private secretary), the relationship with the nanny can help or hinder peace of mind and life-style. If the children are well taken care of and happy, attention can be paid to other matters. If they are not, the rest of life is disrupted. The more care and attention are paid towards the nanny and her concerns—which, after all, are your children—the more you and the children will reap the benefits.

Mother's help   ☐If the parent wishes to be more actively involved in the daily care of the children, a mother's help will be a better choice than a nanny. Essentially, a mother's help is just what the name suggests— someone who will help in all aspects of caring for the children, but will not take complete responsibility. She will not be trained, but she may have had previous experience in helping to care for young children. Many mother's helps go on to become untrained or trained nannies.

Duties   ☐A mother's help assists in everything relating to the children, including shopping, cooking and serving their meals, taking them to school or to other activities, playing with them, reading to them, bathing and dressing them, washing, ironing, mending, cleaning their rooms and playroom and babysitting. She also helps with such light housework as vacuuming, dusting, laying the table, making beds and washing dishes. She is not expected to do heavy housework, such as scrubbing floors, washing windows or moving heavy furniture.

Dress   ☐A mother's help wears ordinary clothes suitable for the care of children, such as jeans or washable skirts and tops.

Hours   ☐Most mother's helps live in and hours are roughly the same as for a resident nanny with twenty-four hours off each week and one weekend a month plus additional evenings by arrangement. She also expects three weeks' holiday a year.

Form of address   ☐There is no traditional mode of address for a mother's help but as she is usually a young girl, often in her teens, she is most often called by her Christian name. She normally addresses her employers as 'Mr' and 'Mrs' (or by title as appropriate) but in some homes Christian names are mutual.

Au pair   ☐An au pair is a girl not less than seventeen, who comes to Britain to learn the English language and live for a time as a member of a resident, English-speaking family. She expects to be treated as a daughter of the house and to help with the children and do light housework in exchange for her keep and pocket money (an allowance to cover entertainment and other small expenses of the kind equivalent to that given to a daughter of the same age).

Duties □She may be asked to perform similar chores to those of a mother's help—taking the children to school, giving them tea, playing with them, making beds, babysitting, dusting, laying the table and generally making herself useful—but for no more than five hours a day. This is in order to allow her time each day to attend English language classes and to study.
□In return, she expects to live as a member of the family, having her meals with the parents or children and participating in family life in every way.
□The Home Office provides a very helpful booklet outlining conditions for both EEC and non-EEC au pairs, with regulations and advice for each.

Hours □These are extremely flexible. The au pair may spend an hour in the morning helping the children to get dressed and making beds and then go to her classes, returning in the afternoon to take the children to ride their bicycles in the park. Another day's schedule might be completely different, but on no day may she be asked to spend more than five hours in chores of any kind. She also receives one full day off each week plus a weekend each month.

Form of address □See 'Mother's help' above.

General considerations □An au pair is not, strictly speaking, an employee, but it is still essential to make clear, in writing, the family schedule and the duties she is expected to

perform as soon as she arrives, or before. Every
family, even in the same country, lives by different
customs to some extent—one family may dress for
breakfast whereas another may lounge in dressing
gowns until after the second cup of coffee—and so
it is often worth listing the day in minute detail. For
example: '7 am breakfast, fully dressed. Lay the
table and make the toast. 7:30 am make the beds
etc.' Many misunderstandings and mishaps can be
avoided by explaining family routine right at the
beginning and if it is possible to explain in the girl's
own language, so much the better.

☐Experienced au pair agencies consider that it
takes three months before a girl is adjusted to a
new family life but only a few weeks before the
children are happy with the stranger. However, the
more that is made clear at the beginning and the
better the communication throughout the girl's stay,
the swifter and smoother her assimilation into the
family will be. The kind of courtesy and
consideration given to a foreign guest in the home
is equally important with an au pair. If time is taken
to find out what she can do best (she may be a
marvellous baker or wash the dog with a minimum
of fuss) she may find her niche more quickly.

Authority
☐It is important for the children to understand that
the au pair is in charge when she is asked to take
responsibility for them. The parents must also make
clear how much discipline she is allowed to impose.
The children must also understand that she is a
student and cannot be at their beck and call when
she is studying.

Family privacy
☐Many families worry that an au pair will be under
their feet all the time, disturbing their privacy. The
best way to avoid this is to help her make friends
and become independent. She will meet people at
her classes, at student parties and also at cultural
events that help bring young foreigners together.
The more active she is the happier she will
be and the more likely she is to go out and about

343

during her free time (instead of sitting at home and possibly feeling homesick and bored). A television or perhaps a record player will help keep her happy and in her own room when she is home.

Boyfriends ☐The other main worry is boyfriends. Many families avoid the problem by specifying that only girlfriends are welcome at their house and if the au pair has a boyfriend, she must entertain him elsewhere. Also, as most au pairs are teenagers, hosts generally feel a strong sense of responsibility and impose a firm curfew to make sure that a young girl is not out on her own late at night. But clearly this is an area where each case must be treated independently and a mutually acceptable arrangement made in so far as is possible.
☐Generally, there are the same worries and concerns with an au pair as with a daughter of the same age.

Cleaner ☐A cleaner may be full-time (eight hours a day, five days a week) or part-time, but the same overall rules apply. She assumes all of the daily chores involved in keeping a house clean, including dusting, polishing, washing floors and surfaces, vacuuming, sweeping, cleaning the bathrooms and kitchen (including the oven), changing beds and airing linens. In some houses she may also be responsible for washing and/or ironing.
☐A good cleaner will organize herself efficiently and allot a specific time each day or each week for specified chores. She will also appreciate a brief from her employer as to which chores are most important at any particular time, for example should a guest be coming to stay or a dinner party planned.

Fares and lunch ☐As well as her wages, which are normally paid weekly in cash, a cleaner is given money for her fares and, if her hours fit, there should be food available for her lunch. (If there is a cook, lunch will be prepared for the cleaner.)

The fully staffed house □There are still a few large establishments, mostly in the country, that maintain a complete household staff, including a footman, parlour maid, valet, chauffeur, and lady's maid. Each has a clearly defined position which has changed little over the years.

Footman □The footman is really an assistant butler. He aids the butler and assumes many of the duties that might be performed by the butler in a smaller house, such as announcing guests, waiting at table, and cleaning the silver.

Valet and lady's maid □The valet and lady's maid are close to the master and mistress of the house, receiving orders only from them, dressing them, caring for their clothes and sometimes accompanying them on trips. In smaller establishments, the butler assumes some valeting chores and it is sometimes possible to find a butler or valet from a large house who will act as valet (polishing shoes and brushing and pressing suits) for other gentlemen in his spare time.

Parlour maid □The parlour maid's post is very similar to the footman's except that she takes her orders from the lady of the house and often helps with bedmaking, mending, flower arranging and other light household chores.

Chauffeur □In addition to driving the car, the chauffeur is responsible for the upkeep of the car (or cars), keeping it clean, in good running order and available to the family at all times.
□Today many chauffeurs are in the employ of a company rather than the person they are driving and in such cases they are, strictly speaking, not at the beck and call of other members of the family.
□It is not uncommon today for those who are being driven, especially if they are men, to sit up front with the driver; the main reason for this quite often is that there is more leg room in the front seat.

TEMPORARY STAFF

☐In houses without staff, or with a 'daily' or nanny only, reliable temporary help in emergencies or for special parties can be invaluable. Generally, temporary staff can be found through agencies or by word of mouth and build up a clientele who depend on them whenever extra help is needed. Most temporary staff are thoroughly professional: experienced caterers, cooks, butlers and waiters with years of training in a variety of situations. But often people who are training in other fields do domestic work part-time: the personable young man washing the windows may be on television next week and the agency babysitter may be an aspiring violinist with the Royal College of Music. Obviously, less experienced help may need some guidance.
☐It is polite, on the arrival of temporary help, or shortly thereafter, to offer a cup of tea or, when appropriate (to a cook for instance), a drink. There is no obligation to keep them company while they drink it.

Form of address

☐As temporary help can come from almost any walk of life there is less room for old-fashioned modes of address than ever. A temporary Jeeves is 'Mr Jeeves' unless he advises you to the contrary. Some waiters or baby-sitters, expecially if young, when asked their names will say 'Harry' or 'Sarah', and if their preference is so stated it should be put into practice.
☐It is customary in all business relationships for employees to address their employers in a formal manner unless specifically asked to do otherwise.

Fees and tips

☐Some employment agencies invoice customers for the occasion at a later date. It is more usual, however, to pay the employee in person and for the agency's commission to be invoiced separately.
☐Bartenders, waiters, babysitters and cleaners tend to charge by the hour; some cooks, however, charge according to how many people they will be cooking for.
☐There is no obligation to tip temporary staff and

it is not usual to do so. But if you think the service
has been outstanding or extra service has been
given in some way, then a tip would not be out of
place. In the case of a cook or other person staying
late, an alternative might be to offer to pay for a
taxi home.

Catering firms   □Unlike employment agencies these firms supply
both staff and equipment—tables, chairs, coat-
racks, china, linen and so on. They are mainly used
for large parties, weddings and dances.

Temporary cooks   □A temporary cook will plan the menu, shop for
and prepare a meal or meals for any number of
people (she will obviously need help for large
numbers). She may be hired for a special dinner or
an entire weekend, a child's birthday party or a
twenty-fifth wedding anniversary, or she may take
over the kitchen for a country house party or stock
the freezer while the mother is away.
□She may be an ex-debutante who has completed
a Cordon Bleu course, the housekeeper/cook for a
family (moonlighting while her employers are away)
or a housewife earning extra money.
□Always take into account the cook's skills and the
household circumstances when planning the menu.
The cook will need to know in advance how many
guests are expected, how formal the occasion will
be, whether she will be required to serve at table,
what she should wear and whether there are
additional staff.

Temporary butlers   □A butler will confer with the host regarding the
wines and other drinks to be served, lay the table,
prepare the drinks cabinet and decant the wines,
serve drinks before dinner and wine with the meal,
serve the meal itself or direct its serving and offer
liqueurs after dinner. He will also open the front
door and announce guests. In addition, he will
purchase the wine or other drinks, if that is desired,
and make sure that the house has all the glasses
needed.

Temporary waiters/waitresses □Professional waiters and waitresses will be aware of how drinks or a meal ought to be served. If, however, the helpers are not professionals, they may require some direction. (see Chapter Six.) If there is a butler or cook, he or she will be in charge of the waiters/waitresses.

Bartenders □If someone is needed to serve drinks, an experienced butler or waiter will generally do the job. However, if more complicated drinks and cocktails are desired, or a wide variety of mixed drinks is to be available, it is essential to specify this and to request experienced help. It is also necessary to confer with the bartender before the event about what will be served and to make sure that all necessary ingredients and glasses are on hand.

Temporary cleaners □Most temporary cleaners will turn their hand to whatever work needs to be done. However, for heavier cleaning (moving furniture, washing windows) a man will usually be necessary. If there is any specialized work, such as ironing shirts or fine linens, this should be made clear in advance.

Babysitters □Most families have a circle of teenagers or older women whom they may call on to stay with their children, but occasionally a formal arrangement with a service may be necessary. Most babysitting agencies have carefully vetted lists that include trained nannies, nurses and other experienced staf but, as always, the more information given to the agency the more easily they can supply the right help. Babysitters generally expect to be given theii taxi fare home due to the lateness of the hours the often work. It is wise to find out the form beforehand.

15 SPORTS AND GAMES

INTRODUCTION □The etiquette of most games and sports is
virtually synonymous with their rules. The greatest
exception is probably field sports because the skills
involved can be practised outside the activities
themselves. People coming new to the hunting field,
or enjoying the novelty of a day's pheasant shooting,
may be fine riders or good shots but unacquainted
with those touches of good manners and safety
requirements that have become formalized into a
set of accepted practices and conventions. This
chapter is mainly concerned therefore with setting
out the largely unwritten rules of these two
increasingly popular sports. Although full of what to
the novice are seemingly unnecessary 'do's' and
'dont's', often concerned with dress and the finer
points of behaviour, they prove, when analysed, to
have been adopted over the years to ensure not
only the success of the day's sport but the safety of
the participants.
□A word must also be said about those games in
which the rules of etiquette are incorporated into
the rules of play. In an age when sport of all kinds
is more and more competitive (and more and more
commercialized), it has become possible to play a
particular game by the actual rules and still
disregard its etiquette. Forms of psychological
warfare, such as personal harrassment or breaking
an opponent's concentration, are increasingly
acceptable in varying degrees in different sports.
Those touches of consideration and good humour that
characterize 'being a good sport', and make
participation not merely an exercise of physique
and skill (however testing and exciting it may be)
but also a pleasant and sociable event, are often
sacrificed to the overriding desire to win. A few
examples are given here to indicate the latitude
allowed in different sports of what amounts to
'unsportsmanlike' behaviour in the interests of
playing (or more correctly winning) the game;
included also are instances where, in well-known
sports, etiquette lies outside procedural rules. Each
assumes (unlike field sports) a working knowledge

349

of the game on the part of the reader.

CRICKET ☐In cricket, a game rich in tradition whose rules delight the initiated and baffle the newcomer, a batsman can technically be given out if he strikes the same ball twice (this is presumably to prevent him in turn stopping a ball that he has hit in such an unlikely way that it will come on to his own wicket, thus making him out). However, batsmen have been known, after stopping the ball, to send it back to the bowler with what is technically a second shot. No one on the fielding side would dream of appealing to the umpire against this, although the umpire would have no choice but to give the batsman out if it happened. Indeed the captain of the fielding side would be placed in a most embarrassing position by such a breach of form. But the game is changing and no doubt one day it will happen; there are recent cases of batsmen at the bowling end being stumped without a by-your-leave by the bowler as they start to follow up towards the batting end in anticipation of a run. ☐Of course, if they are out of their crease they are technically 'out', but the convention is that the bowler must warn a batsman that he is taking advantage of him in this way before stumping him, and cases where it has happened without warning again put the unhappy fielding captain in a terrible position for although one of his team has acted in an unsporting way he cannot countermand the umpire's decision or the rules of the game. ☐But as the rules are constantly being revised they can be stretched, as in the case of substitute bowlers, where a fast bowler can be taken off and rested and a specialist fielder substituted in much the same way as players go on and off the field in American football, even though the cricket substitute rule only exists to provide a twelfth man in the case of injury.

TENNIS ☐Psychological warfare is invading tennis, where arguing with the umpire or the crowd, or even one's

opponent, may well be not only unsporting or
tiresome behaviour but also a method of
interrupting the moment when an opponent is in
top form, cooling him down and making him lose
the advantage of a winning streak. While these
tactics may be hard to quell in a high-powered
match at Wimbledon, they are totally out of place in
a sporting match between friends.

GOLF □Golf, outwardly a calm, relaxing game, is in fact a
fellowship of sufferers where each stroke is a
personal expression of achievement or failure and
no one else is to blame—your opponent, after all, is
only playing in parallel to you. It is considered bad
form to stand around and not help when your
opponent is looking for a badly lost ball, and to
proffer unsolicited advice to your opponent,
however much his game could be improved, or to
enquire from him which club he selected to play a
certain shot (in much the same way as one does not
enquire after a hand of poker whether so-and-so
held a particular card all the time). Nor is it 'the
thing' in golf to talk, cough or jingle clubs while
your opponent is addressing the ball, and care
should be taken to stand in a position where you do
not distract him as he plays his shot—strangely,
this is held to be at 90 degrees to him facing. If you
follow the spirit of golf etiquette in this way you
may slightly reduce your opponent's torment and
make yourself a more agreeable companion at the
same time.

GAMING □Gambling and the playing of games of chance
embody numerous formalities, and much of the
etiquette is incorporated into the rules to eliminate
the possibility not so much of cheating but simply
of doubt when money and reputation are at stake.
□Although you are expected to be familiar with the
rules of the game you intend to play, gambling
establishments and casinos clearly specify their
individual rules of dress and behaviour, and it is left

in no doubt that whatever they offer the gambler in terms of comfort, charm or grandeur such places only exist to match their skills with those of the players in a properly managed effort to increase their revenue.

☐In private establishments and people's homes there is an even greater necessity to remember simple good manners: be sure to acquaint yourself with any variations of rules that may affect the detail of the game being played and do not attempt to play unfamiliar games—as well as irritating the other players and making a fool of yourself, you may well lose money unnecessarily. Be careful with drink, glasses, plates and cigarettes and make sure they do not clutter the table or impede the other players.

☐The amount of coversation unrelated to the game in question ('verbals') is limited and you must be careful not to over-indulge. Above all it is not sporting to query the results of the turn of a card or the spin of a wheel—you have either won or lost, and in the latter case must put a good face on it and avoid showing too much disappointment. (It is of course equally tedious to the other players if you express too much elation on winning.)

Paying debts   ☐As far as paying debts is concerned, it is more than frowned upon not to do so; gambling debts, in many cases, are not recoverable by law and society ostracizes the man who does not pay up, declining to gamble with him on future occasions and recognizing him as a man who has behaved dishonourably.

SHOOTING   ☐Although most active sports have an element of danger, there is no more potentially lethal sport than shooting. After all, a gun has no other function but to kill and will obligingly do this in whatever direction it is pointed. Shooting is in fact so dangerous that anyone invited to shoot who has no experience should decline the invitation. The host will not only understand but will be grateful to have been saved the embarrassment of letting an inexperienced person loose with a gun amidst shooting companions.

Training

☐How does one learn about shooting? Traditionally, boys are allowed to accompany their fathers or uncles on shooting days and it is up to the experienced older man to pass on the necessary information.

☐At first the boy is deputed to carry cartridge bags and other equipment but might in time be allowed to carry an empty gun. There is also the opportunity on an organized shoot for the lad to go with the beaters, gamekeeper and doghandlers and learn to appreciate what goes into shooting behind the scenes, working with dogs and so on. The culmination of such a shooting education is the Boys' Day or Boxing Day shoot when the older guns (as participants are called) traditionally give up their places and let the youngsters have their first attempt at the real thing.

☐Those coming later to the sport and lacking the advantage of belonging to a shooting family would be well advised to visit a shooting school. There are about a dozen in the United Kingdom where not only the skills of shooting are taught, but also the safety rules and finer points of shooting manners— the two being inextricably entwined. The beginner should rely on the verdict of his instructor as to when he is ready to venture forth with a loaded gun, either on his own or in the company of others.

Handling a gun

☐Handling a gun correctly is of course the most important part of shooting etiquette. Obviously a gun, whether it is loaded or not, should *never* be pointed anywhere except up in the air or down at the ground.

☐Carry a gun on the shoulder with the trigger guard *upwards* and grasping the stock or, alternatively hold the gun under your arm with the muzzle pointing at the ground.

☐After loading a gun, close it by bringing the stock

up to the barrels. This will keep the muzzle pointing at the ground and not, inadvertently, at someone else.

☐ As it is impossible to see whether a gun is loaded or not, a convention has arisen of carrying it 'broken', that is opened with the cartridges removed so that others can see that it is indeed safe. This is quite a recent practice, many older guns considering that their training was sufficient to ensure that their gun is invariably empty between actual times of shooting. Be that as it may, with so many people coming new to the sport, this new convention serves a useful purpose.

☐ As a safety measure, a gun is always broken before it is handed to someone and it should be unloaded while crossing fences and ditches during a walking up shoot, even if it means missing a sudden opportunity for a shot. On an organized driven shoot, all guns must be unloaded between drives and it is highly improper to shoot after the signal for the end of a drive has been given, or to go in search of dead or wounded game with a loaded gun. (Signals for the beginning and end of each drive are given by whistle or horn, and vary in each shoot: it is well to enquire before moving off.)

☐ When not actually shooting, the gun should be carried in a leather or canvas sleeve.

The shooting day

☐ On an average day one is invited at 9am for 9.30am with variations of half an hour or so, depending on the time of year, amount of daylight and programme for the day. It is essential to be absolutely punctual for shooting invitations—better to be half an hour early than one minute late. A lot of planning goes into a properly organized shooting day and hosts tend not to wait for late comers for fear of spoiling everyone else's sport. So, 9am for 9.30am means assemble at 9 o'clock to put on boots and other gear and move off at 9.30 to be shooting by 10 o'clock.

☐ As many people drive a long way for a day's shooting, a cup of coffee or tea may be offered on arrival but it is advisable to bring a thermos of your own to be sure of this.

The firing line

☐On an organized shoot the guns stand in a line and the game is driven over them by a team of 10 to 20 beaters, walking in a line towards the guns and driving the game before them. For safety reasons, the guns are placed at least 35 yards apart, usually in positions indicated by a number on a stick or peg.

☐The normal number of guns in a shoot can vary from six to 10: anything over 10 tends to be unmanageable although a very pleasant day can be had with four or five companions. Before moving off, numbers are drawn to indicate each gun's position on the first drive and these are varied throughout the day to provide a chance of standing in the middle of the line of guns as well as at the ends—the middle tending to be the spot getting the most sport. (Normally two is added to your number after each drive, thus four becomes six in the next drive, then eight and so on.)

The bag in season

☐Once the guns are in position, the signal for the drive to begin is given and the game particular to the day can be shot. It is customary for the host or organizer of the shoot to explain the plan for the day before moving off and this will include details of what is to be shot and what is not.

☐Some pheasant shoots tend to begin or end the season by shooting cock pheasants only: some shoot 'cock-hen', which means you can only shoot at a hen pheasant after you have killed a cock. Some shoots leave partridge alone after Christmas and some shoots do not shoot at ground game (rabbits and hares). There are few shoots where wood pigeons are not shot but it is foolish to shoot them at the beginning of a drive as it only alerts the game to the presence of the guns. A host and his keeper will be pleased if guns kill vermin such as jays or squirrels but the shooting of foxes is a delicate point and varies from shoot to shoot, depending on the interest in fox-hunting among the guns and their relationship with the local hunt. If it is agreed that foxes are shot, it is still entirely up to the individual whether he chooses to shoot or not—he may not care to.

Behaviour ☐During the drive, keep quiet and keep out of sight as much as possible. It is of course vitally important not to shoot in the direction of the other guns or in the direction of the beaters (which is horizontally ahead); nor should one swing a gun through the shooting line. Such behaviour is not only ill-mannered but dangerous and a gun guilty of it can, not unreasonably, expect to be asked to leave the shoot. If a neighbour is handling his gun dangerously, the best thing to do is to point it out as quickly as possible, either to your host or, better still, to the man involved, as frequently people are not aware what they have done and certainly will not be able to recall it later. The only result of waiting until lunch time before mentioning it will be to create an unpleasant atmosphere over lunch.
☐During a drive it is important to remember the number of birds killed or wounded to your gun, and to mark them, so that they can be retrieved afterwards by you and the keeper, or by the pickers-up stationed with dogs at a safe distance behind the line of guns. If you think a bird is dead or wounded behind you, do not go to the next stand without making sure that some effort is being made to fetch it.
☐ It is, of course, impolite to dwell on personal scores—if you are shooting well it will be obvious to the other guns, likewise if you are shooting badly. Quite frequently, two guns shoot and kill the same bird simultaneously, the bird flying equidistantly between them and the guns choosing the same moment to fire. To poach your neighbour's birds, that is to shoot at a bird that is patently a better shot for him or is coming to him, is bad form, but if he misses or only wounds a bird it is all right to try to kill it for him. On a shoot with plenty of birds

shown it is sporting to pick the higher and more difficult targets and to leave the low birds for another day. There is nothing very clever about blowing a pheasant to pieces at close range: it is probably a dangerous shot and renders the bird inedible. Likewise, do not shoot at a rabbit or hare if it is being chased by an unruly dog, there are too many stories of dogs being killed in this way.

Driven grouse □Considered by many to be the premier form of shooting, grouse shooting has some peculiarities of its own. The guns are generally positioned in a line of butts built of stone and turf instead of at numbered pegs. The birds fly fast and low, following the contour of the moor and appearing suddenly for a few fleeting moments. The sport is very exciting, and undoubtedly more dangerous than pheasant shooting as the target presents itself at head height. Naturally, it is forbidden to fire in the direction of the other guns or the beaters as they approach the end of the drive, or to swing a gun through the line of butts. Owing to the speed and unpredictability of the grouse it is not so easy to 'poach', that is to shoot at a neighbour's bird; in fact, many experts claim there are no such niceties on a grouse moor. In any case, if you spend time looking out for and shooting at birds on each side, you are bound to miss the best shooting—those birds coming directly on to your butt.

Lunch □An invitation to shoot will specify whether guests should bring sandwiches or whether lunch will be provided. Luncheon arrangements can vary from a picnic taken in a barn or lunch hut on the moors, to a sit-down meal in a pub or the house of the host, when it can be an elaborate affair. Lunch is normally eaten in the middle of a shooting day but it may be decided, for tactical reasons, to 'shoot through' (shoot until all the drives are finished) and have lunch at the end, say 2.30pm. In this case there will be a break at noon for soup and sherry, and for the beaters to refresh themselves. It is quite

357

correct to take a pocket flask on a day's shooting: cherry brandy, sloe gin, whisky and water and a concoction known as 'Rusty Nail' (Scotch and Drambuie in equal quantities) being popular aiming juices.

The bag ☐At the end of the day, each gun is given a brace (pair) of whatever has been shot and the surplus is usually sold to pay for the cost of beaters and so on. (It may be possible to buy extra game at market prices.) On a grouse moor each gun usually receives two brace, one of young and one of old birds—a fact which should be made known to the cook.

Tipping ☐It is customary for those who are not regular guns on a shoot to tip the keeper at the end of any day's shooting, generally when he is distributing the game to the guns. Five pounds is an average tip for a decent day of about 100 head of game. If a loader has been provided, you should ask a local gun, or the host, what the rate is.

Thanking ☐If you have been someone's guest at a shoot do not forget to write and thank them afterward.

Shooting terms ☐As can be deduced from this chapter, a *gun* is not only a weapon but also refers to the individual shooting. A *drive* means each sweep made during a day's shooting and a *stand* or *peg* is where the guns are positioned, *butt* on a grouse moor. Beaters are sometimes called *drivers* in Yorkshire and *brushes* in East Anglia. In Scotland the moor is called the *hill* and a *piece* refers to a packed lunch—'Shall I bring a piece?'.At the end of a drive the keeper will shout '*All out*'. Woods are known as *coverts* (silent 't') and a *covey* is a group of grouse or partridges. A group of pheasants is a *bouquet*; snipe, a *wisp*. The *bag* (game killed in a day) is counted in *brace* (pairs) for grouse and partridges. Pheasant can be counted by the head or by brace. Duck are counted by the *couple*.
☐A *leash* is an old-fashioned expression for three pieces of the same game.

House parties ☐Many shooting days form the basis of an entertaining house party, in some cases the shoot lasting two or three days. In the case of an invitation to stay before a shoot it is as well to enquire whether dinner jackets will be necessary for dinner, as it is easy to forget that this is sometimes taken for granted in the country. On arriving, it may be the practice of the house to place guns, boots, cartridge bag and waterproof in the gun room or, in the case of a grouse moor, in the keeper's care. (These may be taken to the butt on the first drive by your loader, if there is one.)
☐The usual tips for servants in a country house apply to a shooting house party.

Loaders ☐If you are shooting double guns, it is advisable to ask your host if it will be possible to provide a loader since you may not be able to organize a competent one locally. Bear in mind, however, that shooting double guns takes considerable practice and a novice is not advised to do so.

Dogs ☐Dogs add greatly to the pleasure of shooting but they can also ruin a day for everyone. The fact is that on a really well-run shoot it is unnecessary to take a gun dog as there will be sufficient professional pickers-up to recover the game. On a more informal shoot, or in a syndicate, dogs will be welcome provided they are obedient, quiet and perform their duties adequately. Pet dogs, in fact any dog that is not a gun dog, should never be taken on a shooting day. When in doubt, leave your dog at home, however mournful it may look at the sight of you leaving in your shooting kit.

Companions ☐If you wish to bring a non-shooting companion, male or female, always ask first because this is not acceptable on some shoots and it will also affect the arrangements for lunch, transport and so on. In no circumstances can you bring a companion with the idea of him shooting or 'sharing' your gun: it is you who have been invited to shoot.

359

☐A non-shooting companion should be careful to observe the following simple rules. Wear the same clothing as if actually shooting. Do not talk either at the firing point or when walking to your position. Ask the person shooting where exactly he would like you to stand or sit, and stick to this: ideally it will be directly behind the gun and fairly near him. ☐Apart from taking an interest in the sport, there are three things you may be asked to do: hold cartridges ready so that the gun can reload more quickly, hold an unruly dog on a lead, and, most important, mark the position of fallen birds so that they can be retrieved when the shooting has finished. Host and keepers alike will appreciate a guest who can say after a drive, 'There are so many in front and so many behind'.

Shooting kit   ☐Any make of gun is acceptable on a British shoot as long as it is a double barrelled side-by-side model. There is still an unreasonable prejudice against over-and-under shot guns, while automatics and pump-guns are absolutely taboo: if you cannot hit a pheasant with two cartridges, it deserves to get away. English shotguns tend to be more valuable than imported ones, thus making a better investment, and are built to suit the man who does a great deal of shooting. Remember that in December and January in the country there is not a lot of activity on the farm and many farmers and landowners shoot several days a week.
☐For most people, the 12 bore is the favourite calibre but a 16 or 20 calibre gun is equally acceptable, provided you have an adequate supply of cartridges for it. It is, of course, very careless to run out of cartridges in the first place, but it occasionally happens; and while there is no difficulty in borrowing 12 bore cartridges on a shoot you could be caught out with 16 or 20 bore.
☐Other necessary equipment is a waterproof cartridge bag of the Payne-Galway type, and a shooting stick (seat stick) plus a waterproof coat, boots and leggings. (Should the weather not turn

too nasty, it is probable that shooting will continue in the rain.) In the old days no one bothered with waterproof coats and boots, as thick tweeds and brogues were considered quite sufficient and you can still see keepers in Scotland relying on this more comfortable attire to keep them warm and dry. There is however, no doubt that on a cold day, wet knees and water trickling down the neck can spoil one's aim.

□One of the signs of a novice is brand new equipment or equipment of gimmicky design—or simply unfamiliar to regular shooters who tend to adopt the same equipment as one another, it having proved itself. Thus most shooters choose waxed cotton Barbour type waterproofs and green studded rubber boots of the Hunter pattern.

Clothes   □The classic tweed shooting suit with knicker-bockers or plus-twos may look outlandishly old-fashioned to some but it is still the best-designed outfit for cross-country wear. Even its waistcoat is preferable to jerseys or pullovers, as it leaves the wearer's arms free and protects the stomach and the lumbar region, where the cold is often felt most. It is surprising how the wildest tweeds blend at a distance into the natural tones of the countryside, but this is because the individual purples and oranges that may affront the eye at close quarters in a pattern are but the natural colours of heather and gorse, and serve to camouflage the wearer. There is however, no need to wear actual camouflage or military surplus garments. Jackets with too many loops, toggles and leather patches should be avoided too. They have been got up by the makers to look sporty but will only make your neighbours nervous.

□On many shoots, collars and ties are worn, but for syndicates and informal invitations a roll-necked sweater will do. Hats are *de rigeur:* the most acceptable for pheasant shooting is the brown trilby but for grouse shooting something with a lower profile is preferable. In bad weather the tweed deerstalker and the fore-and-aft come into their own.

Words of wisdom ☐Perhaps the final word on shooting etiquette and the concomitant rules of safety is expressed in the well-known poem written by Mark Beaufoy, MP for his son H.M. Beaufoy, on reaching the age of 13.

Never, never let your gun
Pointed be at anyone:
That it may unloaded be
Matters not the least to me.

When a hedge of fence you cross,
Though in time it cause a loss,
From your gun the cartridge take
For the greater safety sake.

If 'twixt you and neighbouring gun
Bird may fly, or beast may run,
Let this maxim e'er be thine—
Follow not across the line.

Stops and beaters oft unseen,
Lurk behind some leafy screen:
Calm and steady always be,
Never shoot where you can't see.

Keep your place and silent be,
Game can hear and game can see:
Don't be greedy, better spared
Is a pheasant than one shared.

You may kill or you may miss,
But at all times think of this:
All the pheasants ever bred
Won't repay for one man dead.

HUNTING ☐Hunting etiquette is the overt expression of the rules of hunting which must be observed to enjoy the day successfully and safely. This is not to say that hunting is a hidebound, restrictive sport: for the

362

horseman, hunting is exciting, even competitive and for the hound man, absorbing and equally exciting, but this combination of fun can easily be spoilt by uncontrolled or ignorant behaviour. There is another important consideration: it is only possible to hunt unimpeded with the permission and cooperation of the landowners and farmers over whose ground the quarry elects to run. This means that a basic knowledge of the countryside and farming is as important as that of hunting itself. So having studied the do's and do not's, the most important advice to those coming new to hunting or wishing to improve their knowledge of hunting terminology and procedure is to keep quiet and keep their eyes, ears and minds open. Always remember that houndwork, i.e. the skill and experience of the Master and huntsman in controlling the pack, is the basis of the day's activity.

Preliminaries □Obtaining a day's hunting is not as easy a matter as might be imagined. People who are not members of a hunt can only hunt by invitation of a member, except with those hunts that accept visitors. (This is indicated in *Bailey's Hunting Directory* and in the sporting press.) Subscribers to a hunt receive all information about its activities from the hunt secretary and are welcome to attend meets and social events, but the number of riding members and their guests is nowadays strictly limited. This is because it is difficult to control fields of over 200 riders, the hooves of whose horses can do untold damage to fields and crops. With foot packs, beagles and bassetts there may not be such restrictions on outsiders but subscriptions will soon be invited from regular visitors.

□Mounted hunts, i.e. foxhounds, harriers and staghounds, are run by masters of hounds, with the assistance of a committee and a chairman, and operate like any club: qualification for admission to membership is related to behaviour on the hunting field, knowledge of hunting and a helpful attitude in times when responsibilities have become shared,

363

which in the past would have fallen four-square on the Master's shoulders.

The MFH ☐Master of Foxhounds (or Master of Hounds) is a title that is much respected in the countryside. The initials MFH should normally be used after the name of the Master when writing to him. As the man who has responsibility for the day, he has unchallenged authority over it and can send home anyone whose conduct or manners are unacceptable. He also has the right to take himself and his hounds home if he feels that events of the day are not up to his standard.

☐The Master either hunts hounds himself ('carries the horn') or has a professional huntsman: if the former, the huntsman becomes the kennel huntsman and may 'carry a whip' on hunting days (assist the Master as a whipper-in). If the Master hunts hounds himself he will be assisted by a Field Master (often a joint Master of the hunt) who will be responsible for controlling the field. When not hunting, hounds are always led by one of the two whips while the master leads the field behind them.

The field ☐This refers to all the horsemen taking part in the hunt, with the exception of the Master and hunt servants.

Hounds ☐The hounds are referred to as *hounds,* not 'the' hounds or, worse, dogs. Collectively they are known as the *pack.* Their tails are known as *sterns* (pronounced 'starns') as opposed to the fox, which has a *brush* and a *mask* (head). Hounds *give tongue* instead of barking and the noise they make in a pack is known as *music,* being an important element in knowing where you are and what is going on.

☐Hounds are counted in *couples* and foxes in *braces.* When hounds are hunting, they are said to be *running* and the direction they take (the *scent* of the fox) is known as the *line.* Hounds live in *kennels* and can be divided for obvious reasons into the *dog pack* and the *bitch pack,* hunting on different days. (A

364

male fox is a *dog* and a female a *vixen*.) As puppies,
hounds are *walked* (boarded out) individually or in
couples with farmers and subscribers until the *puppy
show*, a social event where the *young entry* (the new
hounds) are judged.

Dg **Dress**

□It is important to be familiar with the variations of
dress on the hunting field as they all relate to the
role of the wearer and his position in the hunt.

Master and hunt
servants

□The Master and hunt servants are dressed as
follows: hunting cap, white hunting tie with plain pin
over hunting vest (a kind of woollen shirt with no
collar), waistcoat, hunt coat of a different cut to that
of the members, white breeches, hunting boots and
spurs plus white gloves and a white or light coloured
hunting whip. The hunt coat will be scarlet or in the
specific colours of the hunt and will have a higher
collar and larger skirt than that of the members, for
protective reasons.

Members
and guests

□The correct dress for men is a silk (top) hat,
hunting tie with plain pin, black coat, waistcoat, buff
breeches, black boots, spurs and yellow gloves; or
white breeches with hunting boots (black boots with
mahogany tops which appear unpolished because
originally the brown was the inner side of a turned
down top).
□Male and female members wear the hunt button
and lady members a bowler hat. Ladies wear black
boots without mahogany tops. Those ladies who
choose to ride side-saddle can wear either a tall hat
or a bowler but they should also wear a veil.
□Farmers and their families, by reason of the fact
that it is their land or crops over which the hunt
rides, have the privilege of wearing riding caps
similar to the Master's and hunt servants'. It is not
strictly correct for member's children to wear riding
caps; they should wear bowlers but caps for
children are accepted in some countries. (A country
is the defined territory of a hunt. It can be divided
into 'the Monday country', the 'Saturday country'

and so on depending on the areas where the Master habitually takes hounds on a particular day of the week.)

Scarlet ☐The traditional red or scarlet coat with distinctive hunt collar and buttons is worn by men at the invitation of the Master, except in those hunts where the hunt colours are blue, mulberry, green or some other individual tone. For this reason, there is some difference of opinion as to whether the expression 'hunting pink' is a correct term, referring as it does to a particular cut of coat, Mr Pink being an eighteenth century tailor who was left with a surplus of scarlet military material at the abrupt end of the American Civil War.

Hunting tie ☐The hunting tie (stock) historically evolved to protect the neck from the whip lash effect of fast jumping and can still be used in emergencies as a bandage or sling for people, or as a tourniquet for horses. It is tied in a variety of ways and always fixed with a plain gold pin.

Ratcatcher ☐Ratcatcher is a tweed hacking jacket and breeches or jodphurs and is only worn by little children and for cub-hunting—the days at the early part of the season when young hounds are initiated and litters of foxes thinned out.
☐The Master and hunt staff remain formally dressed for cub-hunting.

Exceptions ☐It is a Master of Hounds' privilege to wear his own hunt colours when hunting with another pack. Bear in mind that these rules of dress represent those in general practice in the United Kingdom and Ireland but that there may be local variations in individual hunts, in particular with regard to evening dress for hunt balls.

The meet ☐Let us now see how the etiquette and terminology are applied to a typical day. The fundamental rule is to remember that it is not you who are hunting the fox, but a pack of hounds under the direction of the Master and hunt staff. Thus it is essential to keep well away from the pack, not to override them and in no circumstance to overtake or ride in front of the Master or huntsman. It is also considered bad form to choose to follow whoever is hunting hounds, although the Field Master will tend to select a line for the field to follow. This, of course, puts a responsibility on him to ride faster and more skillfully than others.

Arriving ☐The day (i.e. the day's hunting and the events leading up to it) starts promptly at eleven o'clock with the *meet*, the location of which is notified to subscribers by postcard by the hunt secretary and also published in the local and sporting papers. People living nearby *hack* (ride) to the meet, while others *box* (use motor horse-boxes). It is customary to make your presence known to the Master with a 'good morning'.

Cap fee ☐For the day's hunting you will have to pay a *cap* to the hunt treasurer or someone deputed to collect it—on no account to the Master or hunt staff.

Moving off ☐When hounds *move off* they are taken to a *covert* (pronounced cover) which could reasonably be expected to hold a fox, followed by the field who are careful to keep well behind.
☐When a fox *breaks cover* the hunt is on, being signalled by short ('gone away') blasts on the horn, probably after a *holloa* pronounced 'holler' from someone who has seen the fox depart.

Gone away ☐You may be well placed to see the fox 'go away', and thus be able to alert the Master about this. What is the correct procedure? A well known piece of advice on seeing a fox is to 'count to ten before doing anything', the purpose of the holloa being not only to alert the Master and huntsman of the fox's departure, but also to indicate its direction. If you can actually see the Master or huntsman, raise your hat in the air and point your horse in the direction of the fox's *line:* this will avoid a lot of screeching which may distract the hounds from picking up the *scent* of the fox. When they are on this the pack will 'full cry' until it *checks,* upon which, whoever is hunting them will make a *cast,* i.e. take them in a circle for them to retrieve the scent. If by chance they pick it up backwards it is known as running *heel way.* The hunt continues until the fox is either killed, lost or *goes to ground,* i.e. disappears down an *unstopped earth* (open hole).

Hunting tips   □A run like the above is, of course, the most exciting aspect of a day's hunting but there are many moments when the field has to wait and watch for a fox to be found or a line to be picked up. Here are some points to watch.

Roads   □Take care not to obstruct country lanes while waiting for something to happen, in fact avoid roads, many fatal accidents to horses, people and hounds are connected with cars.

Kicking   □Many horses kick (a red ribbon on the tail denotes this) and it is as well to keep your distance from other horses at all times. It is also important to give other riders enough room to take a good run at jumps as on a big day it can get congested at jumping points.
□When hounds are passing horses on a road, turn your horse's head towards them to avoid the possibility of kicking one. If a hound does get kicked by your horse, report it to the hunt staff and it is polite to write a note of apology to the Master afterwards.

Jumping   □Never cut in front of another rider who is about to jump. Do not present a horse to a jump until the person in front is safely over. This is the cause of many accidents.

Gates   □Always close gates. If someone gets down to open

a gate for you, it is polite to wait for him to remount before continuing on. Always be ready to open a gate for the Master or huntsman. During a run each rider may push the gate open with the tip of the whip for himself and wide enough to enable the next rider to catch it with the tip of his whip before it shuts.

Courtesies ☐Nowadays, sixty per cent of the field or more may be women and apart from reasonable courtesy it is not necessary to defer in any way to what can hardly be described on the hunting field as the weaker sex. The only exception to this is when it is necessary for one person to dismount, when it is still customary for the man to get off his horse rather than the woman. ☐As far as helping people who have fallen or catching riderless horses is concerned, it really depends on how you would like to be treated yourself: if a general habit spreads in a hunt of not helping others in this way the members are in for some miserable days. Of course, if someone is hurt you must stop and give what assistance you can.

Barbed wire ☐This is one of the most dangerous features of the hunting field, being difficult to see, and you should warn your fellow riders of it if you spot it by calling out 'Ware (pronounced 'wor') wire!'. Similarly, if a rider seems to be unaware of the presence of the pack or in danger of jumping on hounds you should warn him with the expression 'Ware hounds'.

The kill ☐When a fox is killed take care to keep your horse away from hounds and be ready to hold one of the hunt servants' horses if necessary.

Farmer's point of view ☐While the subscriptions to a hunt go largely to the day-to-day expenses of hunting, paying for the upkeep of its hounds and horses and the wages of the hunt servants, a greater proportion goes today towards supporting the hunt's presence in its country; mending damaged fences, paying restitution for crops and chickens or reared pheasants on shoots that have allegedly been 'chopped' (killed by over-enthusiastic hounds), giving suppers to farmers, gamekeepers and supporters and building hunt jumps free of barbed wire to facilitate open runs. □In many cases an individual member of the hunt will take responsibility for a particular job but overall these duties are the responsibility of the Master. To avoid increasing his burden, it is as well to know what fields planted with winter corn or clover look like so as to avoid them: market gardens should never be entered, nor should fields full of sheep or young cattle and, of course, gates must always be shut, however inconvenient this may be.

16 DRESS

☐'A man of sense,' declared Lord Chesterfield, a
gentleman well versed in the subtlest nuances of
modes and manners, 'carefully avoids any particular
character in his dress'. Anthony Trollope, the
Victorian novelist, was of like opinion: 'I hold that
gentleman to be the best dressed whose dress no
one observes.' Beau Brummel, that Regency arbiter
and glass of fashion, considered any item of dress
that excited the least attention to be, by that token,
a regrettable lapse of taste.
☐Even though there is today considerable
flexibility in the degrees of informality or casualness
observed in different groups, on the whole these
maxims still apply to men's dress which has
remained relatively static and slow to evolve
different—and acceptable—styles. It is consequently
more easily regulated than for women by general
opinion as to what is or is not proper.
☐Fashion for women is less mined with sartorial
pitfalls but more difficult to give guidelines for.
Increasingly, since the 1960s, it is attuned to
whims, to revolution rather than evolution, and
often genuine individuality is welcomed rather than
frowned upon in fashionable circles. Errors of
judgement, unless very obviously so, are merely
regarded as evidence of character or a novel variant
on current fashion, rather than serious blunders. By
and large, age and figure are more immediate
concerns for women than social norms. Except on
the most formal or traditional occasions, conventions
scarcely apply.

Motivation ☐People who dress solely to please themselves are
rare; most of us are governed in our style of dress
by the social standards of the group we work with
and the friends we have. And, of course,
conventions of appropriate dress vary from
profession to profession: an advertising agency will
be more relaxed in its attitudes to dress than a
bank or a lawyer's office. An art director for a
magazine may feel positively obliged to express
character and individuality by eccentricities of dress

371

because that is what is expected. He or she lives up to a self image plus an image that is imposed by others in precisely the same way as a bank manager encourages confidence by a more sober manner of dress. Each has a professional interest in promoting one aspect of character over another and dresses to that end.

□More often than not the habits of work spill over into those of social life. We all associate with friends who generally are like-minded in social attitudes and to some extent share common interests, and our style of dress reflects our social choices. This is particularly true of the young (of any age between early teens and late twenties). They dress in a manner that is acceptable to their own friends and these constitute a society as rigid and inflexible as any other tightly-knit group of people sharing largely the same aspirations and views. To force a young person to dress in a manner unacceptable to his or her own society nearly always leads to misery and social isolation. After the mid-twenties, social life tends to formalise slightly, and a few conventions observed by the majority of the adult population are gladly adopted.

□Dress, then, is partly intended to show that the wearer is fit for the particular society of which he or she is, or aspires to be, a member. In such a case, fashion is generally the only dictator of convention and beauty is solely in the eyes of those whom one wishes to impress.

Conflicts   □Group dress is nothing new. We are all familiar with the class conventions that produced folk or peasant costumes and the uniformity associated with schools and military life. Laws have even existed prohibiting people of inferior status and means from wearing rich fabrics such as corduroy (literally, cloth of kings). The fragmentation of contemporary dress habits is mainly based on degrees of casualness and has nothing to do with class in the usual sense. But it does involve exclusiveness and thereby endangers social harmony. For when dress is used, even inadvertently, to constitute a badge of membership, it becomes tribal dress. The mildest confrontation can cause consternation: a stockbroker and his wife, for example, dressed respectively in a three-piece suit and long evening skirt are bound to feel uncomfortable and demoralized at a television producer's party where all the other guests wear jeans or motorcycle clothes. No one can be at ease who is made to feel a caricature or an outcast and as long as sectarian dress exists these social pitfalls are to some extent unavoidable. The considerate host or hostess can help prevent them by indicating as far as possible when issuing an invitation to those who may be unfamiliar with their lifestyle, the nature of the party and the group who will be there.

DRESS FOR MEN □Within the conventional rules of dress, both casual and formal, certain basic rules are observed and these include nuances about such seeming inconsequentials as waistcoat buttons and handkerchiefs. Of course it is perfectly possible to flout the rules and appear in as eccentric or *outré* attire as you like but unless such independence is based on a knowledge of what the proper form is, there is the danger of merely creating a solecism.

Suits □Increasingly, rules about appropriate dress for work are being relaxed, but it is still normal in the vast majority of offices to wear a dark suit. Fashion and figure will dictate whether the suit is single or double-breasted, or consists of two or three pieces. A double-breasted suit is usually more flattering to fuller figures. When sitting down, it is correct to unfasten the lower jacket button of a double-breasted suit to avoid unsightly wrinkling of the fabric. The jacket should be re-buttoned on getting up and on no occasion should more than two buttons be fastened as the top pair are merely decorative. On a single-breasted suit, only one button on the jacket, the middle one, is fastened. □Town suits should be of good quality cloth—

373

ideally all-wool worsted—and subdued in colour.If patterned, the design should be discreet—pinstripes, birdseyes, pinheads or unfussy checks are best—and although oxford grey and navy are the most traditional suit colours, brown is also popular (but would not be worn on formal occasions). Tweed suits, though acceptable, are not often seen in cities, except possibly on Fridays when the wearer is going to the country for the weekend. A combination of sports jacket and flannel trousers in town usually means the wearer is an American or European.

☐Suit jackets should be long enough to cover the seat of the trousers and should hang evenly all round. Jacket sleeves should reach the base of the hand when the arms are straight, and the collar should fit closely round the back of the neck with about half an inch of shirt collar showing above it. Shirt cuffs should show about half an inch below the jacket sleeves.

☐The bottom of the trouser leg rests on the front of the shoe and should be slightly longer at the back. On a well-made bespoke suit, virtually every button will be functional; cuff buttons unbutton, for example, so that sleeve cuffs can be turned back to wash one's hands.

Waistcoats

☐If a waistcoat is worn, the lowest button is usually left undone.

Pockets

☐It is not correct to put things in the top outside pocket of a town suit, this ideally includes handkerchiefs as well as pens. Nor is it correct to put a wallet in the back pocket of trousers. The wallet goes in the inside jacket pocket, as do pens and pencils, and the handkerchief goes in the sleeve of the jacket (tucked in out of sight) or in an inside pocket.

Shirts and ties

☐White, pastel shades, stripes or discreet checks are all correct shirt colours with town suits. With tweeds or casual clothes, patterns may be bolder

and it is not necessary to wear a tie. With a town suit a tie is held to be essential and the general rule is that a patterned tie is worn with a plain shirt and vice versa. Bow ties or long ties are a matter of personal taste but if the latter is worn it should be tied so that the triangle on the front end of the tie overlaps the waistband of the trousers.
□Regimental, school or club ties are most appropriate when attending a function connected with the associations they represent, such as military functions, school reunions, or sporting occasions like a cricket match. But the advantages of 'old school ties' in making business contacts and other useful associations have led to considerable waiving of this convention. It is, however, most incorrect to wear the tie of an organization with which you have no legitimate connection.

Shoes
□In town, oxford shoes are appropriate for wearing with a dark suit. Soft, slip-on shoes are also popular but these should be plain and unadorned with glittering buckles and redundant decoration. With grey or navy suits, black shoes are correct whereas with tweeds and brown suits, brown shoes are normally worn. One woman who is an excellent judge of character claims that she can tell at a glance most about a man by his shoes, and since this may well be the only clothing that he has selected himself, the observation is worth noting.

Socks
□These should be as plain as possible—no clocks up the side—and colours should be dark, though with tweeds argyle socks are often worn.

Hats
□Hats are disappearing. Even the traditional bowler is rarely worn in the City and, except on certain very formal occasions when a top hat is worn (or carried), there is no need to have a hat. Caps are still very popular for country wear. Under no circumstances does a man wear a hat indoors.

Country clothes
□Out of town, away from the office, greater

latitude is allowed. The rule is, as always, to dress 'down' rather than 'up' and many men prefer comfort to any form of convention. Comfort may be a pair of old familiar jeans and an open-necked shirt and sweater, and few attires are better-suited to the needs of ordinary leisure or domestic chores. The traditional alternative is of course flannel trousers and a baggy well-worn tweed jacket and viyella shirt. Sports have their own special attire for which there is often little flexibility since most forms of traditional sporting dress have arisen for sound practical reasons (see Chapter 15).

Scotland □A kilt, black kilt jacket and plain tie is traditional Scottish dress, and a tweed kilt jacket is permissable in the country.

Formal wear □There is still a number of occasions at which morning dress or traditional evening dress is worn, but these are shrinking or the need to wear them is made optional. Court dress, with its knee breeches and buckled pumps, has disappeared completely except for certain functionaries and special events in the legal profession. Full evening dress, or 'white tie', is rarely worn at balls although it is sometimes seen at State or livery company dinners. Dinner jackets ('black tie') appear at very few dinners but are usual at formal dances. Whenever morning or evening dress *is* worn, however, fairly rigid rules apply about what and how it is worn.

Morning dress □This is still worn at investitures, coronations, state openings of parliament, weddings, and royal Ascot as well as other special events. For specific instructions see the particular event.
□The most traditional form of morning dress consists of a black morning coat and striped trousers or, sometimes, black and white checked trousers. A black top hat is essential and yellow chamois gloves are correct, though dying out. Shoes should be black patent leather or calf oxford, and a plain coloured doeskin waistcoat, a white shirt with stiff

collar, a silver tie and pearl tie pin are also worn. ☐At such festive functions as royal garden parties or Ascot—or where morning dress is 'requested'— there is the option of a grey top hat (known as a white hat). Often seen too are grey three-piece morning suits and sometimes these have specially fashionable details, such as bindings on the lapel edges. With a grey morning suit, grey gloves and a grey top hat are worn.

Full evening dress ☐Full evening dress, or 'white tie', is rarely required except on the most formal occasions. It consists of a black tail coat, white Marcella (piqué) stiff-fronted shirt with separate wing collar and a white Marcella bow tie and waistcoat. The black dress trousers traditionally have two rows of black braid down the outside leg. Gold, pearl or mother-of-pearl studs and matching cufflinks are worn and, strictly speaking, shoes should be patent leather court pumps but patent leather oxfords are usual nowadays.
☐Overall, a single-breasted Chesterfield-style coat is appropriate, or a black evening cloak. A black silk top hat, white kid gloves and a black ebony cane with silver or gold knob are elegant extras.

Evening dress ☐Referred to in conversation as a 'dinner jacket' and on invitations as 'black tie', this dress comprises a tailless black jacket and matching trousers. The trousers normally have one row of black braid down the outside leg. The shirt may be either soft white Marcella (piqué) fronted, or pleated in front, and is worn with a black silk or velvet bow tie. If a waistcoat is worn, it too is normally black. The alternative is a black silk cummerbund (waistcoat and cummerbund are never worn together). A double-breasted jacket precludes the necessity of wearing either. Shoes worn with evening dress are always black, as are socks.
☐In hot climates or on summer nights, a white dinner jacket is often worn with black trousers and cummerbund.

Options   □Increasingly, dark lounge suits are worn in place of evening dress and these are becoming more and more acceptable. A black velvet jacket and bow tie or a dark silk suit are often seen too. Plum, navy or figured patterns crop up now and again as fashionable variations on conventional dinner dress, as do frilly shirts, but unless you feel that you or your *milieu* make it possible to carry this off successfully it is good advice to heed the dictums about restraint mentioned at the beginning of this chapter.

Jewellery   □If worn at all, jewellery should be simple and discreet. This is always true if worn with formal or day wear but with casual clothes there is a modern tendency for men to wear more ostentatious jewellery than has been acceptable in the past. It is a matter of personal taste how much an individual chooses to wear and to what degree it suits the type of dress he favours. Sober suits demand sober jewellery, whereas casual clothes may demand or allow rather more emphatic accessories.
□The general rule is that a signet ring may be worn on the little finger of the left hand. A wristwatch or a pocket watch are worn, according to taste. Cufflinks are usually plain or crested, if appropriate, and normally of some precious metal, but many men prefer simply to button shirt cuffs, dispensing with cufflinks altogether except on formal occasions.

Decorations and medals   □Decorations and medals may be worn on those occasions when the person responsible for the function deems it fitting. On such occasions it is indicated on the invitation card. The following is appropriate with different style of dress:

Full evening dress   □The knights of the various orders of chivalry wear a broad ribbon and badge of the senior British order that they have, unless on certain occasions it is more appropriate to wear a foreign order.
□Up to four stars may be worn on the left side of

the dress coat and, in addition, one neck badge on a miniature ribbon, which is very narrow, may be worn under the collar and hang just below the tie.

☐Miniature badges of orders, decorations and medals are worn on a medal bar, except the Garter, Thistle, Order of Merit, Companion of Honour and the Baronet's Badge. These are not worn in miniature. Companions and Commanders of Orders may wear one neck badge, and their other miniature medals on a bar.

Dinner jacket
☐If decorations are prescribed, the miniatures on a bar are worn, and one star may be worn on the left breast and/or one neck badge may be worn on a narrow ribbon under the collar and hang below the tie.

Morning dress
☐The wearing of decorations and medals with morning dress is quite rare and it should be indicated on the invitation to the function. If prescribed, then up to four stars may be worn as described on the dress coat and those full size orders, decorations and medals are worn mounted on a bar on the left side of the coat.

Lounge suits
☐On occasions such as Remembrance Sunday services and Service gatherings, it is customary to wear full size insignia and medals mounted on a bar on the left-hand side of the jacket. On these occasions, one neck badge can be worn but other badges and stars are not worn.

DRESS FOR WOMEN
☐The days are long gone when nearly every hour in the life of a woman of leisure was occupied by her couturier, hairdresser and social life. Gone, too, very largely, is her responsibility to reflect, through her dress and appearance, the status and wealth of her husband. Life today is too full of other occupations for detailed and scrupulous observation of the minutae of social rituals, and clothes, like many another preoccupation, have become simplified

almost in inverse proportion to the increasing complexity of demands made in other areas of a busy woman's life. The rules of correct dress for even the most formal occasions have relaxed considerably.

☐The chief guideline to dress used to be that it is better to be underdressed than overdressed. Given the individual line women's dress has taken, this has to some extent been superceded by the admonition to dress as you feel and match the mood with the clothes, but anyone who is in doubt about the circumstances and style of an occasion is still advised to beware of overdressing. Clothes and social confidence are inextricably linked and to appear in a party dress when everyone at the party is in jeans is a marginally greater *gaffe* than the reverse, since it indicates that too much, rather than too little, has been made of the occasion.

☐The major consideration that all women should—and normally do—make in their choice of dress is that people must look at each other, and it is only polite to make the sight as pleasant as possible. This can be achieved partly through a proper perspective about age, height and weight and a firm policy to avoid slovenliness. Large fat women do not look good in vividly coloured, large patterned, tight dresses, though an amazing number seem to wear them. Frills and furbelows look foolish on the elderly. Fashion trends favour the young and slim, yet the fact that these trends are no longer the dictators they used to be means that it is possible for any woman to develop a style of dress that suits her own age, figure and lifestyle. This is the modern definition of a well-dressed woman.

Individuality   ☐For all social functions, even though wide latitude is accorded the choice of appropriate dress, there is always a norm and, unless you are naturally adventurous—and valued for it—it is not wise to depart radically in your style of dress from those with whom you will be in contact. Dress, as has been said, is partly a badge of membership and

excessive flouting of conventions may say, or be
seen to say, 'You're not my sort' or 'I don't belong
here', things which, even subtly expressed, are an
obvious breach of good manners.

Day wear □What is sauce for the goose is sauce for the
gander, and men and women increasingly dress
alike nowadays. Women often feel more comfortable
in the standard uniform of shirt, sweater and jeans,
or trousers, for walking, driving, shopping,
housework or general relaxation. Many women wear
jeans to work but this of course is governed by the
environment one works in. Working women must
often dress in the morning to meet all eventualities
of the day and evening just as men do; business
meetings, interviews, lunches, welcoming clients or
guests, drinks parties and the theatre or a dinner
party all have to be taken into account. The wisest
course is to dress in something simple—a smart
dress or a tailored suit, a skirt and shirt, or jacket
and trousers. The multiple choices which are open
to women (unlike men) have some advantages and
some disadvantages. It complicates the solution but
also provides a latitude for different modes of life
and personal style.

Trousers □Trousers can be worn *almost* anywhere, but there
still exist stubborn pockets of resistance where
women in trousers are received with less than
rapture. In such cases, unless one is in a militant
mood, it is easier all round to comply, and if there
is doubt about whether or not trousers will be
frowned upon it is worth checking first.

Special occasions □Diaphanous or long dresses may be worn, if you
are determined to do so, to a garden party or at
Ascot, but short dresses or tailored suits are the
norm. Weddings no longer demand elaborate outfits
and hats, and mourning dress is rarely seen. At
funerals, unless you are a member of the deceased's
immediate family, or a very close friend, grey or
some subdued colour is more usual than black. (See

381

also the particular occasion.)

Evening dress

□Where an invitation indicates an opportunity for guests to dress up most women will happily do so. It is a tribute to your hosts to show that you have taken some pains to do honour to the occasion they have been kind enough to invite you to. Balls, galas, and any invitation that stipulates 'black tie' for men, require that women wear something festive. Long or short dresses, or even decorative evening trousers may be worn, according to fashion and preference, but they must be of sufficiently opulent fabric or design to acknowledge the specialness of the occasion.

Gloves

□Once a sign of a well-bred lady, gloves have become optional accessories, largely reverting to their original purpose of keeping the hands warm. But when they are worn as part of a costume then certain rules apply: very long or very short gloves are worn with short-sleeved or sleeveless outfits; and with three-quarter length sleeves, gloves should reach the sleeve which, in turn, should overlap them slightly. Long white kid gloves such as used to be worn to balls, are rarely seen nowadays except perhaps in the presence of royalty, but when they are worn the correct practice is to leave them on when dancing or in a receiving line and remove them entirely when eating.

Hats

□Even on the most traditional occasions hats are no longer necessary, yet most women prefer to adhere to tradition and wear them to weddings, garden parties and, of course, to Ascot and Henley. Indeed it is part of the fun of the event and the decoration of the scene. The only important rule to observe in choosing a hat for a function where others may be seated behind you, is that it is not of a size to block their view.
□Unlike men, of course, women may wear their hats indoors and generally they keep them on in other women's houses.

382

APPENDIX

INITIALS AND ABBREVIATIONS OF RANK, HONOURS OR DEGREES

□'Bt.' or 'Bart.' for baronets and 'Esq.' (for esquire) precede all other abbreviations after names. Other designations follow in the order given below.
1. Orders and decorations conferred by the Crown
2. Appointments in the following order: Privy Councillor (P.C.), aide de camp to Her Majesty (A.D.C.), Honorary physician to the Queen (Q.H.P.), Honorary Surgeon to the Queen (Q.H.S.), Honorary dental surgeon to the Queen (Q.H.D.S.), Honorary Nursing Sister to the Queen (Q.H.N.S.), Honorary Chaplain to the Queen (Q.H.C.)
3. University degrees
4. Religious orders and medical qualifications
5. Fellowships of learned societies, Royal Academicians and Associates, Fellowships, Membership of Professional institutions, associations etc.
6. Appointments (other than above), in the following order: Queen's Council (Q.C.), Justice of the Peace (J.P.), Deputy Lieutenant (D.L.) and Member of Parliament (M.P.)
7. Membership in the Armed Forces

PRECEDENCE

□The tables overleaf are divided according to sex. Women's precedence may be due to achievement (a dame), derived from father or husband, or as a peeress in her own right. A dowager takes precedence over the wife of an incumbent, unless the dowager remarries and the children of an incumbent peer (or baronet) precede the children of the predecessor. A peer's daughter who marries a peer takes her husband's rank, but if she marries the son of a peer she takes whichever rank is the higher. A daughter follows her oldest brother's wife.

Among peers

□Peers and peeresses rank among themselves as follows: of England, of Scotland, of Great Britain, of Ireland and finally of the United Kingdom and Ireland. Within each category they rank according to the dates of their patents.
□Baronets' rank among themselves is based on their patents and without regard to country.

Precedence in England and Wales

The Duke of Edinburgh[1]
The Heir Apparent
The Sovereign's Younger Sons
The Sovereign's Grandsons
The Sovereign's Nephew
Archbishop of Canterbury
Lord High Chancellor
Archbishop of York
Prime Minister
Lord High Treasurer (when existing)
Lord President of the Council
Speaker of the House of Commons
Lord Privy Seal
Ambassadors and High Commissioners
Lord Great Chamberlain[2]
*Lord High Constable (when existing)
*Earl Marshal
*Lord Steward of the Household
Lord Chamberlain of the Household
*Master of the Horse
Dukes of England
Dukes of Scotland
Dukes of Great Britain
Dukes of Ireland
Dukes of the United Kingdom and Ireland since the Union[1]
Eldest Sons of Dukes of the Blood Royal
Marquesses of England

[1] By Royal Warrant dated 18th September, 1952, it was declared that H.R.H. the Duke of Edinburgh was henceforth to have precedence next to H.M. The Queen, thus having place before the Heir Apparent.
[2] When in actual performance of official duty.
*(Above all Peers of their own degree)

Marquesses of Scotland
Marquesses of Great Britain
Marquesses of Ireland
Marquesses of the United Kingdom and Ireland since the Union
Eldest Sons of Dukes
Earls of England
Earls of Scotland
Earls of Great Britain
Earls of Ireland
Earls of the United Kingdom and Ireland since the Union[1]
Younger Sons of Dukes of the Blood Royal
Marquesses' Eldest Sons
Dukes' Younger Sons
Viscounts of England
Viscounts of Scotland
Viscounts of Great Britain
Viscounts of Ireland
Viscounts of the United Kingdom and Ireland since the Union
Earls' Eldest Sons
Marquesses' Younger Sons
Bishop of London
Bishop of Durham
Bishop of Winchester
Other English Diocesan Bishops according to seniority of consecration
Suffragan Bishops according to seniority of consecration

Secretaries of State, if of Baronial
rank
Barons of England
Lords of Parliament, Scotland
Barons of Great Britain
Barons of Ireland
Barons of the United Kingdom
and Ireland since the Union
including Life Barons and Lords
of Appeal in Ordinary
Lords Commissioners of the Great
Seal (when existing)
Treasurer of the Household
Comptroller of the Household
Vice Chamberlain of the
Household
Secretaries of State, under
Baronial rank
Viscounts' Eldest Sons
Earls' Younger Sons
Barons' Eldest Sons
Knights of the Garter
Privy Counsellors
Chancellor of the Exchequer
Chancellor of the Duchy of
Lancaster
Lord Chief Justice of England
Master of the Rolls
President of the Family Division
Lord Justices of Appeal, according
to seniority of appointment
Judges of the High Court of
Justice, according to seniority of
appointment
Viscounts' Younger Sons
Barons' Younger Sons
Sons of Life Peers and Lords of
Appeal in Ordinary
Baronets, according to date of
Patent
Knights of the Thistle
Knights Grand Cross of the Bath
Knights Grand Commanders of

the Star of India
Knights Grand Cross of the Order
St. Michael and St. George
Knights Grand Commanders of
the Indian Empire
Knights Grand Cross of the Royal
Victorian Order
Knights Grand Cross of the Order
of the British Empire
Knights Commanders of the Bath
Knights Commanders of the
Indian Empire Star of India
Knights Commanders of St.
Michael and St. George
Knights Commanders of the
Indian Empire
Knights Commanders of the Royal
Victorian Order
Knights Commanders of the Order
of the British Empire
Knights Bachelor
Circuit Judges in England and
Wales, as follows:
a) Vice-Chancellor of Co. Palatine
of Lancaster
b) Circuit Judges who
immediately before 1st Jan.
1972, held office as Official
Referees to Supreme Court
c) Recorder of London
d) Recorders of Liverpool and
Manchester according to
priority of appointment
e) Common Serjeant
f) Circuit Judges who
immediately before 1st Jan.
1972, held office as Additional
Judge of the Central Criminal
Court, Assistant Judge of the
Mayor's and City of London
Court, County Court Judge,
Whole time Chairman or
Deputy Chairman of courts of

quarter sessions for Greater
London, Cheshire, Durham,
Kent and Lancashire, according
to priority of appointment
Companions of the Order of the
Bath
Companions of the Order of the
Star of India
Companions of the Order of St.
Michael and St. George
Companions of the Order of the
Indian Empire
Commanders of the Royal
Victorian Order
Commanders of the Order of the
British Empire
Companions of the Distinguished
Service Order
Members of the Royal Victorian
Order (4th class)
Officers of the Order of the British
Empire
Companions of the Imperial
Service Order
Eldest Sons of the Younger Sons
of Peers
Eldest Sons of Baronets
Eldest Sons of Knights of the
Garter
Eldest Sons of Knights of the
Thistle
Eldest Sons of Knights of the Bath
Eldest Sons of Knights of the Star
of India
Eldest Sons of Knights of the
Order of St. Michael and St.
George
Eldest Sons of Knights of the
Indian Empire
Eldest Sons of Knights of the
Royal Victorian Order
Eldest Sons of Knights of the

Order of the British Empire
Eldest Sons of Knights Bachelor
Members of the Royal Victorian
Order (5th class)
Members of the Order of the
British Empire
Younger Sons of Baronets
Younger Sons of Knights
Esquires
Gentlemen

LADIES

*If appointments are held by ladies,
e.g. Secretaries of State, they
should be assigned a
corresponding place as in
Gentleman's Table.*
THE QUEEN
The Queen Mother
Wife of Heir Apparent
The Sovereign's Daughter
Wives of the Sovereign's Younger
Sons
The Sovereign's Grand-daughters
(with style of H.R.H.)
The Sovereign's Sister
Wives of the Sovereign's Uncles
The Sovereign's Neice
Duchesses of England
Duchesses of Scotland
Duchesses of Great Britain
Duchesses of Ireland
Duchesses of the United Kingdom
and Ireland since the Union
Wives of the Eldest Sons of Dukes
of the Blood Royal
Marchionesses of England
Marchionesses of Scotland
Marchionesses of Great Britain
Marchionesses of Ireland
Marchionesses of the United
Kingdom and Ireland since the

Union
Wives of the Eldest Sons of Dukes
Daughters of Dukes
Countesses of England
Countesses of Scotland
Countesses of Great Britain
Countesses of Ireland
Countesses of the United Kingdom
and Ireland since the Union
Wives of the Younger Sons of
Dukes of the Blood Royal
Wives of the Eldest Sons of
Marquesses
Daughters of Marquesses
Wives of the Younger Sons of
Dukes
Viscountesses of England
Viscountesses of Scotland
Viscountesses of Great Britain
Viscountesses of Ireland
Viscountesses of the United
Kingdom and Ireland since the
Union
Wives of the Eldest Sons of Earls
Daughters of Earls
Wives of the Younger Sons of
Marquesses
Baronesses of England
Ladies of Parliament, Scotland
Baronesses of Great Britain
Baronesses of Ireland
Baronesses of the United Kingdom
and Ireland since the Union,
including Life Baronesses and
Wives of Life Barons and Lords
of Appeal in Ordinary
Wives of the Eldest Sons of
Viscounts
Daughters of Viscounts
Wives of the Younger Sons of
Earls
Wives of the Eldest Sons of Barons

Daughters of Barons
Wives of Knights of the Garter
Privy Counsellors (Women)
Wives of the Younger Sons of
Viscounts
Wives of the Younger Sons of
Barons
Wives of the Sons of Life Peers
Wives of Baronets, according to
their husband's Patents
Wives of Knights of the Thistle
(see note on Gentleman's Table)
Dames Grand Cross of the Order
of the Bath
Dames Grand Cross of the Order
of St. Michael and St. George
Dames Grand Cross of the Royal
Victorian Order
Dames Grand Cross of the Order
of the British Empire
Wives of Knights Grand Cross of
the Bath
Wives of Knights Grand
Commanders of the Star of India
Wives of Knights Grand Cross of
the Order St. Michael and St.
George
Wives of Knights Grand
Commanders of the Indian
Empire
Wives of Knights Grand Cross of
the Royal Victorian Order
Wives of Knights Grand Cross of
the Order of the British Empire
Dames Commanders of the Order
of the Bath
Dames Commanders of the Order
of St. Michael and St. George
Dames Commanders of the Royal
Victorian Order
Dames Commanders of the Order
of the British Empire

Wives of Knights Commanders of
the Bath
Wives of Knights Commanders of
the Star of India
Wives of Knights Commanders of
St. Michael and St. George
Wives of Knights Commanders of
the Indian Empire
Wives of Knights Commanders of
the Royal Victorian Order
Wives of Knights Commanders of
the Order of the British Empire
Wives of Knights Bachelor
Companions of the Order of the
Bath
Companions of the Order of St.
Michael and St. George
Commanders of the Royal
Victorian Order
Commanders of the Order of the
British Empire
Wives of Companions of the Bath
Wives of Companions of the Star
of India
Wives of Companions of the Order
of St. Michael and St. George
Wives of Companions of the
Indian Empire
Wives of Commanders of the
Royal Victorian Order
Wives of Commanders of the
Order of the British Empire
Wives of Companions of the
Distinguished Service Order
Members of the Royal Victorian
Order (4th class)
Officers of the Order of the British
Empire
Wives of Members of the Royal
Victorian Order (4th class)
Wives of Officers of the Order of
the British Empire

Companions of the Imperial
Service Order
Wives of the Eldest Sons of the
Younger Sons of Peers
Daughters of the Youngers Sons of
Peers
Wives of the Eldest Sons of
Baronets
Daughters of Baronets
Wives of the Eldest Sons of
Knights of the Garter
Wives of the Eldest Sons of
Knights
Daughters of Knights
Members of the Royal Victorian
Order (5th class)
Members of the Order of the
British Empire
Wives of Members of the Royal
Victorian Order (5th class)
Wives of Members of the Order of
the British Empire
Wives of the Younger Sons of
Knights
Wives of Esquires
Wives of Gentlemen

Precedence in Scotland

GENTLEMEN
Lord High Commissioner to the
General Assembly of the Church
of Scotland (during sitting of
General Assembly)
Duke of Rothesay[1]
The Sovereign's Younger Sons
The Sovereign's Nephew
Lord-Lieutenants of Counties
Lord Provosts of Cities who are
ex-officio Lord-Lieutenants
Sheriffs Principal
Lord Chancellor of Great Britain

Moderator of the General Assembly of the Church of Scotland (during office)

The Prime Minister

Keeper of the Great Seal of Scotland (Secretary of State of Scotland) (if a Peer)

Keeper of the Privy Seal of Scotland (if a Peer)

Hereditary High Constable of Scotland

Hereditary Master of the Household in Scotland

Dukes (as in English Table)

Eldest Sons of Dukes of the Blood Royal

Marquesses (as in English Table)

Eldest Sons of Dukes

Younger Sons of Dukes of the Blood Royal

Eldest Sons of Marquesses

Younger Sons of Dukes

Keeper of the Great Seal (Secretary of State for Scotland) (if not a Peer)

Keeper of the Privy Seal (if not a Peer)

Lord Justice-General

Lord Clerk Register

Lord Advocate

Lord Justice-Clerk

Viscounts (as in English Table)

Eldest Sons of Earls

Younger Sons of Marquesses

Barons or Lords of Parliament, Scotland (as in English Table)

Eldest Sons of Viscounts

Younger Sons of Earls

Eldest Sons of Barons or Lords of Parliament, Scotland

Knights of the Garter

Knights of Thistle

Privy Counsellors

Senators of the College of Justice (Lords of Session), including the Chairman of the Scottish Land Court

Younger Sons of Viscounts

Younger Sons of Barons or Lords of Parliament, Scotland

Sons of Life Peers

Baronets

Knights Grand Cross and Knights Grand Commanders of Orders (as in English Table)

Knights Commanders of Orders (as in English Table)

Solicitor-General for Scotland

Lyon King of Arms

Sheriffs Principal (when not within own County)

Knights Bachelor

Sheriffs

Companions of the Order of the Bath

Thence as in English Table

[1]The Prince of Wales

LADIES

The Queen

The Queen Mother

[Duchess of Rothesay] (see Duke of Rothesay)

The Sovereign's Daughters

The Sovereign's Sisters

[The Sovereign's Aunts]

Wives of Sovereign's Uncles

The Sovereign's Niece

Duchesses[1]

Wives of the Eldest Sons of Dukes of the Blood Royal

Marchionesses[1]

Wives of Eldest Sons of Dukes

Daughters of Dukes

Wives of Younger Sons of Dukes
of the Blood Royal
Wives of Eldest Sons of
Marquesses
Daughters of Marquesses
Wives of Younger Sons of Dukes
Countesses[1]
Viscountesses[1]
Wives of Eldest Sons of Earls
Daughters of Earls
Wives of Younger Sons of
Marquesses
Baronesses, or Ladies of
Parliament, Scotland[1]
Wives of Eldest Sons of Viscounts
Daughters of Viscounts
Wives of Younger Sons of Earls
Wives of Eldest sons of Barons or
Lords of Parliament, Scotland
Daughters of Barons or Lords of
Parliament (Scotland)
Wives of Knights of the Garter
Privy Counsellors (Women)
Wives of Youngers Sons of
Viscounts

Wives of Younger Sons of Barons
Wives of Sons of Life Peers
Wives of Baronets
Wives of Knights of the Thistle
Dames Grand Cross of Orders[1]
Wives of Knights Grand Cross and
Knights Grand Commanders of
Orders[1]
Dames Commanders of Orders[1]
Wives of Knights Commanders of
Orders[1]
Wives of Knights Bachelor and
Wives of Senators of the College
of Justice (Lords of Session)
including the wife of the
Chairman of the Scottish Land
Court
Companions of the Order of the
Bath
Thence as in English Table

[1] *As in English Table*

INDEX

Page numbers in *italics* denote illustrations

Index